Therapeutic TAROT

An instrument for Clinical Approach

Sinuhe Ulises García Reynoso

All rights reserved. The total or partial reproduction of this work is not allowed, nor its incorporation into a computer system, or its transmission in any form or by any means (electronic, mechanical, photocopying, recording, or otherwise) without the prior written permission of the copyright holder is a violation of these rights and may constitute a crime against intellectual property

The content of this work is the responsibility of the author and does not necessarily reflect the views of the publishing house. All texts and images were provided by the author, who is solely responsible for their rights.

Published by Ibukku, LLC
www.ibukku.com
Cover Design: Ángel Flores Guerra Bistrain
Graphic Design: Diana Patricia González Juárez
Copyright © 2024 Sinhue Ulises García Reynoso
ISBN Paperback: 978-1-68574-892-0
ISBN Hardcover: 978-1-68574-894-4
ISBN eBook: 978-1-68574-893-7

Index

Chapter 1
Tarot as a Therapeutic Approach Tool 7
   A Historical Journey Through Tarot 7
   Psychology and Tarot 19
   Theoretical Framework 24
   Main Objectives 33
   Epistemological Foundations 38
   Synchronicity and Tarot 44
   Astrology and Tarot 47

Chapter 2
Tarot as an Evolutionary Path. The Twenty-Two Major Arcana 61
   0-The Fool 62
   1-The Magician 63
   2- The High Priestess or Priestess 66
   3- The Empress 68
   4- Emperor 70
   5- The Hierophant or Pope 71
   6-The Lovers 73
   7- The Chariot 76
   8-Justice 79
   9-The Hermit 81
   10- Wheel of Fortune 83
   11- Strength 84
   12- The Hanged Man 87
   13- Death 89
   14- Temperance 91
   15- The Devil 96
   16- The Tower 100
   17- The Star 102
   18- The Moon 104
   19- The Sun 108
   20- Judgment 110
   21- The World 112
   22- The Fool 117

Chapter 3
Tarot as a Guide to Personal Development. The Minor Arcana — 119
- Four Aces: Swords, Cups, Pentacles, Wands — 121
- The Court Cards — 125
- Tarot and Psychological Types — 126
- Tarot: Myth, Symbol, and Dream — 129

Chapter 4
Quantum, Geometry, Number, Color, and Alchemy — 137
- Quantum Tarot — 138
- Geometry — 142
- Number — 146
- Color — 155
- Alchemical Tarot — 157

Chapter 5
Psychotherapeutic Readings of the Tarot — 161
- Tarot Spreads — 165
- Reading of the World — 167
- Reading of Time — 168
- Reading of Emotions — 169
- Reading of Family Constellations — 172
- Birth Reading — 179
- Reading of Destiny — 180
- Reading of Death — 180

Chapter 6
Tarot as a Clinical Instrument — 183
- Individual Fears — 185
- Paternal and Maternal Archetypes as Structuring of Thought and Feeling — 186
- The Five Wounds of the Soul — 187
- A Clinical Approach from Tarot — 192

Final Reflection — 201

Bibliography — 203

Our love for the world remains within us, speaking to each of us individually through our inner child's soul. It is this inner child that tightens our heart when we feel the vast emptiness of life and the pressing need to reconnect with the universe. We all possess the power to connect with our true selves. Real self-actualization lies in the freedom to discover our true identities, which can only be found beyond what we imagine ourselves to be, beyond the beliefs others have projected onto us, and especially beyond the social roles we typically identify with.

To address the current condition of humanity, we must understand that through our imagination, we can heal our inner system and alter reality. By redefining the past, present, and future, we mobilize a significant amount of energy towards our quantum field. Focusing on clear objectives opens up new realities that empower us to make a quantum leap significant for our species' evolution. If we can change our perception of the world, then it is possible for a sufficiently aware critical mass to drive global change. To design a world of justice and equality for all, a collective commitment is required. Unifying our consciousness towards a common goal can translate the future into one word: abundance.

> *In one way or another, we are parts of a single,*
> *all-encompassing mind, a single great human being.*
> Carl Jung

Chapter 1
Tarot as a Therapeutic Approach Tool

A Historical Journey Through Tarot

It is said that tarot originated around the year 1000, but truly nobody knows exactly who created it, where it was born, or how it spread. The meaning of the word "tarot" and the language it belongs to are also unknown. It is believed to be related to Christianity, Judaism, Buddhism, and Islam, possibly forming part of the Western tradition and serving as a feminine counterbalance to the monotheistic imbalance of civilization. Despite its strong spiritual and scientific roots, the tarot was banned by the Church, as it was considered a tool of magic related to divinatory art.

Delving into tarot, we find it closely linked with superstition, immediately bringing to mind themes associated with witches, black cats, and magic, hence the biggest challenge of this work is to unveil the hidden mystery it holds to reveal knowledge that is part of humanity's cultural legacy. Tracing back the origins of the arcana is even more complicated. These symbols were born with human thought and have developed throughout history, traversing various cultures. Their inception is lost in the mists of time, making it challenging to pinpoint their exact origin since they did not emerge at a specific moment but evolved over the course of our civilization's history.

The numerous myths and legends surrounding tarot have not helped clarify its origin, leading to its historical relegation as part of divinatory practices without considering an empirical approach. However, paradoxically, sometimes looking to the past can help us evolve further. From the 18th century to the present, hundreds of stories about the creation of tarot have been invented, attributing it to Atlanteans, Lemurians, Egyptians, Templars, Gypsies, angels, demons, biblical figures, and even extraterrestrials, according to the beliefs and personal fantasies of each tarot reader.

Marinela Rodríguez, a holistic therapist and tarot teacher, states: "The tarot encompasses the hermetic knowledge of great spiritual masters in symbolic images and constitutes the great book of life. In its symbols, influences as varied as Greek rites, Gnosticism, Neoplatonism, the teachings of the Cathars, ancient Arab and Indian philosophies, and the Jewish Kabbalah have been found." Historically, the first decks appeared in the 15th century in northern Italy, with most creators choosing anonymity.

During the Renaissance, particularly, a divine-archetypical figure, Hermes Trismegistus-Thoth, lord of writing, wisdom, magic, board games, and creator of alchemy, astrology, and astronomy, among other disciplines linked to the tarot's genesis, was possibly attributed with inventing the first tarots. This divine figure is credited with writing a collection of philosophical and magical texts that originated the Hermetic tradition, significantly influencing the Renaissance era. Hermes Trismegistus symbolizes a link between Greek philosophical tradition and Egyptian wisdom, passed on to the Romans, Arabs during the Middle Ages, and later to Renaissance philosophers and artists. The Hermetic tradition even reached New Spain and influenced figures like Sor Juana Inés de la Cruz, mentioning a tunnel leading through and beneath the great Sphinx's claws to the Egyptian initiation temple. Here, tablets inscribed with tarot cards depict the soul's initiation journey through life's cycle, referencing the Emerald Tablet's profound alchemical secret for transmutation.

This path was how ancient Egyptian initiates accessed a soul development method, specializing generation after generation in astrology and gathering information about the human soul. In ancient red Egypt, initiates went through a series of classrooms for training in secret knowledge by Osiris' priests. Legends around Egypt suggest that some of humanity's great masters approached the secret sciences granting Hermetic teachings.

Similarly, ancient African culture had oracles recorded, involving a wooden container with two levels inside, where a diviner placed a small mouse or cricket, which, attracted by food scent, moved objects interpreted by the shaman as messages from beyond. In African culture, the mouse, being in contact with the earth, closely relates to the earth goddess, Asyé, wife of the sky god, Niamyé.

In 1120, China already had a game of 32 ivory tablets with figures related to heaven, earth, man, duty, and the citizen's destiny, called "A Thousand Times Ten Thousand," composed of three sets of nine tablets plus three triumphs (9 x 3 = 21), totaling 30, symbolizing the microcosm in the macrocosm. Also, the *I Ching*, known as *The Book of Changes*, can be considered one of humanity's earliest texts, though historically there are earlier Sumerian writings.

Experts agree that the earliest writings of the I Ching date back to around 1200 B.C. For millennia, millions have consulted the I Ching, and though Westerners may not fully grasp cultures outside our own, many great thinkers and philosophers throughout history have been influenced by The Book of Changes. Cultural references in modern media, such as Neo in "The Matrix," Rick Sanchez in "Rick and Morty," and Dr. Stephen in "Dr. Strange," have encountered it. The I Ching is not about clairvoyance or divination but can be seen as an ancient quantum computer using a binary code symbolized by three coins. This source code allows access to concepts and keys for guiding one's life, heavily depending on the user's ability to operate and decode the necessary information for life improvement.

Exploring further into oracular history, we find Mayan astrology, an art that used mathematical language to understand, manage, and explain the surroundings, applied in classifying, ordering, modeling, measuring, calculating, counting, and distributing patterns found in nature. These patterns are fundamental for addressing needs, resolving situations, and understanding daily life surroundings.

Let us remember once again that pre-Columbian cultures viewed life as magical, expressed through the sacredness of nature, where magic meant observing and understanding generation, the growth of a plant, or the animal movements in the sky, especially the correspondence of these vital cycles and their complementation producing universal harmony. (Federico González, Pre-Columbian Symbolism, 2016)

The monocultural and Eurocentric history we're familiar with speaks of the multiple gods of the Anahuac peoples, overlooking the mathematical conception of a Divine Being grounded essentially in energy, a God of mathematical reason, not metaphysics. Ancient Mexico had an oracular system called the Tzolkin, a 260-day sacred cycle, used in pre-Columbian Mesoamerica, similar to the Aztec Tonalpohualli. It served as a cosmological technology for timekeeping, still used in indigenous communities in Guatemala and Oaxaca, known as "daykeepers." Linguistic evidence suggests the Tzolkin was in use by the Maya and other Mesoamerican peoples before 1000 B.C. The culture that developed this calendar remains unknown, with the oldest stelae using this calendar dating back to the Zapotec era in Oaxaca (500 B.C.), found in places like Monte Albán.

Similarly, the pyramid of Chichén Itzá was used as a calendar with 4 staircases, each having 91 steps and a platform at the top, totaling 365 steps, exactly equivalent to the number of days in a Haab calendar year. For ancient

Mexicans, pyramids symbolized their vast astronomical knowledge. Their myths guide the analysis of their geometric and mathematical development. The face of the Sun originates the four directions: east, west, north, and south. In all Mayan languages, the path of the Sun defines space and time. Despite seeming primitive, the concept of unity among man, community, and cosmos was expressed in their daily greeting, IN LAK'ECH, meaning 'I am another you', and the response HALA KEN, 'you are another me', highlighting our interconnectedness. Carl Jung, a psychologist, was a prominent explorer of the rich cultural heritage of indigenous peoples:

> The required reaction of the collective unconscious is expressed in archetypically formed representations. It is the world of water, in which all living things float suspended, where begins the realm of the sympathetic, of the soul of all living things, where I am inseparable and am this and that, where I experience the other in me and the other experiences me as the self. (C.G. Jung, Archetypes and the Collective Unconscious, 1969)

All ancient peoples of Mexico and the world recognized themselves as children of the Sun. The similarity in the symbolic designs of pyramids is a great mystery as to why cultures with no contact expressed similar ideas on spiritual concepts; specifically, on what happens to the human being after death and the relationship between man and the cosmos. The Mexica people identified the Sun (Tonatiuh) as the spirit of life, knowing centuries before Europeans that life on Earth was possible because of the Sun. According to their worldview, the Earth was perfectly positioned to receive Tonatiuh's fertilizing rays and manifest life as we know it today.

Today, the numerical heritage of ancient peoples is more alive than ever. The *nepohualtzintzin* is a tool (calculator), widely used among the Olmecs, Aztecs, and Mayas, and continues to be used today as a mathematical instrument for students with learning difficulties. The *pohuamatime* ('those who know the count') were the wise teachers of Anáhuac who defined zero, unity, and infinity as three manifestations of a single entity, quality. Similarly, cultures that have preserved ancient knowledge exist. For the Huicholes, geometry and color represent the way gods communicate with humans. Their rituals, dances, and art reflect such a worldview.

The ancient inhabitants of the Mesoamerican continent created a common language through play: combined with mathematical science through numbers, colors, geometric figures, and music, they recreated combinations that showed a numerical relationship existing between the human being and the universe, meaning that there is a symbolic connection between the thought and the spirit of the individual. The conception of numbers and geometry represented for ancient cultures a cultural manifestation of great relevance for the destiny of their peoples and were a cornerstone of their iconography.

Continuing our historical journey, we encounter one of the most unique developments of the Greek religion during the Hellenistic period (323-31 BC), a time when a transformation occurred from a more communal religious experience, moving from the polis to a more individual religion, in which emphasis was placed on what happened to the soul after death. This came to be known as mystery religions. All these cults included myths in which a character descended to the world of the dead and returned, as a metaphor for that reincarnation. For example, the Orphic mysteries, of Orpheus and Eurydice; or the Eleusinian Mysteries, based on the myth of Demeter and Persephone. The Eleusinian Mysteries were open to all those who were Greeks, that is, speakers of Greek; women and slaves included. We know there was an ecclesiastical hierarchy, with priests called hierophants and high priestesses. The so-called great mysteries, celebrated in September or October, began with a procession from Athens to Eleusis, a vigil in honor of the myth of the abduction of Persephone.

The mythological legacy of that era endures to the present day in the so-called Greek magical papyri. Since the beginning of the last century, the existence of several papyri with magical content was known, which had been acquired in the same localities of their discovery, especially Thebes and El Fayum, by the tireless seekers of papyri and antiquities. Finally, the papyri ended up in the great museums of Europe—Berlin, Paris, Leiden, London, Oxford, etc.—, where they were cataloged and briefly described. Upon reaching the universities and museums of Europe, the magical texts on papyrus began to be edited, and the scientific production around them grew extraordinarily, now forming part of a large field of study.

As we have seen, from the beginning of time, humans have sought to know their future, reading their destiny in the stars or in coffee grounds. Perhaps it's because today, just like yesterday, we are all equally lost with the big answers of life, regarding what we are doing here or where we are going. Across the globe, we find records of numerous divination sites, such as the Oracle of Delphi (Greece), Amun (Egypt), Nechung (Tibet), the temple of Uppsala (Sweden), etc. Even within the Bible itself, we find records of a varied number of prophetic dreams. The very story of Moses and the tablet of the Ten Commandments has an extraordinary similarity with oracles as a means to contact divine wisdom.

Now that we have a general overview of the different oracles and myths of history, we can turn our gaze to the central theme of this work, which is the tarot. As we can see, it is possible to observe that, beyond the hidden mystery, the figures of the arcana appear as a great historical treasure that can reveal to us the great philosophical legacy that is part of the cultural foundations of current civilization. The tarot allowed our ancestors to develop psychic senses to a high level and they laboriously kept records of their experiments for centuries, just as the ancient Masons would later do for more than 1500 years, and whose records have been studied because they are in the series called Anu-Enlil of Chaldea, which today can be found in the British Museum of Natural History.

Whatever its origin, it is easy to imagine the power that the tarot had as an instrument of profound communication. By handling images loaded with unconscious symbolism, it went straight to the emotions; it was not necessary to know how to read to communicate through the tarot. Considering that by the end of the 19th century barely 30% of Europeans knew how to read, it is possible to suppose that those who tried to understand the spiritual or to access deeper and more transcendent knowledge about their own life made use of, among other instruments, the symbols and images of the tarot. (Beatriz Leveratto. *Tarot 1. Major Arcana, the Archetypal Symbols of Destiny,* 2005)

From this perspective, all primitive mythologies, all pagan religions, and all esoteric polytheistic worldviews can be understood as a symbolic map of the cosmos. In this regard, Joseph Campbell mentioned the following:

> The mystery of the night sky, that enigmatic passage of lights that move slowly but incessantly among the fixed stars, once mathematically charted, led to the revelation of a cosmic order, which in response evoked, from the depths of human imagination, a mutual recognition. A broad concept of the universe as a living being akin to a great mother, in whose womb all worlds exist, both of life and of death, took shape.

The tarot deck consists of 78 cards called arcana, where human life with all its moments: past, present, and future, is captured. In a generic way, the tarot can be thought of as a set of universal symbols that finds its seat in the mind of all humanity. This universal mind was defined by Carl Jung as the collective unconscious. Legend has it that the origin of the tarot dates back to the first decades of the 13th century when Mediterranean merchants traveled the extensive Silk Road through China, Persia, and Africa, bringing among their belongings the first known deck of cards in the West, called Mamluk. Its origin was Islamic and was organized into four suits.

By 1392, Jacques Gringonneur painted a deck commissioned by King Charles VI of France, who suffered from mental insanity, which led some historians to suppose that the tarot was devised to distract the king's madness. Anyway, while the existence of this deck is known from chronicles of the time, it has not survived to our days, leaving the first Duke of Milan, Visconti-Sforza, the right to be the guardian of one of the oldest decks preserved today, which is owned by a limited number of collectors spread between Italy and the United States. This deck is hand-painted and contains gold dust in several of its strokes.

The Visconti-Sforza deck has an enormous historical and economic value, as it was the first to feature as arcana 2 a female priestess, the Popess, who, according to historians, is none other than Maifreda Visconti da Pirovano, sister of Duke Matteo Visconti. This woman was condemned to die at the stake by the Inquisition for being considered a heretic, as she believed in the prophecy of Saint Joachim of Fiore and postulated the idea that the Holy Spirit had incarnated on earth in the form of a woman, and that she had an adult son whose fatherhood was attributed to the King of Bohemia.

The origins of the Tarot of Marseilles, for which there are indications, are mainly from Italy, where a deck of cards was created for the Visconti-Sforza family to celebrate the wedding of the family's daughter, and this deck was given as a wedding gift around the 15th century. It was introduced into southern France when the French conquered Milan and Piedmont in 1499. The number of tarot decks that have appeared since then is incalculable, and it is believed that there are many others for which there is no record. The Swiss psychiatrist, psychologist, and essayist Carl Jung wrote The Red Book, an illustrated manuscript that can broadly be conceived as a type of tarot emerged from Jung's direct contact with archaic knowledge.

There are suggestions that the tarot cards developed from an ancient form of chess. It could also be supposed that chess comes from the tarot. It is not possible to establish whether the cards came from India, Egypt, or China, whether they first arrived in Italy from these countries, were introduced into the West from the East by the Crusaders or the Arabs, or arrived in Europe with the gypsies in the 12th century. The most important aspect of the cards is the antiquity of their symbolism as part of a fusion of different cultural sources.

One of the most popular decks is the Rider-Waite tarot, which was published in 1910 in London. Its cards were drawn by illustrator Pamela Colman Smith under the instructions of scholar and mystic Arthur Edward Waite, and published by the Rider Company. Its design contains alchemical, Kabbalistic, and astrological influences. It originated from the Hermetic Order of the Golden Dawn, founded in London in 1888. Since then, the tarot has been recognized by famous artists, such as Salvador Dalí, who also painted his own deck in 1984, based on the knowledge provided by Carl Jung. Alejandro Jodorowsky is another of the great cultural references who have helped popularize the tarot within current society, performing readings for people such as the former president of Chile, Ricardo Lagos; actress Sara Montiel, or singers Marilyn Manson and Peter Gabriel. Currently, celebrities like David Bowie, Aurora Aksnes, Emma Watson, and Anya Taylor have felt a great fascination for the tarot cards.

(Tarot Mandala Proposed by Alejandro Jodorowsky)

The original tarot cards consist of the minor arcana: the King, the Queen, the Knight, the Pages, and the Aces. The major arcana are 22 cards whose symbolism are closely related to each other. In the cards, the colors and symbols indicate that there is a correlation between almost all the cards in the deck. Those therapists fascinated by Jung's work do not approach the tarot as a divinatory system, but rather from the archetypal perspective, they approach the myths studied by this great sage. Following the line of thought of analytical psychology, it is possible to affirm that those who are fascinated by the world of tarot are immersed in the hero's journey, one of the powerful archetypes that make up the central axis of Jungian therapy and that were studied by numerous authors, such as the anthropologist Joseph Campbell.

Campbell concluded that in the hero's journey there are a series of basic elements that appear in most of the universal myths, fantastic stories, art, films, plays, and that also come to life in dreams. Whether real or imaginary, the tarot is an odyssey from beginning to end. Its central axis is an adventure where the hero leaves his comfort zone to delve into new horizons. The 22 major arcana are products of the imagination, not of logical intellect. They project archetypal situations and represent instinctive forces that operate autonomously in the human psyche.

From this classical mythology, we move forward in time to discover in the early Middle Ages the same Heroes with other faces: Hercules will be Lancelot as Perceval will embody what Perseus was, a warrior hero who no one can defeat in combat, and one more spiritual and pure to reach the Holy Grail. The same happens in the modern audiovisual mythology of Star Wars, whose initiatory adventure personifies the hero as a spiritual warrior called Jedi, knights who are part of a cosmic order that guards the galaxy. All faces of the hero are the same, and their journey is based on an adventure that repeats in its form. This is the conclusion reached by the American mythologist Joseph Campbell in his fundamental book, The Hero with a Thousand Faces (1949).

According to Campbell, this mythical structure is based on the form of primitive initiatory rituals composed of three parts: initiation, separation, and return; which, translated into traditional narrative, we call, setup, confrontation, and resolution. The mythic narratives of the Disney factory (The Lion King, Moana, Finding Nemo) or Pixar (Wall-E, Coco) have become an indispensable reference for what we call storytelling. The simple art of narrating and telling stories is not only part of literature, cinema, or series but is integrated into the world of advertising and serves as a tool for personal growth. We can really trace in almost every artistic creation elements that are part of the hero's journey, as the representation of a psychological dimension that allows us to explore the relationship of man with his inner world.

> The hero, whether god or goddess, man or woman, the figure in the myth, or the person dreaming, discovers and assimilates their opposite (their own unsuspected self) either by swallowing it or being swallowed by it. One by one, resistances are broken. The hero must set aside pride, virtue, beauty, and life, and bow or submit to the absolutely intolerable. Then they discover that they and their opposite are not different species, but one flesh. (Joseph Campbell, The Hero with a Thousand Faces, 1949)

This is the psychological aspect of Campbell's work, which is based on the lessons of his teacher Heinrich Zimmer (Myths and Symbols of India, 1943), who dedicated himself to bridging East and West, and was influenced by intellectuals such as Mircea Eliade (The Myth of the Eternal Return, 1949), and the tradition of Max Müller (The Sacred Books of the East, 1879-1910) and James Frazer (The Golden Bough, 1890), as well as Carl Jung's theory of archetypes. The hero or heroine's journey shows how our lives pass through different stages and trials that we must face and overcome. Among these are the call to adventure, crossing the threshold, the belly of the whale, the road of trials, the deepest cave, the apotheosis, or the crisis of the two worlds on the return. Key figures include the mentor, the helper, the universal protective goddess, or the father as the archetypal enemy, in addition to the internal dragon to be conquered. Probably the most important of all is the mentor with his wise advice—Mr. Miyagi, Merlin, Gandalf, Obi-Wan Kenobi, or Yoda—, who plant lessons for life and in moments of greatest difficulty remind us of the importance of being guided by the wisdom that comes from the heart: "All the gods, all the heavens, all the hells, are within you." (Joseph Campbell, The Power of Myth, 1988).

Despite the influence of these figures, there will come a time when the hero must face their destiny alone. If we enter the forest where there is a path, it is the path of another. Since each of us is a unique phenomenon, it is about finding our own path to happiness. As the epic and emotional song "Heroes" by David Bowie says, we can all be heroes forever and ever; if not, at least, for one day. The hero's journey has also made a long journey within humanistic psychology, coaching, or NLP. The contribution of Californians Robert Dilts and Stephen Gilligan must be highlighted, who, in addition to publishing the book of their method (The Hero's Journey, 1990), have been giving this seminar around the world for years.

Many mental illnesses stem from the way we structure our internal narratives, so these pathologies require creative tools that allow us to edit the storytelling of our lives. To reconstruct our own stories, we have to admit that at some point we all play the roles of heroes, villains, victims, supporting characters. Our mission is to take back the leading role and dive into our own mythology to find a path toward inner healing. Narrative awareness represents the most suitable mechanism for reconciling with one's own history through clinical awareness. The clinical history could be defined as a story that describes the psychological state of a patient and the follow-up conducted by the therapist through their healing process.

In the context of deep analysis, the analyst and the patient rewrite the clinical history together, creating a new story. They create the healing fiction as part of the analytical work. A part of the healing—perhaps even the most essential part—is due to this fiction developed as a team, which helps the patient to describe all the chaotic events of their life in a new narrative. This allows the therapist to help the patient give new meaning to those events that are painful, so that it is possible to project a different image of traumatic events. All superheroes undergo some kind of unfortunate event that gives them their powers and propels them to fight for justice.

Jung said that patients need "healing fictions," but it is difficult for us to adopt this viewpoint if there is not, beforehand, the capacity to modify the internal script. When we use the power of our imagination to rewrite our internal narrative, we gain the ability to modify our inner image of the world. Healing our perception is the path toward expanding consciousness and personality development. Fantasy constitutes an element of the psyche that allows for the remythologizing of consciousness, and that is why we try to encourage this activity by familiarizing ourselves with myths.

> One of the discoveries of psychology in the last century has been to show that myths structure our thinking, whether we are aware of it or not. All of us, as a species, culture, and individuals, have a narrative about the world we live in, the place we occupy in it, and the purpose that guides us. A myth, according to the original meaning of the Greek word mythos, is just that, a narrative that attempts to make life transparent by referring it to an intelligible source. What narratives have in common is that they are always

constructions of the human psyche. Our imagination is capable of recognizing elements of our myths, or of our form of consciousness when we see them in dreams, or in art and literature, but we may not come to understand their scope. A change in consciousness does not seem possible if we do not achieve some clarity about our mythological conditioning. (Jules Cashfor, The Moon, Symbol of Transformation, 2018)

James Hillman suggests that the construction of the soul goes hand in hand with the delateralization of consciousness and the reestablishment of its connections with mythic and metaphorical forms of thought. Instead of interpreting stories through concepts and rational explanations, we prefer to conceive rational explanations as secondary elaborations of basic narratives that contain and provide vitality. Owen Barfield and Norman Brown say, "Literalness is the enemy." Whenever we cling to a literal interpretation, a literal belief, or a literal claim, we lose the imaginative and metaphorical perspective on ourselves and our world. Often, when we interpret religious texts, we lose sight of their main function and become absorbed in their metaphors. Therefore, it is necessary to integrate rationality and intuition to extract the most relevant teachings for our life. This is the key factor that exists between myth and logos, which demands a great symbolic effort to reveal its mysteries.

What are the stories that need to be told to heal, stories that inspire profound change? Our society is currently bombarded by thousands of advertisements, sensational news, tragic events that make us lose faith in humanity, and this over time shapes our perception of reality, until we feel helpless, disconnected, and empty. Religious conflicts arise as an attempt to impose a world image, where everyone fights to prove events that at least from an empirical standpoint are not possible to demonstrate. We will never really know if a snake was the cause of our misfortunes, or if God is a figure sitting on a throne judging us from above, or if a particular prophet really needs us to wage a holy war. Jung referred to the following phrase: "If our religion is based on salvation, our chief emotions will be fear and trembling. If our religion is based on the wonder, our chief emotion will be gratitude."

What we can be sure of today is that without the principles that arise from religious mythology, humanity is doomed to self-destruction by the action of its own ignorance. The lack of mercy and ethical principles to guide our great technological development should be the greatest concern of our species. In this sense, a fantastic story, a literary book, or a movie can inspire us to become better people. When we let ourselves be captivated by a fantastic story, we see traits in the protagonist that push us to be braver, more compassionate, humbler, and this over time has a positive impact on the world. Regardless of whether this narrative born in the imagination is not entirely real, the degree of influence it can have on the viewer makes it something entirely tangible. Because of this, we can see the hero as the prophet of the time with great power to influence the collective imagination of an entire era.

Inside each of us is an internal call seeking expression. The tarot invites us to reflect on the importance of listening to our inner voice and finding a purpose that manifests in our lives. Deep within each of us, there is a profound desire to be authentic and live according to our true passions. This internal call can manifest through our dreams, desires, and aspirations, and it is crucial to pay attention to these internal signals to discover our true path. Life is a continuous exploration of the soul, which requires reflection on the deeper meaning of our existence. According to James Hillman, the soul is the core of our individuality and the engine that drives our actions and decisions. Life itself becomes a constant journey to discover our glorious purpose.

Psychology and Tarot

To support the tarot as a tool for clinical approach, we must provide a broad theoretical foundation. Therefore, the main approach proposed for this work is analytical, archetypal, transpersonal, and existential psychology, defining these models as those that best fit the objective set forth in this work. However, as we will see later, any theoretical model can be valid for working with the tarot. Despite this, James Hillman and Carl Jung are the authors who most intimately express the potential of the tarot as a therapeutic instrument to achieve inner healing.

Analytical psychology can be seen as the evolution of psychoanalysis, offering a new perspective that focuses on analyzing our symbolism to understand the mind. The rift between Sigmund Freud and Carl Jung marked the creation of a new path towards a broader understanding of the psychoanalytic concepts originally proposed by Freud. Freud's conception of humans as beings governed exclusively by an amoral force was expanded by Jung, who argued that libido, in addition to being a sexual dimension, has a spiritual component that is sublimated through symbols. Cultural and religious contents are ways in which this energy has been transformed to shape culture. Thus, humans are not merely a collection of instinctual drives, but within their will, they possess the free will necessary to elevate their animal condition to more spiritual spheres.

Humans have a need for both nature and culture. According to Jung, this is clearly seen in the manifestation of dreams and the myths of various peoples.

The traditional concept of the unconscious was also expanded by the proposal of a collective unconscious, a deeper and more transcendental stratum of the mind where all universal ideas are stored from the earliest times of humanity —Jung called these archetypes. Archetypes are forms of energetic order observable through symbolic representations accessible to consciousness, for example, in the form of the toroidal energy present in planetary vortices, which give rise to the constellations of the celestial vault. These, in turn, manifest as the abstract representations of the Sun, Moon, Father, Mother, Mind, Soul, Nature, and Spirit. All these forms are concepts that provide a sense of reality and are also present in the designs spun by spiders, in the mating rituals of birds, in the shapes of galaxies and hurricanes, and remarkably bear a similarity to the artistic representation of mandalas. For this reason, they are forms in which energy is organized through symbolic representations, which, due to the dynamics between opposites, establish patterns of universal interaction that give rise to archetypal situations.

We could then consider that archetypes, through symbols and synchronicity, function as the elements with which the universe weaves its stories, leading to archetypal situations represented in the myths of all cultures. For example, we could tell a short story using some of these elements: *When the depth of the night reaches its peak, the Moon recedes, and the Sun emerges. At dawn, the darkness is illuminated to announce the birth of a king who will unify the mind and soul of his people, showing a path towards the reestablishment of balance and harmony with the universe...* In this short narrative, we see that there are universal archetypes: the Sun, the Moon, Parents, Children, Youth, Elders, the People, Death, and Birth are concepts that represent the same thing everywhere, hence they are universal ideas, concepts that endure through time and bear an extraordinary similarity across all cultures.

Humans took our first steps believing in gods, preternatural entities that personified attributes, forces, and universal values (Justice, Time, Numbers, Geometry, Colors, etc.). These beliefs allowed us to conceive the cosmos as a theater where these forces interacted, giving meaning to reality and to life itself. Thus, the theoretical proposal of archetypal psychology is based on our affinity for these personifications. On one hand, Plato already spoke of the tendency to rely on universal enlighteners in his theory of knowledge and metaphysics. He thought that the greatest certainty was in those universal elements, calling them archetypes. Centuries later, Sigmund Freud proposed that, when we dream, our unconscious expresses itself through interpretable symbols, endowed with great meaning for us.

From there, Jung discovered the parallelism between these symbolic images and those drawn from ancient myths: the Hero, the Shadow, the Wise Old Man, etc. Therefore, archetypal psychology has a polytheistic facet, and some authors symbolically talk about "gods" to refer to the variety of symbolism. Thus, Hillman, in his book *Puer Papers*, asserts that the gods are part of the existential structure of our species. Whether we are aware of it or not, they are part of the projection of our consciousness onto the external world and, in turn, are part of the introjection of the principles and values that gave us a deeper sense of reality.

Therefore, the therapeutic proposal of archetypal psychology is based on the exploration of images rather than their explanation; on being aware of these images and paying attention to them until they gain as much clarity as possible. Hillman dubbed this therapeutic process "the soul-making," which consists of carefully contemplating our inner images until they acquire meaning. Mythological narratives are always related to certain symbols and a central figure that serves as a mold, what Campbell aptly called the monomyth: the original story of all stories that have been told since the world began, in any situation and in any culture.

One of the key theoretical concepts that reaffirms tarot as a therapeutic art is the representation of the hero's journey, embodied in the tarot as an analogy to the process of individuation described by Jung. He explained that there comes a time in everyone's life when we realize we are more than our body, nationality, social status. We are indeed much more than all we believe ourselves to be, and even more than the things and people around us. When that time comes, our gaze shifts from the external to become aware of the need for an inner journey.

For Jung, the tarot reflected the structure of the hero's journey. Its cards were a guide to achieving the process of individuation. This process is achieved through the evolution of the various mental facets that enable the development of the personality, the expansion of consciousness, and finally the symmetrical integration of all the elements that make up the psyche, whose ultimate goal is represented in the World card as the archetype of the Self. Jung identified up to five fundamental archetypes that are of great interest to psychology as a scientific discipline:

- The Persona: the mask we project to the world to be accepted in society.
- The Animus: the internal male image of the female psyche, logical and rational.
- The Anima: the female image of the male psyche, sensitive and creative.
- The Self: the true essence of being, representing the principle of totality and integration, the magnetic center of personality symbolized by the square and the circle (cross, mandala).
- The Shadow: the lower part of the personality, where all unrecognized aspects of consciousness are repressed, such as instincts, impulses, or attitudes. This force represents a potential for growth hidden in the person that enables reaching the totality of being.

As we have described, the hero's journey is a journey that continues throughout our life and probably beyond it. This journey combines with the cycles of nature and the cosmos. It is the great collective journey, where the human being realizes that they are separated, isolated, divided, fragmented, and for this reason, they must find a direction towards the unification of their being to give meaning to their existence. To achieve such an objective, they must go through a great number of trials, face dragons, meet with masters, descend into the underworld, confront dark and luminous figures. This arduous process allows the hero to free their soul from the bonds of their own mind.

The hero's journey is a great path of ego transformation that primarily involves the five archetypes mentioned. It is a process of evolutionary development that we could define as the art of being happy being oneself. This process unfolds over four phases.

The first step is to recognize that we are not absolute masters of our will and that there are forces operating below the threshold of consciousness that constantly drag us towards irrationality.

The second step involves completing the unconscious and conscious aspects to integrate the opposites as a means toward personal transformation. For this, it is necessary to embark on a long path of self-recognition of both the shadow and the light that exist within us.

The third step occurs in relation to the integration of polarity. In this stage, the dynamics of opposites enable men who are masculine on the outside to cultivate the feminine within, while women who are feminine outwardly can develop masculine traits internally. Women who connect with their interior find logic, competitiveness, firmness, personal power, and reflection. Men who glimpse femininity within themselves show vulnerability, compassion, wisdom, a desire for unity, and tolerance. The Sun and the Moon symbolize these representative qualities of the Anima and Animus archetypes, which allow access to the depths of the mind. If we integrate the qualities of our opposite without division, we will find within us a balanced being.

Once such a feat is accomplished, dark and unknown areas of our psyche begin to be illuminated, something that expands our consciousness and develops our personality, so that, as we expand our consciousness, moments arise when the Self emerges to provide us with clarity. The process is completed when all the conflicting opposites achieve a stable point of unification. The Self is a center of personality where an internal image capable of distinguishing and separating from the world is formed, in such a way that a fully integrated individual emerges through the self-realization of being.

Erich Neumann, in his work *The Origins and History of Consciousness* from 1949, presents the hero's journey as the representation of the process that leads to consciousness and symbolizes the consolidation of personality in the masculine aspect. Through various trials, the hero recognizes himself as a transformer who gains consciousness by developing his own Ego. He goes through three stages: the birth of the hero, the slaying of the mother, and the slaying of the father.

In this regard, Neumann proposes the following:

> Now, the ego is imminently facing what we call "the fight with the dragon," which represents three main components: the hero, the dragon, and the treasure. By defeating the dragon, the hero wins the treasure, which is the final product of the process symbolized by the fight. It is the battle with a mother who cannot be considered a personal figure, but rather the archetype of the mother.

Achieving individuality means overcoming the domain of the mother. For the ego and for the Animus, the feminine symbolizes the unconscious as the representation of the place from where consciousness originates and to which it must ultimately return. In his work, Neumann addresses the myth of creation, which consists of three mythological stages: the Ouroboros, the Great Mother, and the separation of the Primordial Parents. The ouroboros represents the primitive maternal womb, but also the union of polarity. In his book *The Matriarchate* from 1861, J.J. Bachofen explains why the cultures of the Mother goddess and their mythologies are intimately related to fertility, growth, and agriculture.

Sacrifice, death, and resurrection are the focal point of the primitive cults and rituals of humanity. It is a common belief among primitive peoples that the sky and the earth were originally united with each other.

In the mythologies of indigenous peoples, we see again and again the basic symbol, light, which is at the center of creation myths and is the main object of the cosmogonies of all peoples. Through the heroic act of the creation of the world and the division between opposites, the ego leaves the magical circle of the ouroboros and enters a state of tension and anguish. With the emergence of the ego, the paradisiacal situation is disrupted by the rupture of the initial ouroboric state, which leads to the division of the hermaphroditic constitution (masculine, feminine) and the separation of the world into subject and object, inside and outside. Finally, the hero through his journey integrates the polarity between opposites, dissolving the duality through the restoration of unity.

Therefore, for Neumann, the hero's journey is the path that entails the development from childhood to adolescence. In the first stage of his life, he must differentiate himself from his mother to find his own individuality, and at the end of his journey, seek to reconnect with the great mother, who exists beyond time and space. The maternal archetype represents in this sense the force that links him with nature and the cosmos. Throughout his life, this impulse to return to the great mother will manifest in various ways, which escape the threshold of consciousness and are present behind every action. It is an unconscious longing to return to the origin present in every act. Neumann notes that in the process of birth, development, and consolidation of consciousness, the capacity for orientation regarding the external and internal world arises, and for the hero, it represents the scenario through which he must ascend and descend, until finally transcending.

Theoretical Framework

The foundations for conducting this research stem from my own academic training in the field of clinical psychology. My name is Sinuhe García. I was born in Mexico and hold a bachelor's degree in psychology and a specialization in analytical psychology. Over the years, I have managed to expand my vision of the tarot through various courses and workshops. To carry out this work, I set out to find a way to integrate this mystical view inherited over time with key concepts from psychology, such as personality theories, psychometric tests, psychodiagnosis, and research methodology itself.

Therefore, through this book, the aim is to compare that artistic, mythological, and cultural side of the tarot with a solid theoretical framework based on areas of science such as history, epistemology, anthropology, neuroscience, epigenetics, etc.; all this with the hope of guiding an ethical use of tarot in society. Likewise, it is intended to propose a future in which it is possible to conduct formal studies in observation groups, where through static data, the use of tarot as a therapeutic instrument can be correlated with an improvement in mental health and an increase in the quality of life of the consultants. In this way, it is also possible to help promote education and culture as a means to improve the conditions of social coexistence.

To analyze the operative dynamics of tarot, we first must understand that tarot is related to astrology, biology, alchemy, philosophy, psychology, mathematics, art, and mythology —some even relate it to quantum physics—. However, as we have mentioned, the three basic components of tarot are geometry, number, and color. These elements have a configurative effect on the deepest spheres of the mind because they relate to the biological, emotional, and existential aspects of the individual. We can compare their immediate effect on the unconscious to that of advertising, music, or art, which exert a significant subliminal influence through their sounds, shapes, and colors.

Robert Segal has summarized Wolfgang Pauli's view of the reality of the symbol in a simile: "The symbol is both a product of human effort and a sign of an objective order in the cosmos. It contains information about man and his world." The symbol is related to a deeper structure, which goes beyond phenomena, as it constitutes a possible concrete form of manifestation of the archetype. The function of quantum physics in this sense is a real symbol because it expresses the relationship between abstract possibility and the observable event. In physics, the atom has the quality of a symbol, which can be "wave and particle." As Pauli expresses, "It is a symmetrical relationship with opposites and a transcendence of psychophysical boundaries."

With the help of the symbol, it is possible to develop an angle that relates science and spirituality, emphasizing the interaction between the cosmos and the psyche, representing a parallel of concepts in quantum physics and depth psychology. The neutral language hypothesis is based on Pauli's view that the ordering factors that Jung calls archetypes are neither in the psyche nor in matter but beyond both, in a neutral plane. Neutral language can describe processes that are active and observable both in the study of matter and in the study of the psyche. At the frontier between physics and psychology lies the mystery of numbers. Pauli was inspired by Kepler's conception of the archetype as a mathematical and geometrical idea that describes the archetype of the beauty of the universe whose symbolism reflects a cosmic order. Pauli linked this concept with Jung's psychological archetype as the way consciousness squares itself through psychological functions to project consciousness.

In everyday life, we observe that the world is made up of images: letters, numbers, art, cinema, advertising, signs, even body language is part of a visual representation. Practically everything we see in our psychic reality is presented to us as an image: a smile, a cordial greeting, a seductive dance, a play that captivates our senses and evokes an emotional state. For our brain, every act and event represents something on a symbolic level. These interpretations help form an internal narrative and give it a sense of reality. When we feel offended or appreciated, it is thanks to this ability to assign affective qualities to the mental representations we make of the world around us. Jacques Lacan postulated that the unconscious is structured like a discourse. This discourse articulates a sense of reality and functions as a social bond that connects the individual with the external world.

This discourse could well be the set of symbols operating within a logical and abstract dimension of our psyche, which allow us to define a more specific meaning to our actions. For example, when we go to the supermarket and buy a product, it is thanks to mathematical symbols that we can make a successful transaction; when we work and exchange goods and services, we can put a price on our effort, and similarly, we monetize the time others give us, for example, when someone helps us fix our car.

Likewise, when we interact with people, this capacity to structure a sense of logic allows us to relate on equal terms and know, for example, when we have a high probability of talking to a girl we find attractive. All these calculation abilities arise from the observation of a visual representation in our environment, which we interpret as a series of personal meanings. Symbols are also part of the language of science. Anyone who is going to study with a scientific method (biology, history, sociology, humanities) must do so with a scientific method, which requires mathematics to be valid. Mathematics is an expression of the organizing matrices of the universe and helps us get as close as possible to reality by orienting our senses accordingly.

Symbols also have a technical function when we use an electronic device. This is possible thanks to the interaction of a pole (+) and (-) that allow the transmission of energy. Moreover, to turn on these devices, we rely on a symbol that is in turn composed of two others. That broken circle and central line closely resemble a 1 and a 0. Therefore, the vertical bar corresponds to the 1, which means 'on', and the circle to a 0, which means 'off'. When we watch television, we see a series of moving images, which are combined by the interaction of ones and zeros. This phenomenon is related to this world of imagery, abstract and symbolic, offering us the possibility to interact in a reality that goes beyond the material world. It is the main quality that distinguishes us from the rest of the animal kingdom.

In addition to this, symbolic acts have a subjective, metaphorical, and individual component, in line with each person's reality. From a poetic perspective, we can say that there are things whose value goes beyond price, sacred objects not for sale, places that demand honor. Respect for women, children, and the elderly stems from these abstract concepts that have enabled humans to develop ideas such as justice, equality, chivalry, honorability, etc. These ideas have shaped civilization and allowed the emergence of qualities that characterize humanity.

This capability of our language is not the ability to transmit information about objective facts, but rather the ability to convey information about subjective things that arise in our imagination. Legends, myths, gods, and religions appear as the engine of the evolution of consciousness. These fictions become more useful with the founding of large cities with thousands of inhabitants, as, by collectively creating and believing in myths like the biblical story of creation and the nationalist myths of modern states, among others, we are capable of flexibly cooperating; but it also leads us to obey and follow shared rules, norms, and values. Since the cognitive revolution, sapiens have lived in a dual reality: on one hand, the objective reality of nature (seas, mountains, rivers, animals); on the other, the imagined reality (gods, nations, and corporations).

The symbol, in this sense, appears as a connection between worlds, between conscious and unconscious aspects. It is a bridge between the concrete reality and that imaginary world of dreams and visions. The symbol, moreover, through its metaphors, has the great power to unite the left hemisphere of the brain—analytical, technical, hunter, and masculine—with the right hemisphere—intuitive, sensitive, and feminine, where human attitudes are transmitted. We can say that the left brain is responsible for our technical development, while the right has been in charge of transmitting human attitudes. The development of our civilization has only been possible through the evolution of our humanity. For example, with the conceptualization of the symbol of the Sun and the Moon, our ancestors were able to contemplate the cycles of time present in the universe (days, months, years). Thanks to this, they could understand that nature was governed by these cycles (spring, summer, autumn, winter), thus myths emerged as the precursor to current scientific thought.

Our language is made up of symbolic elements. In everyday life, we constantly use symbolic terms to represent concepts we cannot fully define, thus creating symbolic representations. When we refer to the Holy Spirit, we often associate it with the image of a dove. When we talk about innocence, we might think of a little angel playing a harp on a cloud. When we refer to evil, perhaps the first thing that comes to mind is a little devil with horns. When someone talks to us about love, we probably imagine a red heart —although, as such, the heart does not have that shape. Thus, as time goes by, a cultural legacy as a representation of ideas and abstract concepts is created.

Since the appearance on earth of the first hominids, we have gone through three major revolutions: the cognitive revolution, about 70,000 years ago; the agricultural revolution, which accelerated it, about 12,000 years ago; and the scientific revolution, launched just 500 years ago. This collective journey has only been possible through the intuitive sensitivity of our species. The ability to create images through mental maps represented the greatest and most sophisticated evolutionary adaptation that allowed us to shape reality through the emergence of knowledge; however, imagination precedes reason, and for that reason, we can suppose that the unconscious is structured like a system of symbols, just as the operating system of a computer is structured by a series of programming commands (BIOS).

This is how tarot operates within that dimension where consciousness projected itself outward through images and symbols that precede conscious activity, and therefore has an immediate effect on the unconscious. Science has shown that our decisions and actions are driven by factors that escape rationality. Thus, tarot emerges as a tool capable of structuring unconscious disorders by showing us a path towards the integration of intuition and reason.

For ancient wisdom, illness and suffering arise as a consequence of a disconnection between these functions. Evil is the result of the imbalance that comes from forgetting this invisible reality that connects us with the ultra-human dimension. Thus, the knowledge forgotten by modernity is a clear response to why a society focused on strategic thinking has been entirely guided by economists and materialist scientists who have denied the reality of the soul. Science has forgotten its philosophical origin.

According to Jung, from the 19th century amid positivism, a "psychology without a soul" emerged, under the influence of scientific materialism. The soul was renounced as a superstitious concept of no greater relevance to human progress. From that moment on, everything had to be explained as a set of mathematical equations and electrochemical reactions. Only that which could be deduced sensorially was deemed worthy of empirical study. The investigation of the spiritual gradually gave way to the material conception of reality, and so it was for four centuries. The spirit and psyche were contemplated as an epiphenomenon of matter until theorists like Carl Jung, James Hillman, Marie-Louise von Franz, Victor Frankl, Stanislav Grof, Ken Wilber, and various other authors emerged, seeking to rescue the lost heritage that humanity had on these great ancestral knowledge.

James Hillman states the following: "Modern psychology has lost sight of the importance of the soul in human life." Thus, it is proposed that the importance of the soul in this realm has been forgotten, which implies that the need to attend to the spiritual and transcendent aspect of the individual has been neglected. Current psychology has focused mainly on analyzing and treating cognitive and behavioral aspects, relegating to the background that which connects with our deepest essence. It is necessary to retake the dimension of the soul as a fundamental part of our existence and recognize its influence on our psyche and our emotional well-being. Hillman invites us to revalue the importance of the spiritual to achieve a more complete and holistic understanding of human life.

Jung pointed out that a psychology focused exclusively on the study of material phenomena is configured as a psychology without a soul, where we completely distance ourselves from a scientific psychology that explains the world from a perspective of the spirit and does not confuse fanciful imagination with the intelligence that comes from intuition and knowledge arising from transpersonal experiences that allow the transcendence of consciousness. Claudio Naranjo similarly defines in his works how our science is biased by a lack of vision based on a system of equations that does not take into account the human, thus completely separating from the environment, covering the entire spectrum accessible to reason with logic. This has created a society driven by hyper-desire and a culture that interferes with the development leading to maturity.

In a world full of noise and distractions, it is vital to take the time to delve into our inner world and pay attention to what our soul is telling us. James Hillman mentions that we must listen carefully and sensitively to the internal voices that guide us, inspire us, and reveal deeper aspects of our own existence. Only by synchronizing with the language of the soul can we connect with authentic wisdom, such as that content accessible to consciousness that lies beyond intellectual knowledge and connects us with the very essence of our humanity.

The ailment of our society arises as an over-identification with certain masks and character traits that prevent us from recognizing our deeper nature. The wisdom to see things as they are does not depend solely on reason. Such action requires a gestalt ability to integrate the cerebral hemispheres. Therefore, in this sense, tarot is a tool for opening a connection with the soul. As individuals, we are disconnected from the spirit, absorbed in the world of intellect. We live self-deceived by our false conception of intellectual superiority, completely forgetting that to achieve the totality of being, it is necessary to recognize the reality of the soul. The tarot, in this sense, proposes a path that facilitates the recognition of more humane attitudes, which are transmitted through art, sensitivity, reflection, and the contemplation of old concepts forgotten by modernity.

True healing is not limited to treating the superficial symptoms of an ailment or adapting to the social context of the era but involves contact with the depth of our being. We must discover who we are at our core, beyond the masks and social roles with which we usually identify ourselves. Only when we connect with our most authentic and genuine essence can we open the doors to true and lasting healing. When we connect with universal love, love for others, God, nature, and ourselves, we can face even the most difficult situations.

True wisdom lies in the direct experience of the soul. It is through living, feeling, and connecting with our inner being that we find authenticity and a deep understanding of life. Books can be a valuable tool, but they can never replace the richness of what our soul learns and experiences directly. By transcending the ego, we are able to discover and connect with our soul. We regularly spend our lives guided by social mandates that repress us and subject our efforts to be successful, in such a way that we live for money, external pressures, absorbed in the image that our ego manufactures of ourselves. This gradually leads us to ignore the inner voice and project the shadow onto others. It is necessary to recognize that we are not the angels of the Victorian era. Evil truly exists within us, just as the Christ consciousness dwells in each of us. Evil is not a being with goat horns and rooster legs that dwells in hell and incites us to sin, but rather, we could conceive of evil as our own inability to be more compassionate and responsible with our actions. The greatest sin of man is the impossibility to love his neighbor as himself.

If we were aware of the spirit of our times and had a greater historical sense, we would understand that if we give preference to explanations based on the physical order, it is because in the past, the spirit was abused in an excessive way. In the era of religious inquisition, anyone who dared to challenge the sacred texts was severely punished. Currently, however, there exists a scientistic inquisition, and anyone who dares to approach any extrasensory experience does not receive good acceptance by the scientific community, we might say. It is likely that we are now committing the opposite error — which is, at its core, the same —. We overestimate material causes believing to have thus found the key to the enigma, lulled as we are by the illusion of knowing matter better than spirit. We completely ignore the tangibility of the soul. However, we must recognize that it is thanks to the spirit of the human soul that we are something more than automatons or wild apes; therefore, we must broaden our understanding of these topics through a critical look at this scientific scheme of the soul.

We do not deny the close intertwining of the soul and the psychology of the brain, glands, and synaptic connections. We must acknowledge that we are determined by our sensory perceptions. We do not doubt at all that unconscious inheritance imprints immutable character traits, both physical and psychic. We are certainly influenced by the power of biological impulses. But we must admit that the human soul is especially present in its cultural products (dreams, poetry, art, music, religion, myth, etc.)

Scientists study the world by analyzing weight, height, temperature, etc. Psychologists study the soul through the sensitive language of symbolic expressions. Every act is a symbolic representation with a degree of depth and intensity. The soul, in this conception, is an entity that exists by itself, governed by its own language. Consciousness is therefore an expression of the soul itself, which is why all soulless psychologies are psychologies of consciousness, excluding all unconscious psychism. There is not, in fact, one, but numerous modern psychologies. However, there is only one mathematics, one geology, one zoology, one botany, etc. On the contrary, in matters related to mental health, such a large number of therapeutic models are cataloged that it is difficult to propose, despite the differences, a point of union. There are as many psychologies as there are philosophies.

For this reason, this work attempts to approach tarot from a diversity of therapeutic models such as psychoanalysis, humanism, cognitivism, systemic psychology, and Gestalt. This represents an attempt to return the soul to current psychology, and for such a task, tarot is proposed as a tool capable of achieving this goal, regardless of the theoretical approach intended to be used. A single path, the same outlook towards the unification of efforts to help elevate people's quality of life, is proposed.

In this sense, we approach tarot as an attempt to find a connection with the object of psychology, which is the soul. We choose tarot for this task precisely because images are the language of the soul. The archetypes represented in the arcana form the structure of the soul and manifest more tangibly with the earth and the world. According to Jungian theory, what does not fall into the collective unconscious assumes archaic figures that manifest projectively as archetypal forms that ancient religions associated with angels and demons. According to archetypal psychology, it is not through logic or reason that we can access the depths of our being, but through visual representation and the symbolic function.

Hillman stated, "Myth is the way the soul speaks through imagination." Myth should not be seen as a mere fanciful invention, but as a form of communication of the soul through imagination. In the history of evolution, our species spent thousands of years guided solely by its instincts, with no greater concern than mating and surviving. Only when the spark of creativity and wonder about the surrounding world emerged did the faculty of thinking and developing superior knowledge appear, hence we understand that myth was the driving force that steered the great scientific advance of our era. Therefore, imagination precedes reason. It is through myths that the soul finds its expression.

What does the soul seek? Healing stories, such as observing the celestial vault, exploring cultural vestiges, the drawings on the redskins' mantle, the journey with power plants, the smile of the beloved, or the contemplation of a sunset. These are images that have healing effects on the soul that escape intellectual rationality. Archetypal psychology works with images and symbols that generate deep meanings. Hillman proposes the restoration of the anima mundi (internal image of the self and the world) as a supreme source of liberation and mental healing. When we understand our place in the great cosmic plot, we access a privileged space; from that perspective, it is possible to experience the belief that we are something more than just part of a greater purpose that transcends our mere banal existence. Perceiving the world from this deep perspective fills us with great meaning and makes possible the liberation from all those emotions and frustrations that chain us to suffering. When we are dissatisfied or suffer, it is because the soul calls to our heart to allow it to heal and transcend the limits imposed by our ego.

Main Objectives

The main objective of this work is to establish a theoretical framework that allows defining a protocol of intervention in the clinical area, more specifically within the field of psychotherapy, but also to formalize tarot as a tool for assessment and diagnosis of the various psycho-emotional disturbances that afflict human beings. As a clinical instrument, tarot has great utility for therapeutic approach. With it, we can intervene within the various pathologies that affect human beings, while it is also possible to define a series of coping strategies for the different crises a person may suffer throughout their evolutionary cycle. For this reason, beyond the magical spectrum, we can propose tarot as an effective tool for psychotherapeutic work.

The secondary objective of this work is to establish a correlation between tarot and its effects on mental health. The theoretical framework of this work was supported by analyzing a large number of works on tarot, establishing alongside a theoretical framework based on analytical psychology, Gestalt therapy, systemic therapy, and humanism. Within the tarot, there is a point of concordance among the different therapeutic approaches that allows us to establish a high degree of validity and reliability. For this work, authors such as Carl Jung, James Hillman, Marie-Louise von Franz, Erich Neumann, Stanislav Grof, Ken Wilber, Carl Rogers, Abraham Maslow, Victor Frankl, Erich Fromm, Bert Hellinger, and Claudio Naranjo were taken as reference points. The information presented in different schools of psychology and tarot, such as the Eleusis Institute, the Aztlan Cultural Center, or the Lemat School, was collated. For this work, personal approaches of tarot readers like Alejandro Jodorowsky, Cristóbal Jodorowsky, Ismael Sánchez, Carolina Goldsman, Vianey Torres, Victoria Arderius, Encarna Sánchez, and Daniel Rodes, among others, were considered.

The purpose of this work is to develop an application protocol for attending to people in need of psychological attention, using tarot not as a divination tool but as an instrument for clinical approach. The therapeutic process of tarot will allow us to identify projections, establish intervention guidelines, close unfinished cycles, heal grief, repair our family system, and expand our belief system to find a deep meaning to existence. In this way, the work done with tarot can motivate the consultant to develop their full potential.

Through this method proposed in this research project, we seek to establish a scheme in which through tarot, healing, encouragement, and motivation for a person's evolutionary development can be achieved. The final result of this work is to propose a different approach to tarot, which goes beyond mysticism and can serve as a therapeutic scheme that favors mental health, with a high degree of validity and reliability.

Tarot is a superb map for navigating the extensive territory of our three brains: reptilian, limbic, and neocortex. In its images, we see the possibility of achieving a unification of the cerebral hemispheres, allowing us an integrative view between the analytical and the intuitive functions.

In these times, it is necessary to know how to unite what appears to be separate in a manner appropriate to the times, because the great human paradox we live in the 21st century is that, having so much knowledge and technology at our service, we use our fantastic brains very poorly. All of us are cutting-edge technology, an extraordinary biological creation capable of encoding and decoding reality thanks to the magnificence of our genes.

In the field of psychology, there is a vast array of approaches that encompass a series of theories, tools, and studies enabling us to address mental processes, sensations, perceptions, and human behavior in relation to the social context of the time. There isn't a single model for addressing the various mental afflictions that affect human beings. Tarot is an instrument that could well be comparable to projective tests (Rorschach, human figure, incomplete sentences), or it could even be considered an ancient DSM (Diagnostic and Statistical Manual of Mental Disorders) with which we can identify different mental pathologies as a consequence of the incorrect channeling of archetypal energy or the lack of attention to the lessons that the soul must undertake. The paralysis caused by opposites, the denial of the shadow, and the stagnation of the Self manifest in life as an inability to achieve well-being.

James Hillman stated, "Illness is a sign that something in the soul is out of balance." Thus, we must consider that illnesses are much more than mere psychological disorders, but are also manifestations of an emotional and spiritual imbalance. This notion challenges us to look beyond the symptomatology and to search for the underlying reasons that may be contributing to our illness. We must explore our soul, our emotions, our thoughts, and our relationships to understand what aspects of our life may be out of balance and thus find a path toward true integral healing.

Almost everyone experiences, at some point, a period when life loses its meaning or becomes hellish. This span can stem from an external event such as a death, the loss of a job, the end of a love, an illness, or any other unexpected occurrence that leaves us without certainties. These circumstances and experiences often feel like an emotional tsunami where feelings of emptiness, fear, and loneliness predominate, as well as isolation, indifference, loss of energy, and purpose. This process, which many of us go through, is called the *dark night of the soul.*

The dark night of the soul is part of a spiritual transformation, a time of incubation for the caterpillar to become a butterfly, a necessary disintegration for the transformation that propels us beyond our comfort zone. Thomas Moore says we must accept the dark night and live in harmony with it because the soul feeds on darkness as much as on light. The descent into the underworld connects us with the deep and dark, leading us to the emptiness of our being, towards transformation and renewal. In this sense, Jung said that darkness and chaos are necessary processes to learn to live from the soul. In separation, internal urgencies push us into the odyssey, forcing us to distance ourselves from the environment, from home, family, friends. For this, we will have to go through several trials, but there will always appear a pair by our side to accompany us on the route, making the transition lighter, the initiation is the *descent into the underworld,* in which we will go through the worst situations to achieve the knowledge that entails evolution. Jung tells us, "Only those trees whose roots have touched hell can grow up to heaven."

Many times we will be trapped in the underworld of villains until we are forced back. If we cannot return on our own, it is necessary to connect with a higher force that can help us find the way out. This aiding force is properly the tarot. Jung asserted that imagination belongs to both psychic and spiritual life; because of this, the tarot is a great transpersonal tool in therapy. Once we have identified the origins of psychic suffering, we must establish a therapeutic action plan and the techniques that will allow us to achieve such an objective, for which it is necessary to support this plan of action from a theoretical model. The tarot can be approached from various therapeutic perspectives, for which we will propose some with which one can work in the clinical area. The main one is analytical psychology or depth psychology, designed by Carl Jung. Its central axis proposes the process of individuation through work with archetypal images.

Likewise, humanistic theory is highly compatible with tarot. Abraham Maslow and Carl Rogers are the leading exponents of what is known as *the third force in psychology*. Both Rogers' and Maslow's theories focus on individual choices and share with Jung the belief in the growth potential of healthy individuals found in the understanding of the self. Their theory revolves around two fundamental aspects: our needs and our experiences. In other words, what motivates us, what we seek throughout life, and what happens to us on this path, what we experience. From this theoretical model, we can define that the voids, lacks, and fragmentations of the psyche stem from the inability to rationally satisfy biological, emotional, and existential needs.

When we find ourselves unable to satisfy our needs, psychic tension and emotional frustration lead us to a loss of balance and harmony in life. Only when we are able to rationally satisfy our basic and higher needs can we achieve fulfillment and well-being in our lives. To reach this goal, it is necessary to clearly define what we truly need to be happy. Every being has an innate desire for self-actualization, to be what they want to be, and has the capacity to pursue their goals autonomously—if they are in a conducive environment. In this sense, tarot is a tool that allows us to identify and design a path towards the resolution of problems related to health, money, love, and spirituality. Thus, an individual can develop their full human potential and experience the most transcendental aspects of life.

Within the Gestalt model, tarot allows for a symbiosis between the cerebral hemispheres. The logical and the abstract converge at the same point, generating a deeper vision of reality. This perspective enables the emergence of the wisdom necessary to see things as they are. This perceptive ability requires more than reason; it requires a Gestalt capacity. The two cerebral hemispheres process information in different ways, which is closely related to the concept of Anima and Animus proposed by Jung. Tarot offers this possibility of integrating all the parts that make up the whole through the structuring of the four elements: emotion, thought, body, and energy. Gestalt therapy is a form of psychotherapy focused on self-awareness that concentrates on the here and now. The word

Gestalt comes from German and means 'form' or 'configuration'. It suggests the idea that the whole is greater than the sum of its parts. The Gestalt approach helps guide the patient towards resolving unfinished cycles, aiding the person to better understand how they interact with the world and gradually leading them to an awareness of the responsibility they have over their well-being.

Logotherapy is therapy based on finding meaning. It is the approach defined by Victor Frankl as "healing through meaning." Healing, caring, accompanying, guiding the person consulting the tarot to discover meaning in their life, which also involves finding meaning in each moment of their life. Thus, the discovery of the hero's journey enables the discovery of the privileged space we occupy within the cosmos and our individual duty to the collective. Through the development of spirituality, an individual who feels love for themselves and for others is capable of healing. The evolutionary path of tarot offers the recognition of a deeper sense of life and allows us to address the great existential voids of our time, through commitment to life and reconnection with the spiritual dimension of existence.

Neurolinguistic programming (NLP) was created in the 1970s by Richard Bandler, a mathematician, and John Grinder, a linguist, in California. This approach allows us to change the emotional rationalizations correlated with all those beliefs that generate fear, anger, sadness. When these emotions are perpetuated over long periods, they become unconscious beliefs, creating a series of mental pathologies such as anxiety, depression, phobias, addictions, etc. Over time, these pathologies can somatize, generating physiological diseases, as they are stored in a part of the body. Unexpressed emotions can affect the integrity of the organism, as the mind and body are considered as a single system, each directly influencing the other. As a result of repression not only of emotions like fear or pain, sometimes also happiness is inhibited by feelings of guilt, failure, or limiting beliefs, compromising the quality of life. By taking control of the internal dialogue, we can find new alternatives for thinking, feeling, and acting, forming a more functional image of the Self.

Family constellations are a method developed by Bert Hellinger. Its aim is to free people from their tensions/conflicts, which often come from past generations and are rooted in family context events such as wars, family or domestic violence, the premature death of parents or children, abortions, separations, or sexual abuse. This can manifest in the present in the form of problems such as depression, psychosis, fears, migraines, chronic fatigue, or relationship problems. Epigenetics has clearly shown how experiences are transformed into biological information with transgenerational effects. From this perspective, we can use imagination to discover the script that moves our soul and links us to the family and collective history of our era.

Beyond the various psychotherapeutic approaches, tarot has historically been a tool that allows us to listen to inner wisdom. It is a window of access to the depths of the mind, where the lessons of the arcana enable the unfolding of all the possibilities an individual can access. We all live in the world of material illusions, so the soul needs to experience a series of events that allow it to learn. The structure of the tarot consists of a map of all those experiences the soul needs to undergo for its evolutionary development.

These symbolic-abstract forms are seemingly representations of principles, that is, of true archetypes that repeat throughout human history. Jung also discovered the existence of a "divine being" but also a "distributor of destinies." This makes us think of an entity that is separate and at the same time united, guiding us in a predetermined direction, towards our full realization. Jung studied hundreds of his patients' dreams. Within his clinical experience, he began to find similarities among the symbols emerging from the unconscious. These elements are ancient symbols of a mythological, religious, or philosophical nature that the patients themselves were unaware of. The same themes that made up the myths of the past, scorned by Western thought as falsehoods of primitive times. The archetypes would be something like the basic models of behavior. The only existing possibilities, which according to some followers of Jung are twelve main archetypes, which appear over and over again unaltered in dreams, myths, fables, fairy tales, as well as in all the cosmogonies of peoples, and are perfectly well represented in the arcana of the tarot.

Epistemological Foundations

> *Our psyche is formed in harmony with the structure of the universe, and what happens in the macrocosm equally happens in the infinitesimal and subjective corners of the psyche.*
> Carl Jung

It is said that Sigmund Freud himself frequented the Jewish Masonic lodge Benei Berith, where he delved, as a form of play, into the meaning of cards. Later, his disciple Carl Jung legitimized tarot by using it in therapy. Jung was the first professional in psychology to rely on tarot cards to make use of their symbolism. Specifically, the first 22 cards of the deck are of great utility for conducting a psychological analysis of any individual. For Jung, the tarot reflected the structure of a process of evolution of the different mental facets that enable psychic development.

The Jungian model proposes that the unconscious is structured as a symbolic language. Geometric figures, numbers, and colors act on perception, memory, emotionality, intuition, sensation, and the threshold of attention. All these processes are influenced by the imaginary flow present in the collective, which precedes rationality. Jung established that the structures of the unconscious would manifest through archetypes, and these, in turn, through symbolic function, which would represent the way psychic energy is organized into forms. By analyzing behaviors present in nature, we observe that these forms of energetic order give rise to a varied number of symbolisms.

Recent studies have managed to show how crows have mathematical neurons that allow them to understand the concept of the number 0 and use statistics in their decision-making. Similarly, there is a large number of animals that use symbolic function to set patterns of interaction between natural cycles and members of their own species.

Symbols, according to Carl Jung's theoretical foundation, evoke a connection with the ancient qualities of the primitive mind. Moreover, the prevalence of these symbols appears in fairy tales and myths of different cultures.

Analytical psychology proposes in the symbol a function that reduces the tension of psychic energy produced by conflicting opposites (nature and culture). Jung, in this sense, developed a technique called active imagination to connect consciousness with images that arise from the collective unconscious. Carl Jung, in his work *Nietzsche's Zarathustra*, provides an explanation of how the conception of the collective unconscious is not located within the sympathetic nervous system of a specific person but belongs to humanity as a whole. The collective unconscious is inherited just like the prefrontal cortex. Experience is not a particular phenomenon but the phenomenon of life in its entirety. The type of perception that is characteristic of the sympathetic system is beyond consciousness, which implies that it is a universal consciousness located in the body, just as the internet is part of a global connection but in itself does not proceed from a specific computer.

The sympathetic nervous system is the organ that grants the possibility of having similar consciousness. Therefore, it can be affirmed that the collective unconscious is in all the lower centers of the brain, in the spinal cord, and in the sympathetic nervous system as an instinctive mechanism that enabled evolution. As E. Cassirer reaffirmed, man began to cohabit in a world symbolically created thanks to the creative capacity of his spirit. Symbolic forms are the paths followed by the spirit towards the unfolding of its creative capacity. The projection of the spirit occurs through the transcendent function that acts as a bridge of communication between the unconscious and the conscious. But how is this double reunion achieved? Certainly by appealing to the idea of man as a symbolic animal, understanding that at the core of this idea lies a function that allows the reunion both of the different meanings about man and of the different manifestations made over time. The unity that comes fashioned by the origin finds resolution in the unity of the soul and the body, synchronizing with the spirit of the age and depth.

Through different abstract ideas, the symbolic activity of the soul is actualized. In every idea of man, the symbolic function of the spirit is present, which is erected in the principle of the unity of the soul itself. The total energy remains invariant and is at the origin of the Cosmos. According to current science, quantum fluctuations of the vacuum gave rise to the primordial big bang that shaped the dynamics of opposites. From that moment on, the total energy remains invariant and is at the origin of the Cosmos. An important conclusion of the microcosm-macrocosm analogy is that the cosmos can be considered as a whole that is alive and, therefore, has a mind or soul (the world soul), a position proposed by Greek philosophy. New scientific studies point to a cosmological theory that shows that the dynamics of the universe are governed by laws (gravity, quantum) that are very similar to the laws governing neural networks. The universe could well be a giant neural network, capable of learning and evolving. Archetypal psychology, as expressed by James Hillman, focuses on understanding the relationship between the individual soul and the world soul.

In this cosmic order, synchronicity exerts an intrinsic connection with the collective or world soul, encompassing the broader and more transcendent aspects of human experience. Recently, researchers from the University of Ottawa and the University of Rome have presented a methodology for capturing images of quantum entanglement, which has caught the attention of social media users, as the image resulting from this experiment coincidentally bears a resemblance to the yin and yang symbol. The image as such is just a strange coincidence of photon interference.

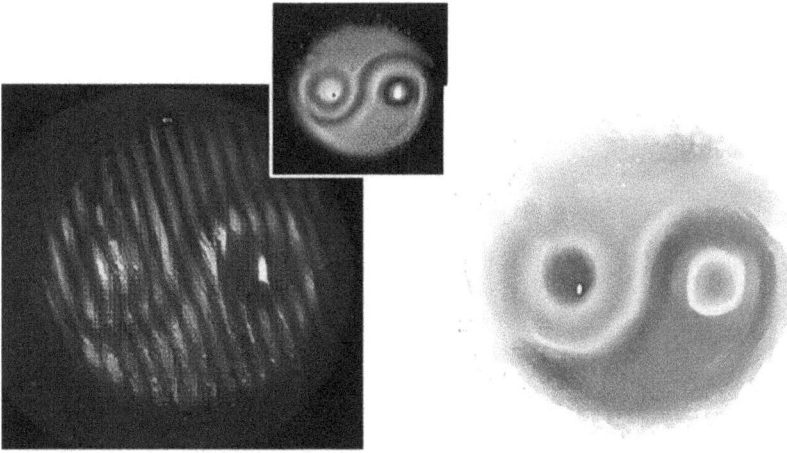

Next, I will attach some photographs by various digital artists who, through their work, showcase the existing correlation between synchronicity, archetype, and symbol, demonstrating the link between the cosmos, nature, and the artistic expression of the human spirit. These images serve as examples of the manifestation of the indestructible energy present in space-time; moreover, upon careful observation, we can discern how through geometry, number, and color, there is a clear relationship between mathematics, art, physics, astronomy, astrology, biology, epigenetics, and tarot.

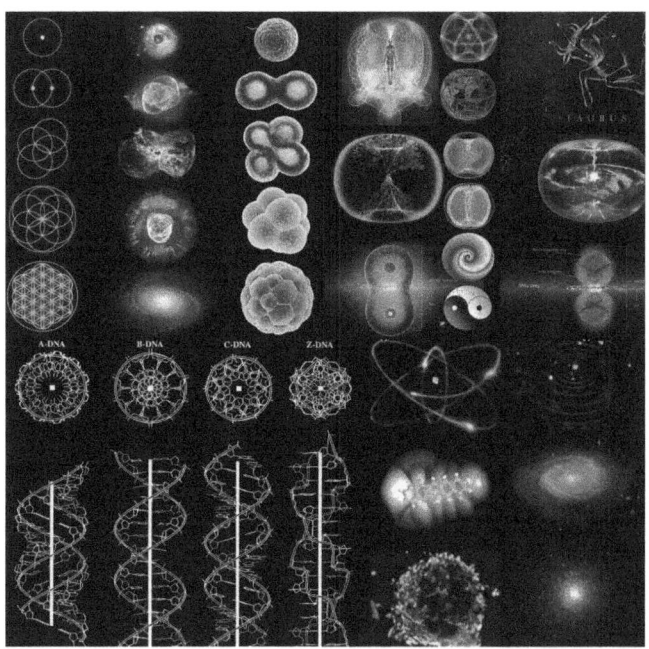

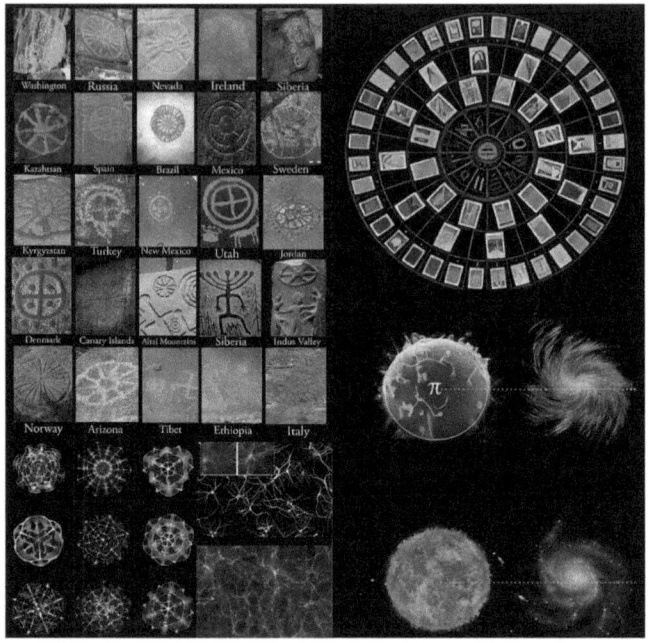

Humans are organically composed of 84 minerals, 23 elements, and 8 gallons of water distributed among 38 trillion cells. Our nervous system has been constructed from nothing with the spare parts of the earth. The cycle of life and death has enabled thousands of thinking beings to be part of a collective journey we call humanity. Life starts according to a set of instructions in the form of a mathematical sequence (cosmic intelligence) hidden in a double helix, small enough to be carried by a sperm. We are solid beings made from fluids and energy. The human experience transforms into biological information and is transmitted through space over time thanks to epigenetic mechanisms.

Our life has been made possible through the recycling of plants, rocks, streams, laws, wolf skins, and shark teeth, decomposed into their smallest parts and reconstructed into the most complex living being on our planet. We breathe the same air molecules as our ancestors, we bathe in the same waters that have flowed through all the rivers and seas of the earth. As Einstein said, energy cannot be created or destroyed, only transformed. The human body uses electromagnetic impulses to generate brain waves and heartbeats. Thermal energy provides heat. Chemical energy transforms food into nutrients that enable the willpower (spirit) necessary to perform extraordinary acts.

In his 1973 book *The Cosmic Connection*, Carl Sagan mentions that humans are made of extraordinary matter: star dust. In our DNA is found the same fiber with which those stars and nebulae that inspire us every night from the infinite sky are woven. Thus, we too are made "to stand out, to shine, and to touch the sky." In reality, this poetic phrase originated in the 1970s. It was the singer Joni Mitchell who, with her inspiring song *Woodstock*, encouraged the generations of that time to shine "like star dust, like glittering gold." According to astronomers, there is gold in our brains. The presence of this precious material in humans would have occurred due to the fusion of stars.

Chris Impey, scientist and professor of Astronomy at the University of Arizona, asserts that all organic matter containing carbon was produced by a very ancient generation of stars; even more, if we consider that all the raw material of the Earth has the same origin, we must assume that 97% of the mass of our body is made up of the material from those distant stars. It's something magical, no doubt. We are made to shine, to gleam like gold, to light up each other like diamond dust. However, if we are children of the stars, guardians of time, representatives of cosmic evolution, why do we feel we do not have a privileged place? Why do we not feel valuable? Why do we feel we are not part of something wonderful? Why don't we recognize our beauty in the mirror? Why do we feel empty? Why have we forgotten to shine? If we are made of stars, why aren't we happier?

With the Big Bang, that initial spark caused a huge explosion of simple hydrogen atoms that gave rise to stars. It was these stars that generated the other elements (carbon, sulfur, iron, helium, magnesium, cobalt, silicon...) that made up inorganic matter, of which life can be considered one of its forms. The random collision of stars that by chance coincided in the same time-space led to supernova explosions. The hurricanes of star dust created galaxies and planets, in a process that has repeated several billion years, until by sheer luck that hurricane of star dust created our planet and made life on Earth possible. Finally, the simultaneity of these events linked by a sense of understanding enabled our species to be aware of such wonders.

Time is an artful illusion of the spirit. In the universe, there are rhythms: the slow revolution of the fixed stars, the ebbing and flowing of the sea, the decline and birth of the living, the ephemeral orbit of the electron in its stationary wave around the nucleus. There are rhythms, but there is no time. Time is an invention of the spirit to make the universe bearable; man needs to measure all things in his image, for this he invents space and time, the clock, and the meter. The symbols of the Sun and the Moon are forms that allowed us to mark the rhythm of existence, to give life meaning thanks to the projection of our consciousness.

Synchronicity and Tarot

The term *synchronicity* was defined by Jung as: "The temporal coincidence of two or more events, not causally related to each other, whose significant content is identical or similar." When a symbol appears in a dream and in daily life, when we think of a person and at that precise moment they call us on the phone, or when we observe a series of recurring numbers that appear in everyday life, we speak of synchronicity, so we can consider it as an order contrary to chance, where a sequence of significant events appears as an interconnection between events that link the internal and external world, and somehow correlate the individual with the world soul.

We can also consider as part of synchronicity all those events that from our childhood are related to our destiny. An example of this was Jung's predisposition towards paranormal themes and Freud's rejection that ultimately led him to develop his own theory. We can compare this force with the concept of the law of attraction or the quintessence of the alchemists. On the other hand, Hippocrates already expressed the idea that there is a sympathy between all parts of the organism, as if all expressed themselves autonomously and strictly responded to a higher order. For Kepler, the universe was governed in all its parts by strictly mathematical laws of nature. Synchronicity would be a geometric principle that occurs in the convergence of the radii of a circumference at a point.

The universe, alien to man and his illusions, rhythmically pulses in a spiral of eternal return and uncertain purpose. The principle of synchronicity proposed by Jung and Pauli postulates that the elements of an improbable coincidence are connected by simultaneity and meaning. If we accept that experiments in extrasensory perception, says Jung, are established facts, we must conclude that, in addition to the connection between cause and effect, there is another factor in nature that is expressed in the structuring of events and that appears as meaning.

The study of ancient oracles from various cultures led Jung to the discovery of synchronicity and prompted him to formulate the theoretical concept of the *entropy of psychic energy* or *libido*, as an analogy to the theory of physics. From this, a very close collaboration between Jung and Wolfgang Pauli developed, culminating in the publication of the book *Nature and Psyche* in 1952, in which they defined the connection between the cosmos and the psyche. This book by Jung is definitively the reasoned and systematic explanation of the prediction of the tarot, or the *I Ching*, methods that assume the possibility of relationships outside of time. The scientific experiment, Jung says, consists of asking a question of nature, excluding all other aspects. When consulting the tarot, what actually happens is an interaction between the individual and the organizing matrices of the universe.

Synchronicity, therefore, aims to discover how meaning can play a role in our physical universe. In this sense, Jung and Pauli presented their conclusions on what they believed was a new principle of nature that would complement the approach of physics. Pauli believed that synchronicity made it possible to initiate a dialogue between physics and psychology, in such a way that the subjective would be introduced into physics and the objective into psychology. These ideas were completed by several followers of Jung and Pauli, such as Marie-Louise von Franz, who considered synchronicity as a manifestation of a much broader principle of "acausal ordering," which is also found in mathematics and quantum theory and represents "acts of creation in time," a sort of acausal connecting principle in our physical universe.

F. David Peat, in his 1989 book *Synchronicity: The Bridge Between Matter and Mind*, postulates how synchronicity could be the missing link between two worlds that seem definitively isolated from each other: on one hand, the immediacy of poetry, music, art, or mysticism; on the other, the discoveries and objective explanations of science. Is consciousness an epiphenomenon of certain complex electrochemical reactions? Is life the product of fortuitous molecular processes? Is the universe an accident or does it have a deep, integral meaning? Synchronicity would be the key that opens a door to the unknown, a window that offers "a view beyond our conventional concepts of time and causality, a bridge that connects the worlds of mind and matter, of cosmos and psyche."

Synchronicities have opened a window towards a creative source of infinite potential, the source of the universe itself, successfully correlating internal occurrences with external events, demonstrating that mind and matter are not separate, distinct aspects of nature but emerge from a deeper order of reality present in the act of observing. Synchronicities suggest that we can renew our contact with that creative and unconditional source, which is the origin not only of ourselves but of all reality.

Genesis tells us: "In the beginning, the earth was formless and empty, darkness was over the surface of the deep, and the Spirit of God was hovering over the waters. And then there was light, and the light was separated from the darkness." It's curious that, despite the thousands of years between Genesis and modern physics, we still lack a definitive explanation of things. Even in modernity, the closest thing to an explanation remains the myth. Both languages have something in common. We do not know why or how it happened, but that's how the Cosmos emerged.

By 1904, the field of physics was already perfectly delineated, and only measurement methods needed improvement; however, Max Planck had formulated his theory, which later led to the development of quantum mechanics. In 1905, Einstein published his special theory of relativity. Both revolutions significantly changed the landscape of physics. In reality, the early 20th century laid the foundations for two different and complementary physics, which to this day have not been unified: relativity or physics of the very large (macrocosm) and quantum mechanics or physics of the very small (microcosm). Both have represented a tremendous advancement in explaining the world we live in.

Jung proposed in his theory how the universe was structured following a sequence of ordering from the general to the particular. Likewise, consciousness followed these ordering principles (archetypal) present in the universe. Jung used the mandala to explain how this symbol appears not only in dreams and myths but is present in the great architectural monuments that characterize man's work on earth. According to Jung, mandalas and the quaternity represent mechanisms of the collective unconscious from the earliest times of humanity on Earth. In "Psychology and Religion," a work from 1949, Jung declared that he had observed quaternary symbols in his patients' dreams since 1914, and they seemed to him representations of God, archetypes of totality. Yet, I cannot help but draw attention to the interesting fact that the Trinity is central to Christian symbolism, though the quaternity is the formula of the unconscious.

Jung's solution, to which he returns in other books, is the following: the Trinity is an incomplete Quaternity with a submerged fourth element. Therefore, the number 3 symbolizes the internal sphere, while 4 represents the external, the way in which libido (life energy) mobilizes towards the interior or exterior, marking the traits of introversion or extroversion in an individual's personality. Meanwhile, unity and duality represent the central sphere where the symbol transforms that energy. These concepts are found in the numerology of the tarot and represent the central dynamics of it as a quality of synchronicity.

The dynamism present in the tarot represents this movement between the macrocosm and the microcosm, between the duality of experience and the unity that arises in consciousness, using the symbol as a bridge between opposites; the real and imaginary are a way of accessing from the macrocosm to the microcosm. Jung defined the symbol as an interface between matter and energy, which shapes the libido in the form of culture, science, or religion. The tarot allows defining the existential relationship of the individual being with universal creation. In its images, we can see reflected the relationship between the interior and the exterior, through synchronistic principles that order the psyche and the cosmos, forming two poles of the same reality. Numerical principles are archetypes that allow structuring reality (time, place, space), in such a way that the situations we approach from the imagination with the arcana transform into situations that change the course of our life and manifest as significant events that shape our destiny.

Astrology and Tarot

> *Man is a gateway through which one exits from the outer world of gods, demons, and souls into the inner world, from the greater to the smaller. Small and insignificant is man; one leaves him behind soon, and then enters again into infinite space, into the microcosm, into the vast inner eternity.*
> Carl Gustav Jung

Jung mapped the psyche, indicating that at its deepest level lies the soul coded through archetypal images that form the collective unconscious. Within the personal unconscious, one would find all the beliefs, habits, customs, and complexes acquired through the context of the era, termed by Jung as the "spirit of the times." The spirit of depth, on the other hand, is assumed as the set of astrological forces operating since the beginning of time, marking the actualizing tendency of our species through different eras. The planets represent the psychoanimic organs of the human being, so we can consider that the entire universe resides within us:

> We are made of Sun's brilliance.
> We are made of pure Moon's emotion.
> We are made of the wondrous Messenger Mercury.
> We are made of Venus's desire and seduction.
> We are made of Mars's action and courage.
> We are made of Jupiter's grand faith.
> We are made of the absolute teaching of the master Saturn.
> We are made of Uranus's infinite inspiration.
> We are made of Neptune's cosmic magic.
> We are made of the flowers that were born in the depths of Pluto.

Everyone carries a bit of the Sun and Moon, a touch of Venus and Mars. The recipe that forms our essence involves, to varying degrees, a certain amount of planetary energy. Everyone has a bit of man, woman, and animal within them, dark and light nuances that are part of a cosmic system that grants us an individual body and a collective body. Everything is energy, everything is mind, everything is consciousness. Each person enters the world with a unique destiny and vocation. And every person embodies many gods worthy of the highest respect. Every human being, regardless of nationality or creed, is made up of humanity, eternity, and divinity.

The Major Arcana are representations of the planets, which in turn have been depicted as mythological gods. They are expressed through symbolic images, and according to Jungian theory, complexes have a planetary archetype or God at their center. Gods are reservoirs of infinite energy that everyone can appeal to, provided they live and think in harmony with them. Within each being exist conflicting archetypal forces with which we must negotiate to free the Self from their effects:

Independent Goddesses:

- Hestia/Vesta, evoking serenity and purity
- Athena/Minerva, intelligence and skill
- Artemis/Diana, solidarity, sincerity, and connection with nature

Goddesses in Relation:

- Demeter/Ceres, giving and the meaning of life
- Hera/Juno, dignity and loyalty to commitments
- Persephone/Proserpina, the ability to integrate experiences, empathy
- Aphrodite/Venus, connection with beauty as an archetype, constant renewal
- Hecate, wisdom in choices, intuition

And the Male Gods: Father Gods

- Zeus/Jupiter, will, generosity
- Hades/Pluto, inner wealth, awareness of immortality
- Poseidon/Neptune, inner knowledge, relationship with the world of feelings

Son Gods:

- Apollo, unity, order, and harmony
- Hermes/Mercury, communication, ability to break circles and toxic situations
- Ares/Mars, nobility, loyalty, courage
- Dionysus/Bacchus, enthusiasm, a deep sense of existence beyond appearances
- Hephaestus/Vulcan, ability to overcome emotional wounds, power to create beauty

James Hillman states:

> From the viewpoint of archetypal psychology, a god is symbolically a mythic perspective, an attitude toward life, and a set of ideas. The gods are within our psyche and manifest in our acts, ideas, and feelings.
> (James Hillman, Puer Papers, 1979)

"A god's form influences our subjective vision so that we see the world according to its ideas." In this sense, Hillman leads us to understand how the other is inhabited by a god that needs to be understood. June and Venus are two different ways of loving, two philosophies of love, derived from different archetypal perspectives that are not always in agreement with each other. Without Eros, there is no thought but tribal logic, calculating and manipulative. Jung would state: "The gods have become diseases; Zeus no longer rules Olympus but rather the solar plexus, producing oddities for medical consultations or disturbing the brains of politicians and journalists, who unknowingly unleash psychic epidemics."

In Jungian psychology, the emotional energy of every complex ultimately refers to an archetype. Indeed, every complex conceals within its core an emotionally cloaked archetype, that is, a universal emotional pattern of the human psyche. In this sense, "it is not true that we possess ideas, but rather that ideas possess us." "We need to know which ideas, which gods govern us so that they do not rule our viewpoints and our lives without our awareness." (Patrick Harpur, The Philosopher's Secret Fire, 2006)

The activation of an archetype is governed by the laws of association: the law of similarity and the law of contiguity. Thus, an archetype is activated in the psyche when an individual is close (contiguity) to a situation or person whose characteristics are somehow related to the archetype in question. Jung created a word association test in which he managed to explain how consciousness is overshadowed by certain contents that emerge with their own autonomy and create a series of disturbances in consciousness, comparing this phenomenon to an eclipse. Following this line of investigation, one of the most popular tests in the field of psychology was conceived, the Sacks sentence completion test. This test helps explore the paternal and maternal complex as well as the individual's own relationship with the internal and external world.

The activation of a complex always signifies a movement of energy in the form of ideas and emotions, clustering around an archetype (mother, father, hero, divine child, god, etc.) that links them together, much like how we group stars into constellations (Big Dipper, Little Dipper) in the night sky. The complexes remain grouped under a thematic knot, through emotionally charged ideas, characterized by having a quantum of psychic energy of an autonomous nature. The more unconscious the complex, the greater its autonomy, and they could well be considered as fragments of the soul with their own will.

Complexes result from the collision between internal and external reality. The core of complexes contains elements from both lived emotional experience and sentimentally emphasized thought, whether positively, negatively, or neutrally. Complexes are a fundamental part of the psyche's makeup. In themselves, they are not pathological; they become pathological the more autonomous they are. When complexes escape the control of the ego, that's when they become pathological.

It is the possession of the ego by these foreign bodies that defines pathology, not their mere existence. Jung compares this autonomous aspect of the complex with the medieval theory of demonic possession that was so frequently used by the courts of the Inquisition. This possessing spirit takes over the psyche, absorbs psychic energy, and manifests intermittently. When possessed by a complex, the personality changes as a whole: voice tones, emotional intensity, and even heartbeats change their rhythm, and the person's will may be usurped by forces operating below the threshold of their consciousness.

Integrating complexes is the main task of analytical psychology. For this, Jung suggests dialogue through images to establish communication between the ego and the complexes present in the unconscious. Many of their manifestations are symbolic representations, expressed in myths and archaic images, present in the world's soul, in the collective unconscious. From this perspective, Jung developed the concept of the collective archetype and the method of amplification. In this way, he could link his patients' delusional fantasies with the mythological representations of ancient peoples. With this mythical amplification, Jung hoped that his patients would not feel so alone and isolated in their delusions, while some conscious integration of these fantasies could occur.

It should be noted that impersonal fantasies also occur in non-ill individuals who are on their evolutionary path, on the path of individuation. Imagination is a gateway to the unconscious. We all have our guests. Some are old friends; others, still unknown strangers. Every being is inhabited by a man, woman, child, sage, animal, angel, devil, king, pawn, jester, magician, explorer, warrior, etc. inside. But there comes a time when we better understand who inhabits our body, who acts in us, and what mental facet we are experiencing in those moments when sadness, anger, jealousy, fear, and insecurities make us feel superior or inferior. When at times in life we feel abandoned, unprotected, devalued, or, on the contrary, when we feel we are saints, heroes, or villains of our own life story, a complex is active in our psyche.

It is precisely the strong tension of confrontation with the complex that presents an opportunity to work through it. It can be said that the possibility of such strong action is precisely an indicator that the complex is starting to lose its dominion over our personality. Then, the ego begins to realize the collective foundations on which its attitudes are based and the alienation this exerts on its personality. With this realization, it begins to free itself from fantasies of power, pleasure, knowledge, and its inexplicable fears. Welcoming these demons and witches into consciousness is where analytical work must begin.

If we wait for the opportune time, as the alchemists did in their work, the little devil and the little angel integrate to show us the truth. We all must negotiate with our gods (laws) and demons (drives) to take charge of our own ego (consciousness). The activation or constellation of a complex is an experience marked by the presence of a strong emotional tone, whether it be love, hate, sadness, joy, or anger. All human beings possess complexes, as they are the structural units of the personal unconscious. In this regard, Jung points out: "Today, everyone knows that people have complexes. What is not known, although it is theoretically much more important, is that complexes can have us."

Similar to instincts, archetypes, writes analyst Anthony Stevens, predispose us to approach life and live it in certain ways, organizing perceptions and experiences to fit a pattern of behavior. This is what Jung refers to when he says that there are as many archetypes as there are typical situations in life. There are archetypal figures (for example: mother, child, father, god, sage), archetypal events (for example: birth, death, separation from parents, courtship, marriage, etc.), and archetypal objects (for example: water, sun, moon, fish, predatory animals, snakes). Each of these archetypes is part of the overall endowment that evolution provides us with as baggage for life; each finds its expression in the psyche, in behavior, and in myths. When the archetype interacts with human experience, the symbol arises as a condensation of the universal and the collective.

Finally, Jung posited that at the top of consciousness lies the ego and the persona, serving as an interface for interacting with the outer world. The persona is the opposite of the person. For this reason, it tends to hide the true nature of the ego, which is the Self, in the shadow. The first complex activated is the ego complex, which begins to function in early childhood. The ego is the center of our consciousness, responsible for our sense of identity throughout life, while the persona is the mask we wear to fit into society.

Typically, the persona performs discreetly well in those contexts, as long as we are aware that it is just a mask, one of our many facets. The problem begins when we fail to make this differentiation and identify too closely with the mask, in which case our growth halts, and we may suffer a disintegration of our identity, leading to a state of chaos and disorientation. The mask allows us to construct acceptable traits in the persona and keep hidden or repressed the traits we consider unacceptable. These undesirable aspects eventually form our shadow, the dark side of our personality, by which we can be possessed at any moment. In those sudden emotional outbursts, the shadow is always present.

When we feel attacked without reason, when something about someone attracts or annoys us excessively, we are seeing the projection of our own shadow. Following Jung's postulates, the unconscious struggles to show itself but is continuously repressed by the ego. Therefore, the shadow is made up of repressed psychic energy that is projected outward. Repressed psychic complexes continue to influence not only the individual but also the collective. According to Jungian theory, the things that are repressed gain more strength.

Jungian psychoanalyst David Cox states:

> The first reason why repression is more bad than good is that it means the loss of some part of oneself. When we completely forget something we have thought or done, or something that has happened to us, it's not just a matter of forgetting that thing, but also rejecting to see that we are the kind of person capable of behaving in the way we did [...]. There may be things that would be so destructive to a man's character if he did not repress them that it is much better for them to remain repressed, and it is true that there are appropriate times for everything, so it could be that it is better not to recover a repressed memory at some particular time.

There are many ways to feed the shadow, the most common being what we know as "striving to be good," because when we identify with a content, we likewise project its opposite. Jung said, "I prefer to be a whole individual rather than a good person."

In the 1993 book *Meeting with the Shadow*, edited by C. Zweig and J. Abrams, a collective shadow is also described, encompassing everything that is collectively rejected. We can observe daily in the news how humanity goes through major psychological crises; racism, discrimination, authoritarianism, terrorism, wars, environmental destruction, senseless murders, and addictions are clear examples of this. The collective shadow is the great creature responsible for the world's misery, an entity capable of possessing men's consciousness and driving them towards the cruelest irrationality.

In World War II, with the rise of Hitler's movement, a regression for all civilization was literally set in motion. For Jung, this was an indication that the god Wotan had awakened. According to Jung, gods, demons, and illusions are names for the inherited inhabitants of the psyche, individually and collectively. He wrote the following on the matter:

> Whether we call them gods, demons, or illusions, they exist and function and resurrect with every generation. They have an enormous influence both on individual and collective life, and despite their familiarity, they are curiously non-human. This last characteristic is the reason they were called gods or demons in the past and are understood in our scientific era as psychic manifestations of instincts, as they represent habitual attitudes and universally occurring thought-forms.

For our modern era, which regards gods as superstitions, the mentioned parallel between Wotan redivivus and the sociopolitical and psychic storm that shook Germany, could at least have the value of an allegory. But, as the gods are clearly personifications of unconscious forces that manifest themselves from the outside, they are considered mere hallucinations, and therefore an unreal phenomenon. Yet, the possibility that there exist psychic contents emerging from the depths of the psyche and possessing men's consciousness would at least have to be addressed as a possible phenomenon, given its effects on humanity's historical events and its implications for the current state of civilization.

It is very likely that the denial of the archetypal methodology and the implicit qualities in the symbol do not allow much progress towards the study of the effects of the shadow on the collective imagination. The myth deals with a timeless truth that never happened, but is always happening. For example, the conflict between Saturn and Uranus represents the eternal struggle between the rational, orderly world that must be preserved (Saturn, consciousness and collective conscience) and the creative impulses that come from the source before time (the synchronistic creative acts of the collective unconscious), but which improbably renews it (Uranus). Time (Saturn) has emerged, from this perspective, from non-time (Uranus), hence Saturn in the manner of a Platonic demiurge imitates eternity trying to perpetuate itself by devouring its children, in the style of its mythical father.

In this example, we observe the archetypal behaviors represented by astrological myths. Thus, Mars evoked the struggle and anger of the god of war, the connection of myths with planets directly establishes a relationship between individual attitude and contents from the collective unconscious. In 1936, Jung wrote an article called "Wotan," warning about the prevailing situation in Germany. Jung had perceived the presence of this archetypal figure in the dreams of his German patients. According to Jung, the ancient god of frenzy and storms was resurging from the mists of the past and mobilizing through the German collective imagination. For Jung, Wotan had also assumed the form of the "Aryan Christ." There was an unresolved dichotomy between Wotan and this Gothic Christianity within Hitler's Germany.

In his 1919 book *Reich ohne Raum*, Bruno Goetz saw the secret of the upcoming events in Germany in the form of a very strange vision. This vision anticipated the conflict between the realm of ideas and life. Jung was in contact with the German Faith Movement, allied with Hitlerism. He knew its leader, Jacob Hauer, who had attended the Eranos Conferences in Ascona, Switzerland, where he had impressed Jung with his talks about racial unconscious, using the concept of the collective unconscious as a basis. Jung had observed that in Germany "an ancient, long-inactive god had awakened, like an extinct volcano."

In his essay "Wotan," written three years after Hitler's rise to power, Jung cites Martin Ninck's exhaustive study on this god. He describes him as the man-beast, the god of the storm, the lord of the dead, a magician, and the god of poets. He also considers his mythical entourage, the valkyries and the morns, as they belong to the significance of Wotan's destiny. Jung continues:

> He demonstrates that Wotan embodies the instinctive emotional part of the unconscious, as well as the intuitive-inspiring: on one hand, as the god of fury and delirium; on the other, as the revealer of mysterious signs and declarer of destinies. Although the Romans identified him with Mercury, properly no Roman or Greek god corresponds to his nature.

When Jung wrote his essay about Wotan, he did so intending to show how his theories on the collective unconscious had been verified, thus explaining the influence of psychic forms on Humanity. In the 60s, Jung wrote a letter to his friend, the Chilean diplomat and writer Miguel Serrano, discussing the difficult modern situation of civilized man.

Jung delved into how our consciousness only imagines that it has lost its gods: "In reality, they are still there, and it only takes a certain general condition to bring them back into the world. The psychic epidemic of Nazism showed the effects of Wotan." Understanding the concepts of repression, the shadow, and the collective unconscious, one begins to see why Jung approached Hitlerism with a hopeful attitude, as it was a manifestation on a massive scale of a potential individuation of an entire nation, which was a clear manifestation of a set of unresolved complexes entering the technological era.

For Jung, the archetypal conjunction revealed Saturn (as the main activating factor) and Pluto (mainly activated, especially by Neptune). When a patient comes to an analyst, they try to bring to consciousness the repressed complexes that are unconsciously influencing their behavior. The same pattern of memories and repressed complexes resides within the collective unconscious of an entire people. Therefore, the possibility of ridding the world of such evils lies in the awareness of one's shadowy aspects. Jung mentioned: "Only the change of attitude of the individual initiates the change in the psychology of the nation. The great problems of humanity were never solved by general laws, but only by the renewal of the attitude of the individual." When we complain about something or someone, we can be aware that we are projecting something of our own. If we manage not to identify with the contents that emerge in consciousness, we can take responsibility for our own conditioning. For this, it is necessary to understand that we all have traumas, fears, frustrations, and broken dreams. Therefore, it is important to free consciousness from the effects of the shadow through the integration of opposites, a process that happens beyond our conscious will.

The greatest danger for a person is to identify excessively with a certain mask by following norms and customs, such as religions or political leanings. A person who plays a specific role is more likely to merge with that role to such an extent that they will lose the vital mobility necessary for evolution. Jung believed that this ego conflict between individuation and separation largely generates our psychic conflicts. The process of individuation allows us to approach the Self by becoming aware of our true essence. In fact, the persona is necessary and acts as a necessary counterbalance for interaction with society. Just as the Anima/Animus are the bridge to the unconscious, the persona is our bridge to the external world. The map of the soul proposed by Jung helps us understand how the tarot moves through this grand cartography of the psycho-analytic realm designed by Jung. If the map of the soul is a plan that allows us to follow a navigation route, the tarot is the ship with which we can sail through the vastness of the psyche.

It is very common to hear about astrology and tarot as a way to know the influence of the stars in everyday life. If we consider hermetic astrology, the human organism is a living zodiac; the planets have movement and progress within consciousness. The solar sign indicates personality traits but also entails a whole complex relationship of forces and energies related to the other planets. The signs they occupy and the geometric disposition they form give rise to the astrological houses. The fire houses represent personal challenges; the earth houses, material challenges; the air houses, social difficulties; and finally, the water houses, emotional learnings. Each arcana is linked to a sign, an element, and a planet. The four Aces of the minor arcana correlate with the four psychic functions: the wands represent the fire element and intuition; the coins represent the earth element and sensation; the swords represent the air element and thought; the cups, the water element and feeling.

The signs of Aries, Cancer, Libra, and Capricorn, which initiate the seasons—respectively, spring, summer, autumn, and winter—are called cardinal. Their influence is related to the processes of creation. In the signs of Taurus, Leo, Scorpio, and Aquarius, the ongoing season reaches its peak; these are the fixed signs, which influence the duration and continuity of things. The signs of Gemini, Virgo, Sagittarius, and Pisces pertain to the end of the seasons; these are the mutable signs, and their influence centers on adaptability. According to Gnostic knowledge, our psyche develops following the same patterns of ordering present in the cosmos. The tendency of our soul is to achieve a universal movement, represented in the astrological mandala:

- The first seven years of life are governed by the Moon.
- The second seven years are entirely Mercurial. Then the child goes to school, is restless, in incessant movement.
- The third septenary of life, tender adolescence, between fourteen and twenty-one years of age, is governed by Venus, the star of love. That is the age of the sting, the age of love, the age when we see life in rosy colors.
- From twenty-one to forty-two years of age, we have to define our life. This era is governed by the Sun.
- The septenary between forty-two and forty-nine years is one hundred percent Martian. And life then becomes a real battlefield, because Mars is war.
- The period between forty-nine and fifty-six years is Jovian. Those with Jupiter well-placed in their horoscope are respected by everyone during this time of their life, and if they do not possess the unnecessary worldly riches, they have at least enough to live very well.

- The life period between fifty-six and sixty-three years is governed by the Old Man of the Heavens, Old Saturn. Truly, old age begins at fifty-six years. From sixty-three years on, each seven-year period will be ruled by Saturn, plus the Moon, Mercury, Venus, etc.

In the Tarot, each card is related to a planet and a zodiac sign. This understanding of planetary energy can be observed in the natal chart and allows us to comprehend the relationship between the zodiac signs and the planets. It's important to keep in mind that each planetary energy can be more susceptible to consciousness or, on the contrary, can remain repressed. The planets have their own quality and shadow, so it depends on each person to reveal their mystery to potentially harness their effects positively. The natal chart reveals a reference point on the internal dimensions where the human being is found from the moment of their birth, thus helping to know the qualities and traits from the different levels of planetary archetypal energy:

- Aries, the Emperor: spiritual authority, mental balance, leadership, mastery of the material and economic world.
- Taurus, the Hierophant: opener of doors for oneself and others, doors of the material and spiritual world. A spiritual guide, a shaman, balance between matter and spirit.
- Gemini, the Lovers: self-knowledge, self-love, great intellect, traveler, internal and external, reconciler with oneself.
- Cancer, the Moon: very emotional, traditionalist, fecundity. Calm, waits patiently.
- Leo, Strength: self-control, mind-body balance, mastery of the Inner animal, overcomes great obstacles successfully.
- Virgo, the Hermit: introspection, closes internal cycles, breaks with the past, closes doors, helps others to close them, heals the past, rational.
- Libra, Justice: communicators to the utmost. Expresses all that is internal through words.
- Scorpio, Death: intense emotions, sweeps away all that is not useful, prepares the ground for changes.
- Sagittarius, Temperance: harmonization and balance of forces, sometimes opposing, distant horizons, philosophical and studious.
- Capricorn, the Devil: professional, responsible, carried away by appearances, loyal, affectionate, risky, rebellious.
- Aquarius, the Star: humanitarian, calm, serene, emotional.

- Pisces, the Hanged Man: sacrifice, daring, has a long-term goal and knows it will be achieved, even if it requires sacrifice and waiting for it.

In tarot and astrology, the knowledge of the collective unconscious manifests through signs and arcana, which are linked to cycles of time and personal life experiences of human beings. Within the cosmic order, the gravitational force of planetary symbols (Sun, Moon, Mercury, Jupiter, Venus, Mars, Sun) are elements that structure the psyche. When we access this knowledge, we can understand which qualities we need to develop, which shadow aspects we need to integrate, and above all, how we can unfold all our possibilities to fully experience life.

Within our inner microcosm, there are various autonomous and self-aware parts of our own inner being. Science demonstrates that in the universe, everything is in constant interaction. At all times, celestial bodies visibly influence each other and also directly influence us—our feelings, our personality, and much more than we can imagine. However, beyond the laws of physics such as gravity and magnetism, there are also invisible influences, hidden from material eyes, as they are of a conscious, soulful, and spiritual nature. The Sun and the Moon have been the most known by all ancient cultures.

At the core of every celestial body, star, comet, or planet, there exist divine intelligences responsible for the evolution of life on that celestial body. These intelligences have been given various names throughout history, such as logos, gods, angels, etc. They represent in the different mythologies of various cultures the spiritual and intelligent principles responsible for the creation and maintenance of the phenomenal universe. They are the elements that update the historical narrative of humanity and civilization itself. An astrological analysis can reveal a deep synchronicity of the influence of the celestial bodies on several revolutions in human history. For example, the last time Pluto was in Aquarius, the French Revolution and the Industrial Revolution occurred, allowing us to understand how the spirit of depth characterizes the evolutionary tendency of the spirit of each era from the beginning of time.

Chapter 2
Tarot as an Evolutionary Path
The Twenty-Two Major Arcana

We are all like this: one part of us lives in the present,
and the other is connected to the centuries.
Carl Jung

The major arcana are our unconscious projections, that is, latent archetypes in the psyche that allow us to develop the full potential of our personality. In this sense, they are mental stages that change as our consciousness develops. They represent all the principles addressed in the previous chapter: synchronic events, numbers, planets, signs, colors, gods, myths, the spirit of depth, and the spirit of the era. All these elements find their symbolic expression in the figures of the arcana, as a representation of the process of evolution of human consciousness. For this reason, each card would suffice to write hundreds of pages, given its complexity and symbolic richness, so we will attempt to refer to the most basic concepts that allow us to have a complete overview of the hero's journey as a path of evolution among the different mental facets that enable man to transcend.

Next, we will briefly explore the general meaning of the major arcana. At this point, it is important to have a tarot deck on hand, to be able to contemplate, along with the reading, the visualization of the images of each card. The most recommended decks are the Marseille and Rider Waite, but any can be of great use. To interpret a card, it is necessary to know its main characteristics and then correlate them with the context of the consultant's question: health, money, love, work, spirituality, projects, travel, changes, etc.

When a card appears inverted or in an incorrect numerical order, for example, 16-21-3, we can assume that there may be poor channeling of that energy or a structural disorder related to the meaning of those arcana. However, for such an assumption, it is necessary to ask more questions and delve deeper with the consultant about those themes. The aim of the method proposed in this work, more than divination, is a scheme to obtain the necessary information to carry out a therapeutic approach. Similarly, when we offer a solution in the form of therapeutic response (metaphorization), we can arrange the cards in order and correctly sequence them, sending a message to the unconscious that, along with the advice provided by the arcana, is a way to structure unconscious disorders.

0-The Fool

Arcane myth: Dionysus or the void. Key phrases: set forth, energy, imagination, creativity, adventure, inner child, stepping out of the comfort zone towards confronting our frustrations.

It represents the hero of time, the innocence of the human spirit wandering the world, the unconscious ego, and all evolutionary possibilities condensed into a single seed. All geniuses who have changed the world were once considered fools. Our true essence lies beyond what we believe ourselves to be. This arcana reminds us of the power of dreams to transform our life. The Fool connects two worlds: the everyday world, in which most of us spend a great deal of time; and the non-verbal world of imagination, which we occasionally visit, inhabited by the characters of the tarot.

The Fool personifies the central core of the psyche, the guiding force, which Jung has called the Self, playing a role similar to our internal locus of control. The World lives in the heart of The Fool, and The Fool dwells in the depth of The World. The Fool moves outside of space and time, connecting the wisdom of the future with the innocence of the past.

The Fool reflects aspects that are present in our being, yet our ego and identity, shaped by socialization, have left out. It represents the same connection with the unconscious that, if navigated wisely, can reveal the hidden treasures of human soul potential; or lead us astray in the psyche's labyrinths if we fail to integrate it. There's always the risk of shipwrecking in it. To achieve our life's goal, we must not let anyone manipulate us; likewise, our happiness should not be conditioned by anything. The Fool symbolizes the soul's constant search and the drive to transform the ego. To achieve this, it's necessary to free ourselves from pain, vices, traumas, complexes, arrogance, and pride. The Fool's action reminds us that we are all part of the same soul present in the world. Its lesson is that we should live with a purpose: to seek meaning in life through spirituality, always pursuing love and happiness.

In the beginning of beginnings, when God created the universe, the spirit floated above the water. Thus, the image of The Fool represents him crossing the ocean as a symbol of our ability to move from one plane to another through the power of our imagination. It's the impulse to move forward with unlimited potential, using the inner senses, shedding the fear of judgment, living without fear, learning to respect everyone's freedom. When we follow the impulse of our spirit, that power leads us towards the realization of paths that lead to integration with the soul of the World.

This arcana represents the spirit of God trapped in matter. Our duty is to liberate it by seeking in our shadow all that causes us suffering and prevents us from evolving. The Fool breaks conditioning and allows us to understand that we left paradise and must return to it as perfected beings through the path and experimentation the journey offers. The path of self-discovery begins by recognizing that we are The Fool carrying a spirit akin to the creative spirit. Once this fact is accepted, you become the beginning: The Magician.

When the energy of The Fool is poorly channeled, we fail to find stability, becoming misunderstood beings, wandering the world without a fixed course, unable to take charge of our destiny. Without a clear purpose, we always risk taking the wrong paths. By not listening to our basic survival instincts, we can get into all sorts of trouble due to our lack of prudence. When The Fool is poorly channeled, we live superficially, not taking anything seriously, and can become perverse beings who obstruct others' paths by committing acts of evil for mere amusement, thus violating, mocking, and hurting others without apparent reason.

The Fool, when poorly channeled, represents illness, paralysis, stagnation, and failure. When we fail to utilize its energy correctly, we cannot clearly observe our surroundings, thus we may rush into danger and miss life's growth opportunities. Misusing this energy incapacitates us to think in the here and now, living with a strong sense of anxiety, wandering between the past and future without taking action in the present.

1-The Magician

Arcane myth: Hermes or the conscious. Key phrases: a beginning to give shape, will, initiative, intellect, formation, planning, effort.

The Magician represents man's evolutionary capacity to be conscious and channel creative energy into culture. It is the evolutionary tendency of our civilization, symbolizing the constant updating of technical and human development. It is the archetype of the craftsman, the artist, and the creator, who through creativity can transform a stone into a sculpture, turn a blank canvas into a beautiful work of art, or transform strings and woods into harmony and melodies. The Fool and The Magician are connected: one is the deep impulse in the unconscious that sets us on the search; the other, the factor within us that directs that energy and can help humanize it. The Magician can initiate the process of self-realization —what Jung called individuation— and can guide our deepest being on the journey to the underworld, to later direct our course through the light of consciousness. The earth reflects the heavens, the external world reflects the internal, the microcosm reflects the macrocosm, and the earth reflects the divine order, thus the Magician comes to represent the ability to act as an intermediary between the higher world and the earthly realm.

The Magician is related to the figure of Hermes Mercury, both in the mystical and in the capacity to communicate, as it is the link between the unmanifested world of infinite possibilities where The Fool dwells and this concrete reality where The Magician acts. The Fool has the capacity to connect with the fertile void, where everything can be (quantum field); The Magician, on his part, can define what he wants to create and where to direct those energies. The Magician is the bridge between the creator and the creation, the instrument that allows the union of two worlds, the unity of all elements, the power, and the connection with the entire universe. He is related to the consciousness that resides in everything, as in the case of Mercury he is the spirit of creation and also the spirit prisoner in matter, he who transforms and at the same time needs to be transformed.

The Magician is immersed in synchronicity and knows that the external world is a result of the internal universe. He represents the origin of the intelligence the soul needs to be born and grow. The Magician reminds us that the infinite power of magic lies in the mind; that with it we can create, transform, and attract into our life whatever we set our minds to. For this, we have all the knowledge and talents of our ancestors, which can help us manage our projects by controlling energy. His table represents the stability from which it is possible to create the reality we desire. His power helps us materialize dreams by controlling the elements (emotions, mind, physical body, and energy). The Magician helps us negotiate, communicate, undertake with enthusiasm, take action using tools. His action allows us to invent, create new paths, use ingenuity for collective benefit, establish a good relationship with money, health, love, and spirituality.

In this card, we see man or the microcosm, the unity, as the beginning of all worlds. The right and left sides of the figure are occupied by the Magician's hands, one of which points to the earth and the other to the sky. The position of these two hands represents the two principles, active and passive, of the great whole. With one hand, man seeks God in the heavens, while he plunges the other into the lower to elevate the shadow unto himself, thus uniting the human, the divine, and the shadowy. This reflects the relationship between the divine, the human, and the material.

The Magician holds the magic wand in his raised hand. Before him are placed the four great symbols of the tarot, which represent the elements that must be mastered and ordered —in arcana 22, we will see these symbols arranged in a cross—. Indeed, we know that the first card of the tarot is completed by the 21st (21 plus 1 equals 22). We then see that, if the first card represents the microcosm, the last will represent the macrocosm. The eleventh card, which serves as the universal link among all the complementary cards of the tarot, will represent the reflected universal current, which serves as a link between worlds. In general, the arcana of the Magician represents the ability to manifest our desires through conscious action and will. In the world of esotericism, the Magician represents all those individuals who have embarked on their spiritual journey or awakening of consciousness.

The Magician teaches us that we live in a world of fantasy or illusion, beyond matter. However, the material world originates from non-physical realities. His wand indicates that cosmic forces are at our disposal. The Magician teaches us that the mind is dual. We have a solar-lunar, planetary-cosmic, divine-animal, human-universal mind. The Magician reminds us to trust that within us lies the connection with the Almighty; we must trust in our strength, fight fear, despair, and the unreal to connect with the reality we wish to live. To do this, we must consciously control our energy to open ourselves to the opportunities life offers. New beginnings allow us to unfold new possibilities to achieve our greatest desires.

When the Magician's energy is poorly channeled, we misuse the elements, living in a state of incongruence without being able to plan the actions we need to take to succeed. Blockages of vital energy, traumas from our ancestors, and illusions of our ego hinder our plans, leaving us unable to find solutions to the most basic conflicts in our life. From this mental state, we become saboteurs, boycotters, deceivers of ourselves and others. We use the power of speech to deceive ourselves, seeking to benefit at all costs. We lie, cheat, and manipulate others, using our magic for perverse purposes.

2- The High Priestess or Priestess

Arcane myth: Persephone or the virgin innocence. Key phrases: heal your unconscious, experience, internal reflection, mysticism, feminine wisdom.

While the Magician was adorned with the attributes of power and placed in the midst of nature, the High Priestess is ornamented with the attributes of authority and persuasion. Within every being exists a High Priestess, a sacred temple, a divine receiver as the image of theoretical intelligence. The Magician creates an effect; the High Priestess invites us to find the cause, through the study of the different laws governing the universe. If we are part of the universe, these laws also apply to us once all information is constantly assimilated. She acts upon the cosmic mind in its aspect of subtle energies that originate matter, this energy that gathers all data in the form of desires, thoughts, conclusions, and sensations. All of this is experienced in the conscious mind and acts as a cosmic ordering principle that transforms experience into biological information imprinted in our DNA.

Everything we think, feel, and do is recorded in our conscious memory and projects into the unconscious, becoming part of cosmic memory. Thus, the High Priestess symbolizes the state of purification that allows us to cut through the ego to unite with the great cosmic mother, the feminine side of God. Therefore, she personifies the Holy Spirit, the Church, the invisible world hidden behind the veil of reality. Her function is to find eternal life through enlightenment, reminding us that we all have the knowledge of universal laws within us.

The High Priestess is the spiritual principle of the feminine. As the great mother, she contains us in her vast womb, where she shows us that polarities are complementary and stem from the same unity. She teaches us that in this three-dimensional plane, there is an apparent duality, a separation, and different forces that seem in opposition, but in essence, are perspectives of the same totality. She is number 2 and represents the duality that encompasses everything, which is represented by the pillars seen in the card. This spiritual feminine aspect—what Jung calls the Anima—is characterized by receptivity and connection with the unconscious.

The High Priestess is the embodiment of spirit in matter, a chaste and pure body, virginal prepared as a chalice to receive the presence of divinity. This chastity does not refer to sexual abstinence or repression of any kind but, on the contrary, a disposition of freedom not to be the possession of any man. She is the woman who is capable of capturing the divine spark within her to produce the miracle of life. In mythology, we relate her to Isis in Egypt, Gayatri in India, the oracle of Delphi, and the figure of the Virgin Mary in the West. She is knowledge, *sophia*, wisdom. She is the power of the Moon, fluid, deep, and passive, that contemplates the mysteries and secrets that the High Priestess can manage and channel.

In the waters of life, two columns of the temple of Isis appear, the white Jakin and the black Boaz, each with four steps, representing the four bodies of sin (physical, vital, astral, and mental). At the top, a Master appears seated between two larger columns. She is inside a temple, facing us, hence the columns are reversed. Arcanum 2 is the High Priestess, the occult science. In the realm of spirit, the One is the Father who is in secret, the Two is the divine Mother, who is the unfolding of the Father.

With the High Priestess, we come into contact with a greater reality of the spirit, the soul, and divine wisdom, emerging from the understanding of cosmic principles necessary to change our behaviors and serve humanity. Intuition and enlightenment arise from the High Priestess to help us free ourselves from suffering. She represents the balance needed to connect with the depth of the mind. This arcana reminds us of the power of the ancestors, the union, and the necessary preparation to conceive of a reality that transcends time. The High Priestess embodies a great mystery: the void. This is deeply felt in both the feminine psyche and the woman's body. Why? The woman has an empty organ: the uterus. It is no coincidence that she experiences sexuality more profoundly: if she lacks a spiritual hint, she empties and becomes only flesh. The void in Spirit is the container, the form of totality, the welcome of being. It is no coincidence that the High Priestess is directly correlated with the arcana of the Moon and the Hermit.

The Inner Voice spoken of in this arcana invites us to connect with our own depth, to dare to make that journey into ourselves that we have long avoided. We must recover the lost memory to remember our mission in this life. The book she holds allows us to know who God is and how the universes work; it contains the hidden codes that God kept for anyone predisposed to cleanse their mind, soul, and body. The book held by the High Priestess represents the hidden mysteries we must uncover about the celestial and earthly laws. Knowing the 72 names of God activates in us a direct connection with the source and allows us to protect ourselves from the 72 antagonist demons of the Goetia described by King Solomon.

It is said that the legend of Solomon's seal developed in parallel within Jewish mysticism, Islamic mysticism, and Western occultism. The myth of the ring is described in various ways as the symbol that gave Solomon the power to command the supernatural. In the Tarot, Hei is the Emperor; Resh, the Sun; Yod, the Hermit. The formula that Moses used to overcome the laws of nature has been hidden in the Zohar for two thousand years. Men who know the deep mysteries of the sacred letters are those who possess the greatest of the gifts the Creator has granted to His creatures. Kabbalah would be the art of reading the Torah, with the help of inspiration from heaven.

When the High Priestess's energy is mischanneled, we become incapable of meditating on our actions, living without regard for others, harming our fellows without consideration, thus becoming insensitive people, closed off, without the possibility of reflecting on our deeds, limited in understanding the sacred principles governing the universe. We completely forget our divine nature. From this mental state, no matter how many verses of the Bible we recite, we lack the power to comprehend what they represent. We remain stuck in patterns of behavior, dogmas, and absurd situations, hindering the opportunity to connect with ourselves. Disconnected from our own interiority, tormented by the past, we find ourselves limited in reconciling the dialogue between the ego and the soul. Suffering and misery arise from this disconnection.

3- The Empress

Arcane Myth: Demeter. Key Phrases: to believe is to create, creative ideas, nature, beauty, fertility, feminine energy.

Let's compare the Empress with her sister, the High Priestess, who is more connected with her internal sensations that come from the divine. The Empress is connected with the external, in her connections with others, with the environment, with the pleasures of the body, sensuality. If the High Priestess is passive femininity, the Empress is action, authority, and feminine sexual power. She is the energy of life, Eros ascending to the heavens from the earth. The Empress is sensual and flirtatious, using seduction as a mystical act to ascend to the divine. Inspired by Venus, she uses her charms with great force, idealism, and youth.

In mythology, she is related to Demeter, sovereign of all nature and protector of all small creatures. She is the great mother who patiently cares for and protects her children. This represents the number 3, related to expansion and creativity. Geometrically born from a third point that is added to the line formed by joining two points, it creates for the first time a body (the triangle), another dimension that opens, interacts, and expands towards infinity (logos).

She represents self-esteem, sensuality, abundance, and prosperity. The Empress symbolizes the impulse towards action, the creative energy that allows bringing our projects to light. This arcana reminds us of the laws of nature, the strength of maternal love, and the power of fertility as a symbol of access to imagination. Thanks to the Empress, we find the ability to visualize ideas and, along with the Emperor, she helps us materialize our desires, concretizing all those projects that allow us to generate abundance and well-being.

The Empress embodies feminine energy, intuition, and abundance. She symbolizes growth and prosperity, suggesting that the querent is in a fertile and productive phase of their life. In the Tarot, the Empress also represents the need to nurture and care for those around us, as well as the importance of connecting with nature and the surrounding world. She relates to a period of growth and development, whether in the personal or professional realm of the querent. She may also indicate the need to pay attention to one's own emotional and physical needs and those of others. Furthermore, she aids in recognizing the importance of maintaining a balance between work and personal life. The Empress lives in the present moment of her life according to natural rhythms. Undoubtedly, through her own power, she has built herself.

The Empress refers to energy and strength. The precise moment, the time that puts everything in its place, her energy refers to vitality, the sexual impetus of youth, the discovery of sexual potential, new pleasurable experiences. Within us, there are two dimensions: spiritual and material, soul and body, a yin part and a yang part, a masculine psychic dimension (Animus) and a feminine one (Anima). Neglecting the shadow of the feminine turns us into prey for the masculine; then it becomes prey for the masculine shadow, thus becoming despotic, aggressive, arrogant (machismo). The same example applies to women. When the Emperor is not heard, he becomes prey to his masculine shadow. Currently, many feminist women become worse than men by adopting aggressive stances, promoted by a society that drives wild competitiveness as the only means to achieve success in life.

In the Kabbalah tree, it is the Empress who connects the Magician with the Fool because she is the sensitive part that unites the conscious with the unconscious; in other words, she gives birth to instinctive understanding. Jung states that the sovereign is such that, after slaying the dragon, he recovered the treasure and re-founded his kingdom in peace. Therefore, the Empress is the active force of maturity, knowing how to manage commitments, confront difficulties, promote peace, maintain order, and grant prosperity. It is this force that allows her to stay grounded (reality) and adopt a realistic attitude—the High Priestess, by contrast, points more to the spiritual world. Becoming the Empress of your life is not the end of the journey; balance is also needed, you must discover and develop the Emperor, you must keep in contact with knowledge (the Magician) and wisdom (the Fool).

When the Empress is prey to her negative shadow, she suppresses the Magician, becomes rigid, authoritarian, despotic, and hysterical, exiling the Fool. The energy of her inner beauty spills outward, characteristic of those who seek only appearances, the vain and egocentric soul, deeply in love with itself—a diva. Her kingdom declines, but she only cares for herself. Her throne is her body, which she undresses, flaunts, empties, obeying her most superficial instincts. Mischanneled energy of the Empress renders us incapable of forming a healthy concept of love. We live absorbed in our image, blinded by vanity, without regard for others, or conversely, live life out of obligation, without desire or dreams, lacking the power of love to find passion in our projects, becoming apathetic, creativity-less to change our situation, unable to materialize our dreams. In such conditions, our life turns into a meaningless routine, confined by surroundings, suffocated by circumstances.

4- Emperor

Arcane myth: Zeus or the patriarchal. Key phrases: manifest your personal power, order, leadership, power, direction, structure, business, masculine energy.

The Empress and the Emperor represent the union of opposites and the manifestation of concrete reality, the interaction between the archetype of Quaternity (projection) and Trinity (introjection), linking heart and mind (thought and feeling). Their joint action symbolizes emotional intelligence, represented by the Chariot card. If the Empress is the maternal archetype, the Emperor symbolizes the father, associated with nature for the Empress and the man-made world for the Emperor, a metaphorical image of civilization carved democratically for progress. The Emperor is the conscious manifestation of order and structures that allow the materialization of desires. Through this arcane, we can establish a relationship with the materialization of ideas, crystallizing in the real world the creative power of the Empress, suggesting that dreams can become reality, but warning of the need to be grounded and rational, utilizing the tools the material world offers to materialize dreams.

James Hillman describes the archetype of the sovereign that represents the Emperor in the arcana. It is the masculine psychic principle within us all: orderly, enterprising, providing stability, embodying order, law, and balance, as captured by the four elements of nature. Ready for action. Without this readiness, one becomes merely political, gossipy, while the Empress turns hysterical, moody, false, mystical, theoretical. The Emperor is the cosmic architect who directs law and order, establishing moral principles within the human mind that allow us to develop a higher intelligence. This arcane reminds us that all work bears fruit. Its action enables taking the necessary measures to build the internal temples and the house of God. Its power allows landing divine ideas. It controls the four elements (mind, body, energy, and emotion). Thanks to this, we can find stability in the planetary order that dominates the material world. This arcane represents governance, inner authority. Its action reminds us that we must be grounded and develop willpower, firmness, and self-confidence to not be influenced by anyone, besides clearly marking the objectives we must achieve.

When the Emperor's energy is mischanneled, we become tyrants, narcissists, selfish, seeking to achieve our plans by force, turning into cruel beings, willing to do anything to achieve our objectives. From this perspective, we lose the compassion and humility necessary for progress on the spiritual path, thus limiting our evolution. No matter how much money, power, or recognition we have, we will live from scarcity because life requires balancing all our needs in symmetrical harmony. One cannot live long repressing guilt, ignoring the voice of conscience, and sooner or later this will take its toll. When imbalance arises, we become unstable, violent, incongruent with our words and actions, lose all that gives us value, and can end up having problems with both internal and external authority.

5- The Hierophant or Pope

Arcane myth: Chiron or the teacher of the gods. Key phrases: communicates divine intelligence, spirituality, authority, power, hierarchy, masculine wisdom.

The Hierophant embodies the correct action and will towards the divine on Earth. The Hierophant or High Priest comes to unify heaven and earth, serving as God's representative among humans. Hence his name, pontiff, for he acts as the bridge between God and men, between the divine plan and humanity. It is the pure and direct communication where one's will is set aside to become the messenger of the kingdom of heaven. To achieve this, he has transcended the ego and transforms into the will of the Father. The High Priestess already accumulates and gestates this connection within her. The Empress expands it with her fertile outburst. The Emperor constructs here on earth and gives shape to this world. The Hierophant goes further: he connects this world with divine ideals, showing us the right actions according to our highest nature.

In this doing, the order of the universe prevails. It leads us to where there are no limits, where the supreme being wants to lead us. The Hierophant dominates the three planes: the spiritual plane, the soulful plane —ethics, morality, consciousness, and order— and the material plane —the perception of receiving order—. The Hierophant represents the five external senses, which we must perfect so that inner wisdom emerges; meanwhile, the Emperor and the Empress represent the material plane, and the High Priestess and the Hierophant represent the spiritual plane —they manage the realm of the soul and impose the dominance of the Self—. Obviously, they pair up to connect them at a practical and psychological level to our internal dimensions, which have both masculine and feminine values: the will (heart) with its feelings (yin) and passions as feminine traits; and understanding (head) with its reasonings (yang) and calculations as masculine traits.

All beings have come to build our temple through the refinement of the spirit. All knowledge must unite into one. The Hierophant looks to the future, indicating he has the capacity to modify destiny. That power lies within us, but we must use spiritual tools to change our life through connection with higher worlds. This arcane joins our intellectual matter with the supra-intelligence, operating throughout the universe.

The mystery of the Hierophant is an alchemical transformation. The divine manifests in us, follows the laws of nature, reflects the laws of the universe, hence the geometric figure that represents it is the pentagram, the number 5. Ether as the fifth element is the opening through which the soul grasps the dimension of the spirit. The power of the Hierophant is to make spiritual reality; indeed, on the tree of life, his path leads from wisdom to love, that is, from theory to practice. The Hierophant symbolizes the key to knowledge for access to the kingdom of heaven, the divine principles that must transform the world through divine will. But what are the keys? Jesus spoke of them as the key of knowledge in Luke 11:52: "Woe to you, lawyers! For you have taken away the key of knowledge. You did not enter yourselves, and you hindered those who were entering." Therefore, having the keys to the kingdom indicates you are responsible for instructing others, educating them, dealing with them, and bringing the truth to light. In this way, the doors of the heart and mind are opened, thus, the inner kingdom.

Within us, we have the ability to create a connection with our inner sage to reflect and connect with the knowledge that allows us to guide and give advice to others. We must learn and teach from the heart, listening to our intuition, purifying the intention of our actions, and acting with faith. To evolve, we must work on all the spheres that make up our being. To achieve this, it is necessary to unite with God and serve His work. We must, more than pray, express our faith through deeds. It is necessary to discover new possibilities and knowledge not found in books, guiding ourselves by ethical principles, honoring the divine hierarchies, respecting the rules and laws that allow us to live in harmony.

When the Hierophant's energy is misdirected, we become antisocial, dogmatic, fanatics of principles we are incapable of internalizing. In history, holy wars and the inquisition were motivated by this fervent desire to serve God from a dark aspect, without understanding that no action arising from a pole different from mercy corresponds to the creator, therefore, when this supra-intelligence is lacking. We can commit irrational acts thinking that we are good by judging others as bad, according to moral principles. These acts, in which we seek to supplant the authority of God, are contrary to divine wisdom, for Christ did not come to this world to judge sinners but to offer his sacrifice as a possibility of salvation for humanity through the knowledge of the kingdom of heaven.

Therefore, we must never forget that our nature is imperfect. For this reason, we should not repress our emotions and impulses, nor criminalize others prematurely; only God has that power, and everyone will have their time to be judged. But that is not up to us. As humans, our greatest duty is not to be victims of indiscriminate hatred and to understand that we are all imperfect. Each being is on a path of personal evolution at their own pace. Respecting the free will of others is the only way out of human suffering and represents one of the fundamental traits of divine wisdom.

6-The Lovers

Arcane Myth: The Judgment of Paris, Apollo. Key phrases: knowing how to choose, relationships, union, love, eroticism, sexuality, passion.

This arcane represents the archetype of choice, free will, the symbol of the harmonious union of two beings, Adam and Eve (Anima and Animus), and the possibility of returning to the lost paradise. The power to recover the responsibility for our own destiny lies within ourselves. This card speaks of a duality and the mind-spirit relationship. It's the unification of two opposing energies in harmony. It reminds us that we can't have everything in life and that we must choose. The conflict between obedience and disobedience is one of the central themes of the biblical narrative. And it is one of the most crucial issues in the individuation process that leads to the debate about sin, guilt, and evil.

In Jungian theory, it is argued that the Anima opposes the persona. The persona adapts to the external world, the world of social conventions and customs. The Anima, on the other hand, is rebellious, unconventional, and inclined towards individuation. The first mention of the Anima in the Bible is in Genesis, with the name of Eve. Adam, who represents the persona, is obedient to the commands of external authority. The serpent, representing the deepest laws of the unconscious, approaches through the Anima. In this drama, Jehovah is culture, and the serpent is nature. The resolution of the story of Adam and Eve and the Garden of Eden comes when Jehovah finally places Eve under Adam's authority. It is proposed that the masculine element is clearly to govern the feminine and the feminine to submit to the masculine; until later chapters where the figure of Christ emerges to balance and restore the lost harmony as a way of resolving the original sin.

The alchemical marriage or the fusion of bonds represents refined desire. In this number, Raphael, the angel of air and communication, is implicated because the lovers are a dialogue. This number implicitly includes the apple, for it is the knowledge obtained from oneself, i.e., the divine fruit through the bond with the other. There is passion that transmutes both into one, they are two poles of the manifestation of a totality. The card of the Lovers represents the decisions we must make to create a future of abundance. To overcome uncertainty, we must choose a path, and this path must be chosen from the heart. The arcane of the Lovers symbolizes the union of heaven and earth, family, marriage, affective relationships, the cultivation of humility and charity that connects us with our spiritual family. Love frees us from suffering, allowing us to achieve fulfillment in every sense.

The arcane of The Lovers tells us that only true love yields enduring fruits. It is a constant reminder that the way back to Eden can only be reached through this path, for which we must develop compassion, communication, and assertiveness as a necessary mechanism to heal our relationships. Learning to love ourselves, others, and, in general, all of creation is an essential step towards healing. For this, it is necessary to love from freedom without attachments, being responsible with our neighbor, seeking to take action in the creation of a better future, committing ourselves to collective well-being.

The Lovers also speak of a strong sexual connection between them that goes beyond instant gratification or the lust of the moment. It marks the deep desire and passion that exist between two beings, as an entity full of affection and commitment. The energy of the arcane of The Lovers, on a psychological level, is the inner struggle we all have to balance the choices between what our head tells us and what our heart dictates: Eros tends to oppress the ego, because this way it does not have to tire itself out thinking, and rushes to the most immediate, which is passion, desire, pure will without motives.

The risk is high when making decisions from a pure heart because you follow emotion without logical reason; that's why we live passion in nature, a bit like animals, a bit like gods. The opposite is when the ego tends to repress Eros: in this case, choices are made only in the head without listening to the heart. In this case, the price to pay could be very high: we become narrow, rigid, tasteless, odorless, without passion, moralistic.

When our ego integrates with its spirit, then passions become authentic, balanced, conscious, we know how and when to let ourselves be overwhelmed by passion without neglecting our own commitments. Whatever the choice, it can lead us back to the correct end. Even the same wrong choice serves us as an experience to learn that the ego kills Eros. But blind love is equally harmful, only the balance between ego and Eros ensures the freedom of the spirit in a relationship that first arises from self-love. Subsequently, this love can be harmonized in a mutual space.

The true choice is to embrace our dual nature and know how to harmoniously integrate duality. We all have another half, which is also a wild, natural instinct; it is part of us as animals. On the opposite pole, we find the purest, spiritual part. Both are part of the being. Only arduous internal work enables us to unify in this dual nature. But for this, it is necessary to exercise free will and make the right decisions. In this card, we see reflected the harmony between the inner and outer life. It speaks of the union of opposites, balance, and overcoming trials. Openness to inspiration, overcoming challenges, connection, and closeness. The lessons of this arcane invite us to be open to love, both to give it and to receive it, listening to our intuition in the search for connection. It is an invitation to be flexible and creative in our relationships, avoiding adopting rigid expectations.

The poorly channeled energy of The Lovers symbolizes the myth of the fallen angels and the expulsion from paradise, in the biblical story. The temptations that come to human beings through the serpent result in the loss of innocence and the emergence of suffering. The negative energy of The Lovers represents a lack of self-love, the incapacity to create a true connection with the other and therefore to commit in a relationship based on respect, communication, and mutual interest. Today's society is characterized by a voracious love born out of needs, lacks, and childhood wounds. The current concept of love is guided by the influence of narcissism and idealism. These forms nullify any possibility of real connection. When the energy of The Lovers does not flow correctly, there is no deep connection at a biological, emotional, mental, or spiritual level, which often makes relationships superficial. Over time love is lost and they become a routine of monotony.

When we are not able to listen to our heart, we fall into infidelities, love triangles, toxic relationships. When the energy of this arcane does not flow correctly, disorders of love occur in the form of codependency, attachments, jealousy, promiscuity, manipulation, romantic idealism, superficiality, family conflicts, incest, transgression of limits, etc. The problems arising from the inability to conceive heavenly love as a sacred force that flows throughout the universe are a clear incapacity to act from the heart, and manifest in the lack of responsibility towards our environment. Wars, violence, environmental destruction, the deterioration of the social fabric, and addictions are the clearest symptom of this lack of love.

7- The Chariot

Arcane myth: Prometheus or the entrepreneurial warrior. Key phrases: evolution in balance, intelligence, will, control, determination, diplomacy, dynamic mobility.

The Chariot arcane represents the power of action and the intelligence of one who has been able to mobilize their will, thoughts, words, and actions in the same direction, in such a way that the congruence between their internal and external world grants them the power to act with intelligence. Its qualities are self-control, self-esteem, discipline, and leadership to guide others. It represents action in society, public image, and the development of inner strength. The Chariot's lessons allow us to overcome fears, surpass vanity, assimilate success and fame, recognizing them as gifts from heaven that must be shared with others. The Chariot controls the four elements, is a guardian and representative of the gods, has the capacity to direct superior energies, unifying directions, setting clear objectives.

This card represents self-control, objectivity, and diplomacy as necessary traits to transmute temperamental states through the use of emotional intelligence. Those who master themselves can emerge victorious in the face of any adversity. When we consciously direct our will towards a goal, we can have the determination necessary to achieve our objectives; otherwise, we will be dragged into irrationality by the energy of our unresolved conflicts. The Chariot is a structure that grants a sequential and ordered direction to all the psycho-animated movements we perform during our personal growth, enabling the capacity for self-regulation. It represents, therefore, the internalization of intelligence in action.

The Chariot does not speak of a vehicle towards the Self, where one can travel both in the external world and the internal world. Every journey we make in the world is a journey towards ourselves. It represents movement and having a clear direction, a decision, a will to achieve, aligning the body, energy, emotion, and mind towards where the being wants to go. It is being on the way to achieving what the soul proposes. The Chariot is considered a seed, like the Wheel, Death, the Tower, and the Sun. It gives us the possibility of new beginnings and renewing energies.

This card symbolizes two opposing powers that must be mastered in order to advance triumphantly in life, without falling into excesses and ruin of one or the other. With this arcana, we achieve success over personal weaknesses and triumph over internal struggles, maturity, and the stellar vehicle that allows establishing a connection with God. The solar Chariot allows going beyond the world of the ego towards the spiritual planes. With it, one can navigate through light and darkness, exercising dominion and power over oneself, developing celestial mandates on earth, transforming reality for the better, becoming a spiritual warrior maker of divine principles.

The Chariot always suggests movement, vibration, a path to embark on towards constant mutation. This constancy is stability amidst movement, stillness in change, peace in war, joy amidst sadness, order in chaos. The arcana of the Chariot is the image of progress. Intelligence mobilized in the dual world is the arcana that puts us on the path, in the progress of existential development. The Chariot is symbolically the driving force within us, and if you look closely, although we say that love is the engine of this world, on the other hand, it is sex that ultimately moves every human goal. Only those who can free themselves from this impulse can direct their love and sexuality towards the same objective.

The Chariot is symbolically a force (motive) that pushes us and leads us to conquer a celestial dimension. It is also a chariot of war, in the sense that we must fight against all the adversities that we will encounter on the spiritual path. In this archetype, we see it in the *Bhagavad Gita,* with the hero Arjuna, or in the hero of Troy, Achilles. They are young warriors who are going to win their soul on earth, through a fierce battle; however, they know that they carry their goal, the soul's maturity. The prince of the Chariot has not yet become king, but faces the battles of a warrior tempering his blood to reign in peace once crowned. There is nothing that limits him in achieving his objective, no matter what obstacle they encounter. It is the punch between the sacred and the profane, heaven and earth, the source of all changes since every change implies action in itself, fulfilling the transmutation of reality by facing reality, changing the act into action itself.

Man realizes that he lives in various worlds and that his role is to unify them, like a plant that sinks its roots into the earth and raises its stems towards the infinite. Man himself has roots that extend into the outer world and direct certain energies towards his inner being. Inside him is another world, or even several worlds, in which he lives more or less consciously. If he is unconscious, he no longer knows who is steering his ship, who holds the helm of his destiny. The Chariot symbolizes the *Merkabah,* the vehicle of divine energy, constantly spinning, harmonizing, balancing, flowing, moving, and expanding in all four directions, always supporting you wherever you want to go.

In ancient Egypt, it was said that the Sun's boat, Ra's boat, had to be created by the initiate, meaning it is up to man to create his boat with the higher teachings he receives from tradition. He must take all the elements to create his boat, his life, his body of immortality. Man comes to this world in the womb of the mother, but it is through the eye that he is fertilized. The eye is the lake or ocean of life, and the boat is the body, the guardian of cosmic wisdom. Man navigates within himself and carries with him a world that must be led to an ennoblement of the Light. If man forgets his purpose, he strays from his purpose and loses his worth.

When the energy of the Chariot is misdirected, we can feel blocked, restrained, frustrated, disconnected, without control to direct our impulses, without the power to think and act intelligently. From this incapacity to control our thoughts, words, and actions, we become overbearing, arrogant, belligerent, trying to exert power selfishly, causing conflicts in our environment. When the energy of the Chariot does not flow correctly, we are dominated by our impulses, leading us into conflictive situations, getting ourselves into all kinds of trouble.

When the arcana of the Chariot influences us negatively, we are dominated by desires; our spiritual power is absorbed by worldly desires for control, power, fame, and wealth, completely forgetting our divine nature. In these circumstances, we are subjected to anger and the need to dominate others, so we become fixated on certain social roles, completely forgetting our life's purpose. From this incapacity to connect with our own interiority arises evil as an over-identification with character traits, masks, and social hierarchies. When the energy of the Chariot does not flow correctly, we are incapable of conceiving a reality beyond the material, becoming cruel to ourselves and our fellow beings.

This arcana is related to what the Greeks called hubris, which was an ego inflation in which, by identifying with the archetype, one could transcend human nature, but also feel superior to the rest and become intoxicated with one's own ego. This is the case of the myth of Apollo's chariot: his son Phaethon, not knowing how to govern his father's chariot due to his recklessness, ended in a tragic fate, as he was punished by Zeus with a thunderbolt. This invites us to humility and the recognition that the Chariot, being a neutral power, can be used for both good and evil.

8-Justice

Arcane myth: Athena or justice. Key phrases: any personal judgment on others is foolish, balance, harmony, fairness, values and principles, assertiveness, laws, karma, action and reaction.

Justice represents personal sovereignty, balance in all aspects, harmony in the cosmos, the search for personal balance, Justice as a mathematical expression of equality, balance, order, and harmony. Only by being just can we reach dignity. To help others, we first have to help ourselves. There is no love purer and more sincere than self-love, therefore we must be just in the order of giving and receiving. Balance is not a goal, but a means to perpetuate eternal movement. True balance is a constant state of progress.

The arcana of Justice represents the order present in the universe, the law of cause and effect, karma, inner justice. Its field of action is related to legal matters, contracts, and verbal agreements. Everything we experience is the consequence of our actions. Its energy indicates that we must act in life with principles and values. We should not wish harm on anyone; we must conduct our path being upright, just, respectful, honorable. When we acquire the ability to self-regulate, we can direct a company with the power of discernment.

The arcana of Justice reminds us that we should not carry guilt; we must let everyone be responsible for their learning. There is a divine plan that seeks to harmonize and balance individuals within societies. To transform the world into a fairer place, we must treat everyone equally. To act consciously, it is necessary to constantly monitor our thoughts, listen to the voice of conscience, and act justly. This card also represents maternal authority and the principles that govern our belief system. To evolve in life, we must be fair to ourselves and others.

The action of the Justice arcana helps us balance the masculine and feminine, the mind and heart, to make a correct judgment. Justice and legal processes have always been closely related to divinity, considered to be part of the demands that God imposes on men. However, if we recall the act that allowed humanity to access salvation, it was an act of sacrifice: Jesus was judged as a thief, and his crucifixion was the payment for humanity's sins. This act represented the rescue of the soul, trapped in the depths of shadows. This is a reminder of how justice, when exercised from reason, can be used conveniently. Only divine justice emerges from mercy as a mechanism to elevate the condition of the most needy. Humility and compassion are the fairest ways in which, regardless of our position, we are in conditions of equality. No one is superior or inferior; in the eyes of God, we are all equal.

When the energy of Justice is mischanneled, we manifest imbalance in our life. Blinded by dogmas, we become inflexible and authoritarian, thus tending to polarize our thinking, becoming cruel due to a lack of discernment in our reasoning and actions. When we are intolerant of others, paradoxically, we act wrongly. Often, when the energy of Justice does not flow correctly, we can become too demanding of ourselves without considering our limitations, thus idealizing concepts that make us suffer. From this excessively rigid internal demand, an unconscious impulse to punish ourselves for not being perfect can arise, leading to the belief over time that we simply do not deserve to be happy.

Justice is often blind, as it acts from thought. Only when intuition and feeling are balanced can we feel good about acting correctly. Justice is not only about punishing the wicked but also about assisting the unprotected, protecting the weak. Helping to reduce the world's inequalities is an act of divine justice. True clarity for judgment arises from reasoning with the heart. When justice is devoid of enlightenment, it becomes a blind observer of the law that borders on fanaticism. Often, legal loopholes are exploited to carry out actions that harm people with little knowledge of legal matters, therefore, legal and divine justice often take different paths. It is well known that there are innocent people in jail, or that people have been condemned for stealing a bit of food, while white-collar thieves and criminals who destroy the environment evade justice thanks to the authority conferred by money.

9-The Hermit

Arcane myth: Saturn or the Lord of Time. Key phrases: the ability to silently observe who we are, the power to self-transform what we are not, meditation, introspection, self-knowledge, wisdom.

The Hermit, preceding the Wheel, has the function of seeing where his own spin will stop to transcend one cycle and move to another. The Wheel is fast. The Hermit makes a balance (Justice precedes him). His staff will be inserted and will propel him forcefully into another story. The patience and wisdom that all our ancestors and elders have are given as a result of multiple conflicts they had to face in the past. The Hermit, in this sense, reminds us to stop and keep silent to listen to our inner voice, which often gets lost amid the noise of the rest of the world. Experience must be transformed into knowledge; knowledge must be flexed to a point of introjection; reflection should prompt us to modify our behavior; finally, with a bit of luck, wisdom arises when we act congruently with the knowledge derived from experience.

The Hermit advances amidst a dark night. As he traverses this great shadow, he illuminates his steps, reflecting the process of fertilization, gestation, birth, moving from the abstract to the concrete, from the minuscule to the great, or perhaps the other way around, from the macro to the micro. The Hermit teaches us to navigate in the darkness, hand in hand with our shadow, while holding the focus of a small flame, bringing forth a third lesson: we can only know the shadow that effortlessly arrives at our enlightenment (understanding), and thus, knowing the shadow consists of accepting our inability to encompass the entirety of its mystery. However, by observing in a single focus, what is manifested before our gaze will be as immense as what we can comprehend. Because, just like a starry sky, with a single atom, we have the key to access the entire helix of our cellular library.

The Hermit represents the wisdom gained from life experience, which allows us to discover the things that are truly important. He is the inner master carrying the light that illuminates our steps towards the inner path, through which we can develop our soul. The Hermit is the activator of divine energy in our life. But this enlightenment can only occur through the path of austerity; we should break the silence only if our words have a positive effect. It is preferable to have peace than to be right. We should not argue over superficial matters. Only prudence will allow us to overcome difficulties without straying from the path. The Hermit brings the energy of heaven down to earth. It is the action of God's pure love. Thanks to the union with the father, we all can access inner wisdom, culturally represented by the popular knowledge of grandparents and great sages, who have brought enlightenment to humanity.

This arcana allows us to understand that we must free ourselves from mental schemas. Only by opening our minds can we understand from the heart. The supreme truth cannot be comprehended through logic. It must be felt, not reasoned, to let intuition flow. To heal, we must first illuminate our wound; to act with prudence, we must first cautiously observe our surroundings. Only then can we make the right decisions. The Hermit symbolizes a period of introspection and reflection to analyze life experiences and conclude cycles. It is personal growth, which can only come through personal contact and the integration of light and shadow. Like the Hermit, there often comes a time in life when we need to slow down and go inward to find our life's purpose. When you withdraw to explore the mysteries of your inner life, you become open and innocent like a child. On the other hand, this process also demands the absolute mastery of the higher side of personality over passions and instincts. It is necessary to find common sense, sensibility, caution, and all the rational and reflective values. Its action exalts introversion and inner life. Through a hermetic life and renouncing material pleasures, one can know oneself and achieve spiritual peace. Such a task becomes impossible amidst the hustle and bustle of everyday life. The straightness of the staff symbolizes justice in the face of errors all humans make. The Hermit represents the ability to use knowledge as a tool to reach the highest levels of consciousness.

Jung refers to him as the archetype of the wise man, the seeker of truth. It is that inner dimension that takes us away from the mind, towards the realm of the soul. But many, in confusion, not knowing what the soul is or where it is, search for it fervently outside, in religions and philosophies, in books and social standings. Eventually, the identification with the mask of luminous beings projects outside of us the gateway to the internal reality. Therefore, the Hermit reminds us that we must seek integration with the soul of the world through the recognition of our darkness, which we must find in silence, in the cultivation of dreams, in the recognition of symbols and signs that indicate the way.

When the energy of the Hermit is poorly channeled, we isolate ourselves from human connection, fall into confusion, into great voids, not knowing where to go, lacking light, becoming depressive, pessimistic, lazy, arrogant, incapable of following ancestral wisdom. When the Hermit's energy does not flow correctly, the inner journey can make us so detached from reality that we feel alien to this world. Therefore, instead of transforming into a solitary sage, we become a grouchy old person, a neurotic, due to the presumption of having absolute truth; we turn into a false mystic who believes themselves to be superior to others. It is here where we confuse fireflies for lanterns. In this mental state, it is not the inner voice that guides us, but uncontrolled imagination that drives our visions. Eventually, the light that was supposed to illuminate our steps ends up blinding us, diverting us from the path of spiritual progress.

10- Wheel of Fortune

Arcane myth: the Moirai or Fates (the spinner, the allotter, and the unturnable).

Key phrases: involuntary change, learning to enjoy the here and now, destiny, life cycles, changes, acceptance, evolution.

The arcana of the Wheel represents the law of cycles and changes. In nature, the universe, and the life of a human being, there is a continuous movement, driven by cosmic forces beyond our control. Life and death remind us that our earthly existence is temporary; but our soul is eternal energy. Our duty in this life is to flow with the changes, to recognize that in every end there is a beginning, that in all chaos there is a cosmos. Evolution and fortune depend on our ability to recognize our mental patterns. Within us exist both animal instincts and spiritual impulses. In the world, matter and spirit combine all those experiences that enable us to grow. The Wheel indicates that we must integrate the internal with the external, that we should contemplate the four elements as a path towards harmony between body, mind, emotions, and spirit.

The only certainty in this universe is change: the good can turn bad and the bad can turn good. For this reason, it is necessary to develop a neutral attitude towards events we consider positive or negative (blessings, curses). We must remain neutral towards praise and insults. To face changes in life, it is necessary to recognize the causes and effects of our words, thoughts, and actions. We must be unflappable and understand that, although we may not comprehend it, everything has a reason. To evolve, it is necessary to navigate through trials, navigate through difficulty, face situations, and learn from our failures, so as not to repeat the same mistakes. Our mission in this life is to rise beyond our beliefs, to unite with the spirit that dwells outside of time-space. Within us, there are different mental states, so life's situations push us towards constant learning through the different life cycles (child, adolescent, adult, elder). During these vital cycles, we have to develop a series of traits and qualities necessary for our evolutionary path.

The Wheel, in addition to being related to the circle as a perfect figure, shows us that we must remain stable while we move constantly; a conviction so powerful that it acts as a dike to the sea of superfluous ideas and thoughts that invade us from morning to night. The Wheel, therefore, embodies two universal principles: everything transforms (spins like the wheel) but there is always something stable (the center of the wheel, its pivot). A bit like us: our soul remains the same, from the innocent child to the wise elder, the essence of being remains. We must cultivate a flexible attitude and openness to change. The only thing we can control are our intentions and reactions to life's events.

When the energy of the Wheel of Fortune is poorly channeled, we come to believe that we have bad luck, that we are cursed, bewitched. For this reason, we feel paralyzed, in chaos, without joy or strength, losing the power to act or think about change. When the energy of the Wheel does not flow properly, we lose vital mobility and lose faith in our ability to act. The Wheel marks the cycle as a symbol. Everything in life completes a cycle, the eternal return. Everything comes back if it does not evolve. Everything repeats without transcendence. Often there is a risk of falling into the whirlwind of the Wheel, characterized by fatal routine. We are the ones who turn it with our actions, repeating the errors over and over without the possibility of understanding, believing it is our destiny to suffer and live in scarcity, repeating negative patterns without being aware of the causes of our mistakes. For this reason, we lose hope in humanity and in ourselves. From this mental state, we completely forget that we always have free will at our disposal; with it, we can mobilize our resources and change our destiny whenever we wish.

11- Strength

Arcane Myth: Hercules or healing irrational fears. Key Phrases: becoming realistic, purity of intention, overcoming, determination, self-control, resilience, mental power.

The spirit dominates matter, intelligence overcomes brute force, the inner strength allows sustaining an action over time, the control of the shadow grants us the ability to subdue the impulsive aspects of our personality. This card represents internal forces, struggle, courage, and character, which play an indispensable role in facing difficult times. However, it is not always about an active fight. Patience is the determining factor to endure battles, it is courage and faith that can overcome obstacles, conquering the objectives we set for ourselves. Strength symbolizes the ability for self-mastery and control of instinctive energy. It is the ability to turn aggressiveness into willpower. It represents taming through the word of God, gentleness, and understanding of our nature.

We all have within us a divine impulse that allows us to master passions and instincts through awareness, without repressing or denying our wild nature. Thanks to this ability, we can overcome our weaknesses and obstacles, through the strength of the spirit, which allows us to solve problems through dialogue, finding clear answers to the challenges we face. Strength represents the feminine part of God, the pure love capable of transforming savage animality. In the history of humanity, the development of civilization was possible thanks to the alliance of humans with certain animal species (horses, cows, cats, etc.). Specifically, the domestication of the wolf allowed humans to overcome their biological limitations in the midst of a hostile environment full of dangers. Thus, the special alliance forged with the dog conferred on this being the role of the guardian angel of the human soul. This is expressed in different mythologies. From a medical point of view, literally interacting with a dog protects our heart, thanks to the hormonal secretion of oxytocin, so evolutionarily the possibility of controlling and dominating our wilder side represents one of the biggest pillars of evolution. Some consider the dog as God's representative on Earth.

When we learn to manage external strength, it projects inward; but here it becomes gentle, calm, constant, a breeze that turns mountains to dust, a drop that erodes stones, a seed that blooms in the desert soil. This is how libido is transformed through the symbol. If strength does not keep the lion in balance, then it prevails, and we become prey to our passions and instincts. When earth and fire are in balance, the earth sprouts, hence our energy rises (the air, the breath of the lion with its mouth open). Only this breath or air, being balanced and healthy, can generate rain, like the air in the sky; therefore, water and emotions. It requires great power to love without judging, to be compassionate and humble with everyone and yet face any difficulty with courage.

Strength is a virtue that arises from working with one's own shadow, from the integration of those parts that make up the totality of our being. Thanks to this, we can connect with our cosmic essence to achieve our greatest objectives, having at our disposal an unbreakable willpower. Power arises from knowing how to direct our energy consciously. The brute force with which humanity has evolved has been entirely masculine; therefore, the feminine is a type of energy that balances and enhances personal power. Often strength is needed not to act violently, not to explode in anger, not to say what one thinks, not to harm others, not to get angry or boast. How much strength is needed to tame one's own ego and not to give oneself too much personal importance... Strength is never enough to control our wildest instincts. This kind of fortitude is a quality not only physical (muscular strength) but above all spiritual (the ability to endure pain, suffering; the ability to withstand time with perseverance, etc.). It's no coincidence that the tree of life is found parallel under the Empress, it is her reflection, her inner soul strength.

The beast she tames is the earth's instinct, materiality, because that is the indispensable condition to then be able to transmit that strength to the higher planes and maintain the balance of opposing forces: light and shadow, joy and pain, unconscious and consciousness, etc. But the lion is fire, while she is earth. This contrast creates deserts, a way for people to enter into spiritual life. All great thinkers, enlightened individuals, geniuses, started in the desert (even sometimes physically, like the hermits who go up the mountain to reach the desert of the heart and mind).

Strength teaches us to recognize the enormous energy we have. The way to use it consciously is by guiding it towards creativity, towards the construction of what we desire in our life. It reminds us that our instinctive side is a source of vitality, beauty, inexhaustible energy, and provides us with the resilience needed to overcome obstacles and solve difficult situations.

When the energy of Strength is misdirected, we become weak, insecure, insensitive, explosive, abusive. When our will is subjected to our impulses, we lose control at any provocation. This is reflected in a volatile personality, dominated by anger, desire, envy, lust, etc. These are resources of the ego to deviate us from the light and enslave us in its domains. The only truth is love. When you allow passions and excessive emotions to condition your life, they dominate your world. When passions and desires lead you to voracious consumption, against reason and even more so against the spirit, true satisfaction is not manifested. All this translates into imbalance and emptiness, which evidences a loss of energy, where irrational passions, rigid positions, and obsessive possessiveness predominate. In any case, it is a situation of compulsive struggle to satisfy illusory desires, to connect with symbolic needs invisible to the ego.

This translates as the unconscious impulse to restore the connection with the soul of the world. From this state, the existential voids of today's society arise as an inability to connect with our true needs.

12- The Hanged Man

Arcane Myth: Prometheus or self-discipline. Key Phrases: knowing that we are a solar being whose purpose is to bring light into darkness, confrontation, self-detachment, sacrifice, patience, compassion, empathy, altruism, courage.

The Hanged Man refers to duty and renunciation, the stopping of passions and instincts, the non-identification with mental projections. Responsible for his process, he prepares for the death of his ego, from which the solar consciousness will emerge through sacrifice. The hero voluntarily hangs by his foot, fearlessly, with serenity to be able to observe the path from another point of view, to be motivated and predisposed to change. He will let himself be carried away by what happens to him internally. This arcana indicates that we must die on the cross of tribulations to shine with the glory of divine understanding. At this level, the human being has climbed the six rungs of the tree, therefore having to learn to know its six levels: physical, emotional, vegetative, mental, causal, and spiritual. When reaching the sixth level, the spiritual, one no longer has personal will, but acts according to divine will. This symbolizes that at this level of consciousness the human being identifies with divine consciousness. The Hanged Man stops seeing bodies and starts seeing souls and energies; begins to connect face to face with divinity in everything around him and starts to see the world upside down, a world governed by ego and superficiality where the Hanged Man contemplates reality from the depth of the soul.

The Hanged Man represents the ability to reflect on our actions, face destiny, and accept circumstances. Its action tells us that we should not fear pain or pressure if we wish to evolve—that it's necessary to accept sacrifice, renounce our own ego, and detach ourselves from everything that ties us to the earth; only then can we achieve the realization of the soul. Life is a duality in a world lived from the ego. Prioritizing the reality of the spirit is an act of rebellion. To harvest, it is necessary to sow; to receive, we must first give, and above all, be willing to devote ourselves to others through unconditional love. The Hanged Man reminds us that patience, meditation, and inner search are the elements that will allow us to undergo a profound change. Only then can we break free from stagnation and liberate ourselves from the blockages that tie us to suffering. There are moments in life when we must remain hidden, inaccessible to others, to transform into a new being. The image of this card indicates that its head is in the roots, representing ancestral memory, hidden knowledge accessible only to those willing to renounce everything.

The arcane of The Hanged Man represents the archetype of the hero. It is a symbol of entrance to another dimension, where things, seemingly upside down, acquire a different perspective: the view from below, from the unconscious. Christ was also hanged. It is a passage to an alternative psychic world. They are awakened, conscious individuals who are often considered inadequate by society, insignificant, and therefore guilty (asocial), hence their sentence to live hanging from the soul in an upside-down world where all those who live from the ego are competitive, intelligent, and cunning. The executioner's gaze is the intuition of the unconscious and the instinct of the heart. In myths, it is represented in the person of Prometheus, condemned to the darkness of a slow and never-achieved death. It is the descent to the spirit and the suffering of clairvoyants and enlightened individuals, people who feel they die every day. Like Prometheus, the Enlightened in some way have stolen the fire from the gods, the mystery of life; but those who understand suffer. Remember, in the myth, it was Hercules who saved Prometheus.

The image of Prometheus is a symbol of that part of us that has the foresight to understand that it is necessary to go against the current to find the origin, clarity, or truth at the source. It's an inevitable crisis. Western mystics call it "the dark night of the soul." In The Hanged Man, it is the ego that is finally turned upside down: it does not die, but it no longer has the advantage of always standing upright, it can no longer rise above the spirit. The Hanged Man is, therefore, the renunciation of the ego, a sacrifice that grants light and peace—in fact, Prometheus, once freed from these chains, becomes immortal. This figure of The Hanged Man is very particular. Generally, while he is hanged, gold coins fall from his pockets, representing the material dimension that is left behind, abandoned. Spiritual gravity leads to detachment. Here, however, the coins have another symbolism: they are words, truth, beliefs. When you go through a spiritual awakening, you also lose the sense of things and even of life, but you learn to appreciate what is truly valuable in this world, to clearly differentiate the price from value.

When the energy of The Hanged Man is misdirected, we do not accept others, we live trying to change them; therefore, we live frustrated, victimizing ourselves, feeling inferior, paralyzed by circumstances, we judge and project our own conflicts onto others. When the energy of The Hanged Man does not flow correctly, we feel misunderstood, we do not accept our true nature and fall into positions where we seek the approval of others at any cost, losing the value of our own individuality along the way. From this mental state, we live angry, frustrated, dissatisfied, full of reproaches and feelings of guilt that lead us to harm and sabotage ourselves, blocking our own access to our soul through the wrongful action of our own ego. When we suffer mental blockages in our life, we are not able to act in any scenario. This generates powerlessness and uncertainty. We become victims of external factors. Stuck in our lack of progress, we project feelings of resentment towards the world and others.

13- Death

Arcane Myth: Hades, Lord of the Underworld, or drastic change. Key phrases: self-transformation ability, change is life, flowing with the cycles of time, rebirth, sowing spiritual feelings, lightening the load, moving forward.

The Death arcana represents the learning that arises from difficulties in all pain, in every illness. There's a hidden lesson that enables our evolution. We must learn to empty ourselves, connect with the deep unconscious, and flow with the energies that govern the universe. Death is as important as life. We must honor the memory of all those who have passed away by living fully, cutting ties. Death reminds us that we must harvest, gather the fruits, and move on, stopping to see things superficially, internalizing the true value of everything. We must be willing to leave behind old thought patterns, to let our ego, pride, vanity, and personal importance die, remembering that we were born to die. Therefore, the only thing we will take with us are the memories we leave in the people we love. We must manage fear, develop an awareness of death, and not be swept away by irrational violence. To love life is to accept it as a passage to another plane of existence.

What frightens humans the most is falling into a crisis because it reveals everything that is unresolved: dependency, need, lack. Nothing deep can be resolved except through a crisis, as it itself contains the elements of healing. In Jungian theory, crises are a necessary part of our transformation and should be faced as part of the path towards psychic integration. Every crisis is a growth opportunity that allows us to go beyond our comfort zone. Death symbolizes the worn-out parts of our psyche that we also find painful to leave behind. The alchemists already knew this reason. Thus, the skeleton also symbolizes the need to lose the identification of oneself with one's body.

They also recognized the need to make conscious the conflict between the spiritual man and the natural man. Jung says, "By doing so, the alchemists rediscovered the ancient truth that every operation of this kind is a figurative death, which explains the violent aversion that everyone feels when they have to pass through their projections and recognize the nature of their Anima."

Death takes care of returning all nutrients to the earth when we are finally ready to transition to the next plane of existence. Man is born biologically, develops symbolically, and finally, when death appears, there is the possibility of being reborn spiritually. When everything seems to be against us, death reminds us that nothing else matters except its touch. All spirituality is a struggle that the human being creates to combat death, to solve this enigma that ends all sense of our existence; however, we can all overcome death through spiritual rebirth, which is why it is important that all our actions in life are directed towards the recognition of that essence that connects us with a reality beyond physical existence. Nothing is created or destroyed; everything is transformed. The universe is governed by interconnected cycles where the decay of the dead serves as fertilizer for the living.

Thanks to Death, time cycles can allow space to renew itself again and again. Without it, our own life would not be possible. Therefore, through the action of death, we have the opportunity to conceive the great variety of beings that have nourished the advancement of our civilization. Every being that has contributed its consciousness to humanity is part of a great legacy. We are all part of the collective journey of the soul, as part of the spirit that dwells within each being. Death is intimately related to wisdom. People who have had near-death experiences undergo radical spiritual transformations that forever change their way of seeing life. Material and egocentric positions lose meaning when we accept the changing nature of the universe. The archetype of death and life are symbolically united, representing the void from which we emerge and to which we will finally depart, the tribute of pain for love, and the connection with the cosmic forces that regulate time through space.

When the energy of Death is mischanneled, we experience losses with great attachment, thereby remaining tied to suffering, grief, disillusionment, and destructive emotions. In this mental state, we are unable to accept reality, to flow with changes, to move forward quickly, and to live fully. When we lack awareness of the eternity to which our soul belongs, we become ghosts unable to transition to the beyond, fixated on the earthly dimension. When the energy of Death does not flow correctly, we are unable to transform. We live so attached to life that fear leads us to commit terrible acts. Paranoia and mistrust prevent us from living fully, thus we remain immersed in an eternal place of perdition, unable to flow, advance, or evolve.

Resistance to change, a result of attachment, only produces pain and anguish, while hindering true freedom. When something is changing and you're unable to prevent it, but also unable to accept it, everything becomes heavier: circumstances, thoughts, emotions turn into a burden. Attachment, fear, and a sense of emptiness cloud the consciousness of those who refuse to see that a cycle ends and things change. However, despite this denial, we cannot prevent what must end from ending. We cannot hold on to what must leave; we can only delay it or not see it. This card is often associated with pathologies such as grief, suicide, eating disorders, or life crises.

14- Temperance

Arcane Myth: Archangel Raphael or spontaneous healing. Key Phrases: moderation and adaptability, Higher Self, calmness, stability, serenity, sensibility, self-regulation.

After death comes renewal, the pact between heaven and earth that offers us the opportunity to enter the higher realm of consciousness. Alchemy means to combine, mix, balance, integrate opposites, disintegrate the unnecessary. When we achieve congruence between feeling, thinking, and acting, we develop inner vision. The process of inner work allows the recovery of the balance of vital force through an energy movement across all functions and their intellectual, emotional, psychomotor, and sexual centers.

The Temperance card is an archetypal force that complements the arcana of Death. Temperance is responsible for crossing souls to other planes of existence. Its action allows us to move from the dream world to the waking world. It represents the vital breath, the incarnation of the soul in the world, the unification of subconscious lunar energy and solar consciousness, which allow us to receive the necessary information to correct our life. It represents chastity, but not as a repression of sexuality, but as a playful libidinal use. Sexual energy roots us to the earth, which is sacred energy, and to the spirit, which is divine energy. When these forces unite and travel through our energetic points, they allow us to advance, create, and materialize our desires in this material plane. Through this connection, we can attract energy to ourselves to transmute, resonate, and create a connection with the creative energy present in the universe.

The thoughts and feelings of most people consume the majority of the energy from the first three energy centers of the organism, which are related to survival mechanisms: procreation, consumption, and the fight-or-flight response. Meditation exercises allow the heart to open so that the energy stored in these first three centers can flow towards the higher centers. Each energy center of your body has its own biological composition. They have their own glands, hormones, chemicals, and individual mini-brains (a set of neurons). When consciousness activates the neurological tissue, it creates the mind.

To better understand your body, we must imagine that we are a pyramid or a building: at the base or first floor is the physical body and, at the same level, the energetic or electromagnetic body; on the next floor is the emotional and mental body; finally, on the last floor is the soul. Most of that energy stored in the body has to be released and returned to the brain. The cerebrospinal fluid is made of proteins and salts in a solution, which have a negative or positive charge. When you begin to inhale and draw that cerebrospinal fluid towards your brain, you accelerate those charged molecules. With breathing and meditation exercises, all that energy from those lower centers begins to move towards the brain. When that happens, suddenly, all the energy you use in a stress response, instead of being chemically released into the organism in the form of cortisol, is being drawn into the brain. All that energy goes directly to the limbic brain and hits the pineal gland.

Now, when you modify your electromagnetic field, you become more conscious and capable of transmuting anger, fear, and guilt, and the release of that energy from this center to the upper part of the brain begins to create a powerful polarity, with the positive charge in the head and the negative charge in the tail. Once the pineal gland receives a signal, it sends a direct signal to the pituitary, which starts to release two very powerful metabolites called oxytocin and vasopressin. Oxytocin sends signals of nitric oxide. When you feel love and gratitude, you enter a receptive state. Then there is a reverse field that begins to come from another direction. This is vasopressin. Both neuropeptides are involved in social recognition, pair bonding, cognition, and aggression. Once the energy begins to move and travel up to the brain, we can modify the internal resonance frequency to modify your reality. For Descartes, the pineal gland is intimately related to the soul; in turn, serotonin and melatonin are directly related to the wavelength of visible light. This means that the pineal gland is responsible for producing the images of our three-dimensional reality.

In the ancient mysteries, the Alchemical Cross appears in the work *The Book of Hieroglyphic Figures* by Nicolas Flamel. In it, the images of a coiled or nailed serpent on a cross are described, symbolizing the sublimation of the vital force, victory, and control over the lower powers, which is projected through a vertical axis, *axis mundi*, always taking the idea of the cross as a representation of the transmutation of polarities in the human microcosm. It is the representation of the glorious body or tree of life ascending from the root of a *cruciferous* globe, a symbol of royal blood and supreme power. This represents the transmutation of *darkness* (representation of chaos) into *light* (symbol of harmonic order). This emblem is a biblical allegory that connects the crucifixion with the ascension and the repolarization of opposites.

Within mythology, kundalini is the most powerful force in our universe. It resides in each one of us. It is the vital force of the Holy Mother Sophia/Shakti and the supreme cosmic energy, bringing enlightenment to ourselves and the world. It is the source of all healing, creativity, and manifestation. This mystery was transmitted symbolically through the myth of crucifixion. The Gnostic knowledge says:

> In the skull, right in the middle of the head, there is a place called or known as the Holy Cloister because there a cerebrospinal fluid is produced, which is actually an oil. That is why it refers to the Secret = Secretion, which in antiquity was known as Christos, coming from the brain directed towards the spinal cord, reaching the sacral plexus or coccyx, the second group of most fused vertebrae of the spine, crossing the 33 vertebrae.
>
> This oil is created every month when the Moon is in the same position as when one is born, occurring twelve times in a period of a year. This fluid or oil, on its journey to the sacral plexus, passes through the solar plexus, also known as Bethlehem where the seed or Christ is born. This seed will have to return from where it came, the midbrain. The midbrain or mesencephalon, in union with the limbic system, is known as "the Holy of Holies." It is the structure that joins the posterior brain with the anterior, conducting motor and sensory impulses between them. Its correct functioning is a prerequisite for conscious experience. The brain located in the posterior part is also known as the small brain, associated with the posterior part, called prosencephalon. It is the most developed, evolved brain structure, with higher organization and complexity.

> These two correlatives are associated with the constellations of Taurus and Aries.

Before being sent through the spinal cord, the oil is differentiated into its electrical and magnetic parts. Flowing through the Ida-Pingala nerves, descending to the sacrum, the first energy center, of several through the spine. Ida and Pingala are two energetic channels found in the human body, which are subtle conductors of libidinal energy.

> The Moon moves in Ida and the Sun in Pingala. The former is cold and flows through the left nostril; the latter is hot and flows through the right nostril. This structure will be differentiated between the brainstem bridge and its function is to connect the spinal cord and the medulla oblongata with the superior structures of the cerebral cortex hemispheres or with the cerebellum. The entire network of nerves, glands, and organs along the journey of the seed = Christic consciousness is known as the tree of life, having implicated important consciousness functions.

Among the main energetic tubes is the kundalini, which is the serpentine or dormant Shakti power. It has 3 and a half turns and is located at the base of the spine, looking downwards. The task will be to elevate it through breaths and exercises. If through habits of caring for nutrition, meditation, and care of the bodies (physical, emotional, mental, and spiritual) we can transmute this seed along the journey of the tree of life, the inert egg called crucifixion will be reborn, raising the vibration, reaching the optic thalamus and pineal gland, a place that was known as "the light of the world," since the upper part of the torso was known as "the heavens."

All this serves for the physiological regeneration and the ascension of consciousness. According to kundalini, when the initiate manages to bring the sexual energy to the heart, then he goes through the symbolic death and resurrection of Jesus Christ. From that moment on, the initiate lives the entire drama of Christ's Calvary in the astral body. This is one of the greater mysteries of ancient initiation, which is consummated in us with the death, burial, and resurrection of our Christs. This process of purification, sanctification, and healing is found within the tarot symbolized in the arcana of Temperance, the Emperor, Death, the Tower, and the Sun. It represents Christ's journey for the activation of the seed of life in the pineal gland and indicates to us that the tree of life, the tree of good and evil, as well as the possibility of returning to Eden, are found within us.

To achieve returning to Eden, we must develop the virtues of the soul, center our libidinal energy from the heart to elevate our consciousness.

Additionally, in the tarot, there are four angels linked to the cycles of different times (chronological, universal, natural, and spiritual). Dawn is symbolized by Judgment, where life metaphorically begins through a resurrection.

Midday, represented by The Lovers, depicts the Sun at its highest point, with feminine and masculine energies illustrated in their fullness.

Twilight or dusk is represented by Temperance, where the Sun sets on the horizon and feminine and masculine energies alchemically transmute into Lion and Eagle.

Finally, the Devil (the Fallen Angel) corresponds to midnight, symbolizing the descent into the underworld, where feminine and masculine energies are chained to matter. It is here that the hero descends to embrace the shadow and ultimately achieve the process of individuation, forming the archetype of the Self.

This arcana symbolizes balance in all senses: good and evil, matter and spirit, heaven and earth, masculine and feminine, sex and love, mind and soul. This symbolism represents the victory of light over corruptible and impermanent matter.

Temperance is the ability to maintain balance in madness, for we know well that sanity is illusory. When we sleep and dream, our perception of reality is completely altered, so we can consider that the mad are merely people who dream intensely, while neurotics are those who have lost the ability to believe in their own dreams.

When the energy of Temperance is misdirected, we become extremists, fanatics, uncompromising, unable to dialogue. Therefore, we are overwhelmed by our own emotions. From this mental stage, we often become intoxicated by our own emotional states. Emotions can heal or poison us, depending on how we utilize emotional energy, for or against ourselves.

Our ability to use intelligence to manage our emotions determines the quality of our life. When what should flow becomes stagnant, it creates discomfort.

The body's memory somatizes due to unexpressed, denied, or repressed emotions. Lust, gluttony, and disordered desires give rise to a spiritual blindness that incapacitates the possibility of obtaining spiritual goods. Instead, sobriety makes us capable and predisposes us to the spiritual life, where moderation and harmony grant us the power to elevate consciousness and transform into better human beings. The soul does not die because it lacks something but because something poisons it, and that something could be translated as the ability to transmute emotions through the development of consciousness.

15- The Devil

Arcane myth: God Pan or lack of self-love. Key phrases: feeling tied to concepts and beliefs that are not one's own, attachment, vices, greed, animality, materialism, obsession, ignorance, internal demon, shadow.

This arcana represents the arduous inner work that allows us to free ourselves from the chains that bind us to suffering, to overcome Satan, to overcome our shortcomings and fears. To do this, we must control our thoughts, open consciousness, travel to the depths of our inner selves to discover the light of knowledge that allows us to face our shadow, assume responsibility for our actions, stop projecting the shadow outward, and recognize our animal side. All this grants us the necessary inner strength to overcome ourselves. Evil arises when we let ourselves be dominated by fear, when we identify with certain roles that imprison our soul within the rigidity of thought. The torch is an emblem of spiritual enlightenment and knowledge and is often depicted in monuments, such as the Statue of Liberty. In this case, as a psychopompic character, the Devil is not only the guide of souls to hell but also emulates Prometheus who frees chained souls from ignorance. While the uninitiated relates the Devil to vice and sin, the adept advances toward their own underworld (subconscious) guided by a mythical bearer of light.

The story of good and evil has been the process of mastering and controlling our darkest side through time until our true self can emerge. This arcana indicates that there is an essence deep in our minds that must be released. It is the hero who descends to the underworld to elevate their shadow to consciousness and thus achieve the totality of the soul. Christ represents this action, reflected in the symbol of the cross and the various mythologies of peoples. During the winter solstice, the image of the Egyptian god Horus was taken out of the sanctuary to be publicly worshipped by the masses. He was depicted as a newborn child, lying in a manger, with golden hair, a finger in his mouth, and the sun disc above his head. The festival of the birth of the unconquered Sun (*Dies Natalis Solis Invicti*) indicated that a new sun was born that conquered darkness, and from the end of the winter solstice (December 21), the days would become longer. This festival ran from December 22 to 25.

The Devil represents the ego as a cruel jailer that chains us in our own mental prisons; however, its true function is to transform into a guardian. The shadow represents the set of wild instincts that allowed us to come this far; without it, we simply would not have been able to survive. The serpent, Satan, who is not the enemy of man, but the one who made men into gods when man ate the forbidden fruit of the knowledge of good and evil. He truly assumed his role as God by judging others through moral judgments. From that moment on, the shadow was projected outward, and evil ceased to be perceived within.

In Baphomet mythology, the Androgynous, which is the hieroglyph of arcane perfection, is a demon represented as black brass, but not by nature, but inherent due to mistakes made. The alchemical task is to polish it, to make it white again. There are two arcana that open the doors to the lower triangle of matter in the Tree of Life: Death and the Devil. When the card is negative, then evil acts as always, either by default or by excess: by default one is drained, apathetic, there is no purpose in life, the past is a well where one has remained meditating and lamenting; by excess, it is a destructive force, evil is chosen pathologically, such as ignorance, illusion, deception, attachment, greed, and lack of compassion.

If, on the other hand, we walk the central path, the Devil would show us our limits and thanks to him we could discover our dark side. Not facing the demon that everyone carries within themselves means excluding ourselves from the possibility of fully knowing ourselves for what we are, imperfect, which is why we recognize that evil is within us. The aspect of this arcana in general is bestial, animalistic. This makes sense if we understand the Devil as the animal instinct, the maddening nature. That is why sometimes it is related to the Greek god Pan, a god who is dominated by a primitive instinct, reproductive, hunger, anger, and a desire both sexual and for power.

Within mythology, we also find the relationship of the demon with Abraxas, who is considered the main God of the ancient gods reigning in the chaos of the universe. This word is found in Gnostic texts like the *Sacred Book of the Great Invisible Spirit*, and also appears in *Greek Magical Papyri*. It is related to the seven planets. Some believe that its name is directly related to the word *abracadabra*. This God is often associated with Osiris, Harpocrates, Pantheus, and Hecate. In the book *Esoteric Course of Kabbalah* by V. M. Samael, we can read:

> "The key is found in the Serpent. The Gallic feet of the Abraxas are a double snake tail. There is the tempting serpent of Eden and Moses' copper serpent, intertwined in the tau, that is, in the sexual

lingam. The serpent is normally enclosed in the Muladhara chakra (Church of Ephesus). It slumbers in that coccygeal center. The serpent must inevitably leave its Church. If it ascends through the spinal canal, we become angels; if it descends to the atomic hells, it turns us into demons."

In another excerpt from another book, it says: "The soul is between two paths, that of light or that of darkness, and the problem is absolutely sexual. The key is found in the sacred serpent."

Jung, in *The Seven Sermons to the Dead*, borrowed from the Gnostics the thought in paradoxes. He used Gnostic terminology like the word *Abraxas* to refer to divinity. In this book by Jung, we can read the following:

"Abraxas is the sun and, at the same time, the eternally overwhelming abyss of the Void, of the Devil. The power of Abraxas is ambivalent. What the Sun God says is life. What the Devil says is death. Abraxas, however, speaks the worthy and condemned word, which is both life and death. Abraxas produces truth and falsehood, good and evil, light and darkness in the same word and in the same act. Therefore Abraxas is fearsome. He is proud like the lion at the moment he overcomes his victim. He is beautiful like a spring day. He is the fullness that unites with the void. He is the sacred copulation, he is love and its homicide, he is the saint and his traitor. He is the clearest daylight and the deepest night of absurdity. Seeing him means blindness, knowing him means illness, praying to him means death, fearing him means wisdom, not opposing him means salvation. God lives behind the sun, the Devil lives behind the night. What God begets from the light, the Devil drags into the night. But Abraxas is the world, its becoming and ceasing to be itself. With every offering to the Sun God, the Devil presents his curse. Everything you ask of the Sun God produces an act of the Devil. Everything you create with God gives the Devil power of action."

Matter has a gravitational force that attracts us downward, to the earth. When we surrender to material temptations and do not develop spirituality, we lose the power to elevate ourselves. Remember that the tarot also functions as a reflection of our unconscious, and the Devil, being part of it, indicates that we all have a shadow that is always there with us, and it is in our dark side where he resides with a force that imprisons us to matter. He is very important in the deck, as he is the main character we must know to overcome our weaknesses. If humans remain on the plane of matter, they remain at the level of the animal, without the ability to see beyond the realm of the earth. The shadow gains its power, and man becomes greedy, corrupt, selfish, evil. It resides in the darkness that comprises hatred, pride, greed, and everything that enslaves you and distances you from the light of God.

In the Sun card of the Marseille tarot, we see the two characters together showing affection because love unites, God is love. The Devil referred to in the tarot is not a being in the air or underground; it is a psychic instance present within us. No wild predator has the capacity to do as much harm as humans themselves. Humans are the only animal species that can willingly jeopardize the continuity of their own species and the planet.

The Zohar poses a very radical question: "Who expelled whom from the Garden?" The Zohar teaches that it was actually man who expelled God from the Garden. It is as if we are still in the Garden, but we do not realize it. Because we have expelled God, that is, we have lost contact with the spiritual dimension. And the challenge is to regain some awareness, some intimacy with the divine. It is man who turns his back on God, not the other way around. The miracle is constant; it is us who turn our backs, and in doing so, we fall. When we project blame onto others, be it the woman, the Devil, or anyone who is blamed for our sins, we evade the responsibility of dealing with our own darkness.

When we reject divinity, the Garden (Sophia) sacrifices her own freedom and descends with us, remaining beneath our feet, always providing a home for our ongoing evolution. And as She will never leave us, when we choose to rise, She ascends with us and, in this way, is restored to her celestial throne. Divinity never rejects us; we reject it, and when we tire enough of the Hell we have created, She always embraces us again. Sophia represents the Universal Mother; she is truth, strength, unwavering dedication, and loyalty. A Hermetic principle states: "The further creation is from the center, the more it is bound. The closer it reaches to the center, the freer it is."

In the Gospel of Thomas, it is mentioned that Christ rejects temptations but tells the Devil, "Accompany me so that together we may bring consciousness to humanity." We must understand that the true sin of man is the inability to love responsibly. Love and responsibility go hand in hand because they require us to measure our behaviors much more to promote the well-being of what is important to us. Love makes us responsible for our thoughts, words, and actions to ensure the well-being of everything we value. Responsibility and awareness are two fundamental gears of emotional health. As Da Vinci said, "You cannot love what you do not know, nor defend what you do not love."

Material goods are only a vehicle for higher learning. Adam and Eve can always remove the chains that bind them to suffering, but to rid ourselves of evil, it is necessary first to ask what it is. What knowledge do I lack? What ignorance am I suffering from? How do I relate to money, use money, or let money use me? How do I manage my love? How do I relate to my health, diet, sexuality? If we were only material beings, we would live in animal tranquility; we would not need culture, deep bonds, or existential transcendence.

The book of nature is open every day before us; we can learn from this book the wonders of the eternal wisdom that the Creator has inscribed upon every stone, every flower, every star. If our eyes do not see and our ears do not hear, it is because we are still preoccupied with worldly activities. When we choose to sacrifice certain pleasures of our own accord, we unleash our potential. At that moment, our eyes and ears open so that the book of nature may be revealed to us. The arcana of The Lovers, Strength, Temperance, The Devil, and The Star are closely linked to the actions of consciousness through the integration of the shadow.

When the energy of the Devil is mischanneled, we become beings enslaved by instincts, incapable of loving ourselves and others, projecting our flaws onto others, and seeking to blame others for our unhappiness. Petrarch said, "Five great enemies of humanity are within ourselves: greed, ambition, envy, anger, and pride. If we rid ourselves of them, we shall enjoy the most complete peace"; "Pride, envy, and greed are the dark forces that corrupt men's hearts." Mischanneled Devil energy represents instinct, power, and appetite not only sexual but for any egocentric and ambitious desire for superiority, anger, vengeance, dominance, or pride. Fear, cruelty, attachments, greed, misery, and all that causes suffering in the world can be understood as a poor flow of this arcana's energy. To overcome the Devil, it only takes to act responsibly and illuminate our own shadow.

16- The Tower

Arcane Myth: King Minos and the labyrinth or the Tower of Babel. Key Phrases: everything built from the ego will collapse, life crises, mental states, changes, ego projections, arrogance, pride, the end of something, the need to evolve.

This card has an apocalyptic representation, representing disastrous events that break in from the outside by all kinds of forces beyond man's control. Although the word apocalypse is often understood as final destruction, it actually means 'to uncover' or 'reveal.' During the Middle Ages, apocalypse was taken as a synonym for revealing, that is, removing the veil. We all live deceived by illusions created by our senses: what they communicate to us, our mind assumes as an intangible reality, although these perceptions are often nothing more than unequivocal interpretations of the world that need to be updated. The apocalypse is the act by which we remove the veil of the senses that hide the truth. It is a way to access hidden treasures that often can only be revealed in moments of great difficulty. In every suffering, there is involuntary growth that reveals unknown aspects of ourselves.

This arcana represents the opportunity arising from crisis, the unexpected events that scatter the seed of transformation and open a new stage in our lives, the destruction of old belief systems. When the mind and heart are in disunion, the purifying fire breaks in to renew us and free us from the negative energies we have built through irrational beliefs. Its action always indicates that it is time to renew ourselves, change habits. The Tower represents the force of the universe operating synchronically to lead us towards growth. Jung defined the mana archetype related to phallic symbols, representing the divine power that frees us from the mental prison forged by the ego. The soul is immersed in these structures, and its vehicle of expression will always be the symptoms. As long as the ego tries to maintain an image through the mask, the soul seeks to express a truth through human vulnerability.

This card indicates that we cannot continue with certain lifestyles; we must break free from the structures that hinder our evolution. The Tower is the prison we have built and in which we live isolated, full of insecurities and fears that imprison us. This construction represents dogma, from which we cannot escape by our own will, living surrounded by a strong wall of prejudices and limiting ideas. The lightning represents uncontrollable fate, events that seem to come out of nowhere and force us out of this self-imposed prison, to overcome accumulated fear through uncertainty and leave the walls behind, being displaced by destiny towards the void influenced by the forces of constant change. The crown in this case represents attachment to material, there are two that fall, one who detaches from everything to save themselves and the other who clings to pretension and possessions. Just like the myth of the Tower of Babel, everything man builds based on pride and ignorance will collapse.

When the energy of The Tower is mischanneled, we find ourselves trapped in suffering, as a consequence of the inability to learn the lessons we need for our evolution. Jung said in this regard: "Those who learn nothing from the unpleasant facts of their lives force the cosmic consciousness to reproduce them as many times as necessary to learn what the drama of what happened teaches." Resistance to change is a comfort zone that limits our evolution and immobilizes us. When achievements are created solely from the ego, this act condemns us to the misfortunes of life. The human soul cannot be boxed in by dogma for long, as its possibilities for manifestation are infinite and it will always seek to make itself known. Man's activity on earth has created civilization. Despite the positives of this, our technological development has led us to an imbalance by ignoring higher forces. Man has competed with God to dominate creation, until finally his inflated ego is punctured by the lightning, which comes to free him from dogmas and prejudices. The lightning also symbolizes creative ideas that emerge from nowhere to provide creative solutions through flashes of genius (*eureka*).

The development of science has been extremely materialistic. Our civilization has fallen into an inflation of the ego, believing ourselves to be the owners of the earth, forcing higher powers to correct our erratic course. Crises like the COVID-19 pandemic mark a before and after that reflect on our way of relating to the environment. The climate crisis is a consequence of man's arrogance over the earth; we must evolve and improve our relationship with it. The universe demands our commitment. We must make changes, politically, educationally, in health, and in business. In the card of The Tower, the lightning strikes the crown, symbolizing the ego inflation complex. Misfortune forces us to release the identification with our ego. Nothing belongs to us except our own sense of humanity.

17- The Star

Arcane Myth: Pandora or the naked truth. Key Phrases: inspiration, talent, humility, inner search, honoring ancestors, renewal, hope, communication.

After a crisis comes calm through order in manifested processes, attunement with cosmic forces, understanding of our role in the universe, and the willingness to serve a higher plane. After chaos comes order. The Star reflects tranquility, trust, and surrender that follows the symbiotic union with the inner world. Temperately pouring two vessels balancing the content of the mind, returning the water to the source, from water life is born just as the ego emerges from the unconscious every day, towards death and rebirth, which are part of the cycle of life.

The Star represents the great universal cosmic mother, which allows us to receive the manna from heaven, the energy from our solar center that connects us with the earth. Its action enables us to awaken stellar consciousness, necessary for healing and regenerating the world. In its womb, a new world is gestated representing the sacred feminine part, the force we must develop to balance civilization. It is the tree of knowledge that allows us to read the symbolic language with which we can conquer death through a new way of acting, recognizing that we truly are divine, pure, and innocent beings.

This arcana allows us to develop creative and artistic intuition, teaching us to use the force of synchronicity to attract the situations and people we need to grow. Its action reminds us of the humility we need to put our gifts at the service of humanity. To see things as they are, it is necessary to cleanse our soul of impurities, seek the help of spiritual guides, and rid ourselves of old concepts. We must receive cosmic energy and deliver it to the earth to help create a new world. This arcana teaches us to flow with life, to wait with humility, to recognize our ancestors, to conceive the celestial worlds. It represents hope, the love of Eve (Anima), the reception of light that illuminates our illusions and helps us cleanse the mistakes of our past.

Traditionally, the figure on this card has one foot on the ground and the other in water, thus bridging the gap between form (earth, body) and substance (water, soul). To see the stars, however, we must stay in the darkness. This path requires and calls for meditation, into oneself. Only then do the sparks of truth shine, in the unconscious of the soul's night which is the inner life. This path is, therefore, marked by constant meditation. In its darkness, our inner dimension is illuminated. The arcana of The Star is opposite or reflective to The Lovers because it marks the transition from one initiation phase to another. Indeed, if The Lovers mark the transition from theory to practice, then The Star indicates how the mystic's soul, guided by the light of the stars, passes through a silent wisdom like the inner light.

It's important on this path to listen closely to the world of our dreams. The Stars indicate the importance of sleep and our dream world. In this tarot card, Venus is the goddess of love, the star that guides our dreams, hence the symbol of the bird of dream reality. The water pitchers are always the search for balance between heaven and earth. The star is present in almost all mandalas. Jung describes this symbol as the rebirth of God in the soul. For Jung, the star is a symbol of "the coming" and is one of the central themes of The Red Book. In Symbols of Transformation, Jung refers to the water symbol as "the waters of the flood, as a symbol of new creation." Water is a symbol of life, symbol of emotional flow. The unconscious is considered the mother of consciousness, hence the figure of the Sun and the Moon have a close relationship.

When the energy of The Star is mischanneled, we seductively use our charms to satisfy selfish desires, leading us into despair and abandonment due to the loss of connection that unites us with others. This represents a source of disillusionment, hopelessness, failures, disharmony, and illness, limiting the capacity to develop those virtues that enable the evolution of our entire human and divine potential. Often, we forget that on this planet Earth, we owe our life to a star called the Sun. While spiritual life is active, it is due to a star that shines with its own light, that is, inner enlightenment. The process of becoming a star, Jung called "individuation." When we are unable to follow this evolutionary path that pushes us forward, life loses its shine, the dreams that should inspire us become nightmares, and we see the world as a cruel and dark place, completely fragmenting ourselves, losing sight of our power to evolve.

18- The Moon

Arcane Myth: Hecate or the great mother and the secret of the witches. Key Phrases: uncertainty, illusions, mirages, subjectivity, shadow, unconscious, right hemisphere, inspiration, intuition, sensitivity, dreams, soul, fantasy, art, femininity, humanity.

The Moon card represents the emotional and spiritual dimension of the human being, the dream reality, the world of images, the phylogenetic heritage, the collective unconscious, the primordial waters from which life emerged thanks to the energy of the great mother queen of hidden mysteries. Light prevents clear seeing when it opposes darkness, darkness clouds when it opposes light. Behind the lunar brightness lies the Sun. Behind what lies hidden in the mind is the hidden Sun, that is, consciousness, which allows one to see clearly what remains hidden in the mist of the unconscious.

In legends and mythology, the energy experienced by women during their menstrual cycle was described as a rhythm of four stages reflecting the phases of the Moon. The Virgin and the waxing Moon represented the phase extending from the end of bleeding to the beginning of ovulation. The energy corresponding to this phase resembles that of a young maiden. On the other hand, the Mother and the full Moon represent the period of ovulation itself.

The energies in this case bear similarity to those of motherhood. The diminishing light during the waning phase reflects the reduction of physical energy from ovulation to menstruation, as well as the increase in sexuality, creativity, internal destructive energies, and awareness.

The New Moon and the Dark Witch represented the menstruation phase, in which the Witch embodied the woman, who withdrew her physical energies from the earthly world to focus her consciousness on the spiritual world. If we compare the lunar cycle with the feminine cycle, the waxing and waning phases are moments of change and correspond to the stages of the Virgin and the Sorceress, while the full Moon and new Moon are periods of balance, similar to the phases of the Mother and Witch. In this sense, the Virgin phase is an ascent towards the clarity of the external aspect of feminine nature, while the Sorceress phase is a descent into the darkness of her inner aspect.

The cycles and female archetypes, the role of women, and their connection with the cosmos, nature, and rhythms have played significant transcendent activities, neither lesser nor more important than those of men. Women gained great knowledge, which granted them much power and ultimately led to the creation of religion, understood as the gathering of people with a common spiritual goal, which, given the conditions of that time, was uniquely and exclusively to preserve life by offering love and protection among them, developing eroticism and sexuality, assuming a stance of individuality and responsibility.

The feminine nature is changeable and subject to intrinsic (internal) and extrinsic (external) stimuli. It is known that a woman's hormonal period is divided into four stages, a fractal of the four seasons of the year, the four cardinal points, the four states of matter, and the four elements. Natural cycles, seasonal changes, the phases of the Moon, and circadian rhythms show that there is a clear relationship between the four elements. When we observe planetary orbits, precise and proportional geometric patterns emerge, reflecting mathematical harmony and a connection between terrestrial and celestial phenomena. Our ancestors were well aware of this relationship between the cosmos and women.

From an energetic perspective, the Moon radiates yin polarity energy, energy with centripetal force, moving from the external to the internal, from light to darkness, from micro to macro, from unidirectionality to multiple possibilities. Goddess woman, creator, Priestess. This is how all cultures from different geographical points knew the woman. In many cultures' sources, the universal feminine force is represented by the Great Goddess, also named Gaia, where three figures of a woman coexist, the Maiden, the Mother, and the Witch, giving rise to the Triple Goddess. Alongside this life cycle, we find the one represented by the Moon, where four cycles are symbolized: the Maiden, the Mother, the Sorceress, and the Witch. If in the first we find the strength of the creative energy, in this we find the mutability and cyclicality of all that is created.

The Witch represents wisdom, imagination, the gateway to death. The path to the powers of the inner world makes the shadow of the waning Moon complete, turning it into the hidden aspect of the New Moon. It represents the reflective phase of the cycle, winter, carrying within it the energy of transformation and the first day of menstruation. True to the significance that art, and more specifically art therapy, holds, this type of expression is a method for treating neurosis resulting from the internal split between opposites. The conflict arises between the sensual and spiritual parts, between the ego and the shadow, between consciousness and the unconscious. In the Moon card, we see a figure of the Sun and Moon integrated as a representation of the totality we must achieve through the restoration of the bond between our mind and our soul.

The Moon is the most unconscious and introspective arcana of the tarot. It is always present but not always visible, it does not have its own light, it is the truth of the Sun that makes it shine, like the truths that lie in our psychic shadow. Just as children have imaginary friends, adults have virtual lovers, ghosts of desires, nocturnal shadows in the dreamer's heart. These are the shadows of the Moon in the darkness of our silent nights, a mirror where we can see the reflection of our unconscious and the projections that arise from the world of illusions. This card is a good representation of the shadow in which our unconscious is submerged, which, unless we elevate it to the light of consciousness, will continue to affect our existence.

The shadow is the effect caused by the light of morality in the form of religion, values, norms, laws, and traditions, which have been projected onto us with a darkening effect on that lower and irrational part of our personality. Today, the shadow holds great power over our civilization and, even with all our intellectual rationality, its power is capable of dragging men towards the most cruel irrationality. However, when we introject the figure of the Sun and Moon, not as something external in the higher realm but from an inner dimension, from the center of our heart, the assimilation of spiritual principles enables an integration between light and shadow, described by Jung as "the hero's journey," which, by descending into the underworld, manages to elevate its shadow towards solar consciousness, repolarizing the opposites, transmuting its flaws into virtues.

For the Maya and the Mexica, eclipses did not symbolize a dance between the stars but rather a war between the Sun and the Moon. When there was a solar eclipse, it announced drought, war, and changes, and lunar eclipses caused problems for pregnant women since the Moon represented fertility. That's why obsidian stones were placed around the belly. The fight between the Sun and the Moon represented rebirth, the battle of darkness against light, a battle won by the Sun. Symbolically, it makes us reflect on our internal battles between our darkness and our light. Pre-Hispanic ceremonies during solar eclipses were to feed the Sun so that it would win the battle. Dances, fires were made to help it conquer the darkness, and songs to help it wake up faster. Feeding the light of our hearts through compassion would be an important symbol. This leads us to the reflection that humanity must overcome its cruelty by nurturing its kindness.

This card is associated with the symbol of the ouroboros, the serpent that devours its own tail, and represents the universal polarity between the masculine and feminine principles that also takes place within every man and woman. We are the union of an ovum and a spermatozoon, we have male and female hormones. Within every cell exists a positive (+) and negative (-) pole, which enable synapses. Similarly, the Anima and Animus represent the polarity of psychoanimic energies present in consciousness and the unconscious. This duality is represented in culture as 0/1, everything/nothing, matter/energy, light/darkness, square/circle, inside/outside, sun/moon, sky/earth, separation/union, mind/soul, spirit/nature.

The masculine polarity implies movement. It is the action of begetting, of penetrating, the ability to explore the world and go in search of what one wants. It is initiative, logic, the mind. The feminine polarity is the capacity for surrender and receptivity, tenderness, fecundity, contemplation, and intuition. The body versus the spirit. The work of integrating both polarities is called "inner marriage" or "alchemical wedding," which consists of uniting and balancing both complementary principles within oneself to become complete. The Anima and Animus are the archetypes through which we communicate with the collective unconscious in general. It's important to make contact with it. It is also the archetype responsible for our love life. As a Greek myth suggests, we are always searching for our other half, that other half that the gods took from us. When we fall in love at first sight, it's because someone has filled our particular Anima or Animus archetype exceptionally well.

When the energy of The Moon is mischanneled, we might use our gifts to manipulate for hidden purposes, dragged by the uncontrolled tide of our own emotions, which overflows and leads us to take actions that often bring negative consequences to our lives. When we do not connect appropriately with lunar energy, we feel incomplete, empty, and therefore become jealous, neurotic, deceitful, lunatic, people without control who harbor grudges and repeat self-destructive patterns in their lives. Misusing the energy of The Moon arcana, our imagination takes us through dark places, diving into projections, illusions, delusions, and hallucinations due to the misuse of our imagination. When lunar energy does not flow properly, we constantly find ourselves submerged in the dream realm, completely darkening our ability to think clearly. The energy of this arcana can be related to perinatal mental health, epigenetic factors, personality disorders, neurotic and psychotic states.

19- The Sun

Apollo and his twin, Artemis. Key Phrases: union of opposites, communion of the physical with the soul, vitality, objectivity, consciousness, left hemisphere, waking world, logic, order structure, confidence, discipline, fraternity, joy, flourishing, civilization.

This card represents light, joy, fraternity, innocence, knowledge, and intelligence. It relates to the photons of light, which grant us vitality, and symbolizes the integration of the brain hemispheres that allow us to synchronize human thought with the supraconsciousness. It's the connection between the spiritual father and the inner Christ, the alchemy that occurs in the solar plexus, resulting in the solar vehicle with which we can transcend the cycles of time, contacting the source of eternal life. The Sun arcana allows us to overcome duality, the false self, and find our true essence, capable of flourishing in all its splendor. Therefore, it signifies the development of our entire human potential on earth and in heaven.

The conscious mind grants us the clarity to steer the course of our life, taking responsibility for our actions, acting with congruence. This card represents the healing of our inner child, the abandonment of masks of pain, and the acceptance of the father in the heart. Jung states that the child archetype is a representation of forgotten aspects of our childhood, the preconscious aspect of the infancy of the collective psyche. Despite what we believe to be, deep down, we are always children. The Self-symbol originates in the depths of the body and participates in this materiality as much as the structure of conscious perception and the collectivity itself.

The child is both a being of the beginning and the end: the initial being was before man, the final being is after man. Psychologically, this statement means that the child symbolizes the preconscious and postconscious essence of man. Its essence is the unconscious state of early childhood. The postconscious essence is an anticipation by analogy of what comes after death. In this idea, the omnipresent essence of the soul is manifested. Totality is never confined to consciousness but encompasses a reality that goes beyond time and space. Mind and soul need each other to transcend; one is the key and the other the door.

This card reminds us that we all carry an eternal child within us, a being made of innocence. This symbolic child also leads us and carries with it the record of our formative experiences, our pleasures, and our pains. The inner child manifests in fantasies, dreams, art, and myths from all over the world, where it represents renewal, vital enthusiasm, the capacity for wonder, curiosity, courage, spontaneity, and immortality. All children are born scientists. Scientists are children who explore the world around them in search of truth with wonder.

Wordsworth said, "The Child is the father of the Man." The child is the father of the whole, complete, and rounded person. Our child possesses the spirit of truth, spontaneity, and authenticity. Its actions manifest the naturalness within us, the ability to act appropriately, and the aptitude to solve any situation. When we listen to the voice of the child within us, we feel authentic; creativity allows us to flow with life. The child is the authentic part, and the authentic part within us is the one that suffers. Many adults split this part of themselves and chain that part of their own soul, therefore not achieving individuation, as the inner child is the key that allows us to reach the full expression of our individuality.

This infant entity, the being we truly are and have always been, lives with us here and now. The inner child carries our personal history and is the vehicle for both our memories of the real child and the idealized child from the past. In his book "Jung's Map of the Soul," Murray Stein distinguishes between contrasts with the shadow and contrasts with Anima-Animus, as each of these facets expresses itself differently within us. The author addresses the psychic emergencies we may encounter, making it clear that it is not easy to emerge victorious from a contrast with Anima-Animus without first having negotiated with the shadow. It is even more difficult for the person to understand what individuation means in a society governed by a principle of normality that leads us to fit into certain behavior parameters to achieve the status of success.

When the energy of The Sun is mischanneled, we become blinded by our intellect, denying intuition, becoming arrogant and prideful. Overconfidence prevents us from seeing clearly the most appropriate way to act. Sometimes the clouds that seem to cover the Sun are unconsciously created by ourselves, clouding our field of vision. In that case, the barrier preventing us from seeing clearly lies in our own inability to recognize the truth. We lose the optimism necessary to motivate our actions, excesses harm us, fatigue us, and make us lose energy. Serenity and good judgment are required not to overdo it and to see in the midst of light without being dazzled. When we are exposed to the Sun's light, there is always the risk of being blinded. Circumstances demand remaining conscious of our own being so that clarity prevails without blinding us.

When the energy of The Sun does not flow correctly, we see ourselves as wounded abandoned children, dominated by the fear of rejection, feeling vulnerable, and falling into childish attitudes. For some people, abandonment constitutes a wound to the child-self that results in a restrictive adaptation, whereby the child is deeply buried under layers of resentment and claims. From this mental state, the individual fails to connect with their inner child, therefore a part of their soul is fragmented, and if not recognized as an existing entity, it loses the shine in their life, their own ego abandons them, and they become an orphan, unable to evolve or transform into a hero. This makes them dependent on circumstances, waiting for an external force (God, UFOs, leaders) to save them from their own state of abandonment.

20- Judgment

Arcane Myth: Anubis or the psychopomp. Key Phrases: emerging from the unconscious, rebirth, healing and being, forgiving and self-forgiveness, understanding, maturity, renewal, mission, vision, awakening of spiritual consciousness, mental clarity, connection.

This card calls us to a new life, a spiritual rebirth through the renewal of our lives. It is not a judgment of condemnation, but the awareness of a deep truth. Judgment is the result of the straight path that led to understanding and unification of opposites. We all come into this world with a mission: to develop our spiritual nature, awaken the inner child, unify the brain hemispheres to access the gifts of language, words, mantras, celestial music. We all carry the inner gold, the hidden treasure of the soul; therefore, we must seek the inner light to have confidence in ourselves and overcome the fear that drives us to want to control everything.

The qualities of the spirit allow us to heal, open up to new ideas, elevate our consciousness, and communicate with our higher self. Freeing ourselves from the need to judge ourselves and others is the only way to evolve. Within us lies the power to reach heaven on earth through our actions; within us lies the power to overcome difficulties. Judgment represents the birth of cosmic consciousness. The process of individuation leads us to the recognition of the true nature of being. At the end of the path, the evolution of consciousness is possible when the shadow and the Self integrate into the same image.

The Judgment arcana reminds us that, regardless of the suffering we have endured, there exists divine Justice, which is manifested in daily actions. Kindness, love, fairness, and solidarity are God's attributes in men; the closer our life is to these attributes, the closer God is to earth. Therefore, we must be capable of reflecting on our daily actions and whether their value is positive or negative.

When we are capable of meditating on our actions, we can forgive those who hurt us, free ourselves from resentment and pain, return to the family that abandoned us or we abandoned. The action of this arcana indicates that we have the power to modify our life story. We are the judge of our own actions, but to do so, we must act with honesty. We must turn our heart into the Grail to receive the light of eternity. Judgment has one of the best vibrations, those of rebirth, of the future Self, of the divine call.

The Judgment arcana transmits the strength of the phoenix to be reborn from our ashes. It represents the law of realization, which consists of the consequence of the experience of the fourth dimension (integration of soul and body): unity between the observer and the observed is achieved, the last enemy —death— is conquered, and from that moment on, the being is no longer subject to time. All biblical characters are archetypes that live within us as potentialities, thus it is our duty to awaken or activate them, which means we should ask ourselves what area of our life or being we should and can resurrect today.

When the energy of Judgment is mischanneled, we seek to control everything compulsively. Our obsessions turn us into overly severe people, judging others through moral judgments. We become closed off to new ways of thinking. We are unable to communicate assertively, to dialogue, work in a team, or conceive anything beyond our personal benefit. For this reason, we are limited in our field of vision and stumble over our own flaws. We remain locked in our beliefs, without even opening a possibility to contemplate new options or see the conditions of our life with renewed values. Rigidity becomes a pit, a tomb from which we cannot escape. Trials multiply, and pain prolongs. When you only see suffering and losses, you are incapable of understanding the essence of life. If you do not accept a painful reality out of fear of the unknown, if you make endless excuses just to not change your life, sooner or later everything will collapse, and in the long run, the pain will be greater. If you do not leave the pit, you will remain in the shadow and suffering. We always have free will at our disposal to choose which paths to take in life. This card is a reminder that in every act and every decision, there is at least some element of control. Even if some external event is beyond your control, the decision of how to react to those events is always within our power.

21- The World

Arcane Myth: God Himself or enlightenment. Key Phrases: Enlightenment after a spiritual awakening, inner paradise, peace, psychic integration, fulfillment, abundance, growth, success, inner image, center of personality, union with the soul of the world, elevation of consciousness.

The World arcana is the material representation of the queen of the heavens. This card represents the possibility of freeing our soul from the prisons of the ego, the end of a cycle, and the beginning of a new stage in life, the end of a process of perfecting our personality and the start of a new state of consciousness through the mastery of dark forces, the knowledge of truth, and triumph over earthly life. This arcana grants us the power to become creator beings. Its image symbolizes Shiva Nataraja or the Lord of the Dance.

Analyzing the image from a geometric perspective, we can observe the symmetry of the four elements and the *Vesica Piscis* or Fibonacci spiral, which completes the triad of Creation: an arithmetic constant, a geometric figure, and an algorithm. This almond or fish-shaped form (*Vesica Piscis*), an archetype impossible to ignore or evade from the beginnings of human sexuality, omnipresent in art, architecture, and religious or mystical iconography, is considered the origin and mother of sacred geometry.

The Vesica is a symbol made with two circles of the same radius intersecting in such a way that the center of each circle is on the circumference of the other. It was a symbol known in ancient civilizations of Africa, India, America, Europe, Mesopotamia, and Asia, in almost all cultures since prehistory. Research indicates that the term arose during the early days of Christianity when it was used as a key for identification. It symbolized *Ichtus* ('fish' in Greek). Christians associated it as an acronym for the phrase "*Iesous Christos Theou Yios Soter*," meaning "Jesus Christ, Son of God, Savior."

In the Pythagorean school (540 BC), the Pythagorean mystical pentagram or five-pointed star symbolized the PHI constant ($\Phi = 1.618...$). One of the Pythagorean topics that has had the most influence on art, mysticism, biology, and even magic has been the golden ratio or divine section. Pythagoras said, "Limit gives form to the limitless." This also speaks to the great harmony achieved through mathematical knowledge and love; because Cosmos means 'order,' and order is harmony. All of this was called symmetry and synergy, which equals the proportion or measure between the whole and the parts.

The golden ratio and the Fibonacci series are the greatest exponents of mathematical-geometric measurements demonstrated in the growth and evolution of all creation. Pure geometric forms are not stagnant in a static formula but are in constant generation, connection, evolution, and involution, transitioning from one form to another, each at different frequencies and speeds, whether in our body or in every living being, material or immaterial. This continuously creates three-dimensional, living, and changing mandalas, because they perpetually evolve into infinite concentric geometric patterns that unfold in a constant spiral called the "golden proportion spiral." Our thoughts, emotions, and feelings also produce an infinity of geometric mandalas.

Even if our reason doesn't grasp it, this geometry has a powerful effect on our mind and physical body. It is a symbol of the harmonic proportions of geometric and mathematical configuration, a symbol or analogy of the spirit in matter, because it interweaves the material and etheric dimensions. It's the arrangement or correspondence of the parts of the whole or of things related to each other. The function of art transcends communication and delves into the disturbing landscapes of suggestion, poetry, magic, where messages acquire unlimited meanings, and countless subtle worlds unfold in the profound experience proposed by the work. Art delves into the dizzying complexity of symbolic language and, with it, into myth, metaphor, invocation, in the constant reinterpretation of reality in pursuit of a higher experience of ourselves.

In The Red Book, Jung describes the three diseases of the human soul: the first is blindness, represented by Salome, which reflects our inability to see all the unconscious aspects influencing our life; the second is division, arising from the deep division between consciousness and the unconscious, represented in the opposites of the Red and the Ascetic; the third is paralysis, which occurs due to the tension between opposites that generate a crisis seeking to restore psychic balance produced by the one-sidedness of consciousness, that is, the tendency to repress psychic contents.

Jung used the technique of active imagination as a method to heal the division between consciousness and the unconscious, by establishing a communication bridge that facilitates a change in the patient's attitude towards their unconscious through deep dialogue with the symbolic images that emerge from the collective unconscious. Jung says, "The creative process consists in unconsciously vivifying the archetype and shaping it into the complete work. [...] Therein lies the social importance of art: it brings to the surface the figures that the spirit of the epoch most lacks."

Alchemists used the term magnum opus to describe the process of creating the so-called philosopher's stone. Through a laborious process (nigredo, albedo, citrinitas, rubedo), the alchemist managed to realize their complete work through art. The origin of this process can be associated with the figure of Maria the Jewess, the first female alchemist. The 8th-century Byzantine chronicler George Syncellus mentioned her as the teacher of Democritus, whom she met in Memphis (Egypt) during the time of Pericles. The Roman philosopher Morienus called her "Maria the Prophetess" and the Arabs knew her as "the daughter of Plato," a name reserved in Western alchemical texts for white sulfur. Maria is considered the founder of alchemy and was known for her axiom: one becomes two, two becomes three, and through the third (logos) and the fourth (sacrifice), it achieves unity. This represents Paradise, Sin, Salvation, Paradise.

Marie-Louise von Franz also offered an alternative version, stating: "From the One comes the Two, from the Two comes the Three, and from the Third comes the One as the Fourth." Jung used the axiom as a metaphor for the process of individuation:

> One is the unconscious totality; two represents the conflict of opposites; three, the points for a possible resolution. The third is the transcendent function, described as a psychic function that arises from the tension between consciousness and the unconscious,

supporting their union; and the one as the fourth is a state of transformed consciousness, relatively complete and at peace.

In the psychology of transference, the progression from 4 to 3 to 2 to 1 can be interpreted as an alchemical analogy of the individuation process from the many to the one, from undifferentiated unconsciousness to individual consciousness. This is reflected in the Christian cross as an alchemical formula that provides the vital mobility necessary to free us from all the internal blockages that prevent us from evolving.

To transcend, we must descend into the lower part of our personality, that hidden place where our shadow resides. Only by accepting our wild and unconscious nature can we elevate our consciousness. For Jung, The World card represents a mandala where the archetype of the Self is symbolized, which represents the principle of totality and integration. In this card, we observe that the figure is within a mandorla, a symbol of the union of opposites. The figures in the corners are associated with the four elements, related to the suits of the minor arcana. They symbolize the first being that emerges from the center of a cosmic egg engendered by time. It is associated with the light that, through union with the night, created the heavens and the earth.

The seven principles or axioms described in The Kybalion are: Mentalism, Correspondence, Vibration, Polarity, Rhythm, Cause and Effect, and Generation.

In the arcana of The World, we can delve into the fourth law, which defines the principle of polarity: everything is dual; everything has two poles; everything has its pair of opposites: likes and dislikes are the same; opposites are identical in nature, but different in degree; extremes meet; all truths are half-truths; all paradoxes may be reconciled. The fifth principle of The Kybalion is the principle of rhythm: everything flows and ebbs; everything has its periods of advance and retreat; everything rises and falls; everything moves like a pendulum; the measure of its swing to the right is the measure of its swing to the left; rhythm compensates. That's why, when we've reached one extreme of the pendulum, we must now swing back in reverse. We conclude with the arcana of The World and The Fool who waits to take us on a new adventure, to a new beginning.

In this part of the journey, our essence of the fool transforms into a naked young woman, symbol of innocence and the feminine potential, giving birth to a new stage of life. The naked woman performs the dance of her great liberation. With the help of the Eye of Horus, she has seen beyond the nature of limitations. Equipped with this penetrating ability (symbolized by the sickle she still holds in her right hand), she makes her way through the web of entanglements. Even the great serpent of transformation has lost its function. Its powers of seduction, which make possible the necessary experiences of learning and practice, are no longer needed, given the power and the new quality of metamorphic energy.

The 22nd card of the tarot carries the number 400, which results from the sum of the number 22; 4 multiplied by 10 squared, that is, by 100. The letter TAU. The number 4 encloses the divine denouement of creation, the number 10. Because, adding the figures up to 4, we get 10 (1 + 2 + 3 + 4 = 10). The numerical value 400, the figure 4 joined to the double 0, symbolizes all material creation, the entire universe with the creator, with God. The woman, the feminine visage of God, God in his quality of mother, Isis or Kali, represents in this card the figure 1 and the crown, the infinite circle, the universe. But behind the woman, the visible aspect of God, nature, we also feel the masculine principle of God represented also by the symbol of the cross and the mandala. Jesus, Buddha, and the other giants who reached the goal were not painters, sculptors, musicians, poets, nor dancers; yet, their life is an artistic representation from the heart that represented a divine manifestation on earth.

Jesus Christ and Buddha were historical figures of great relevance to history, but they are also considered archetypal states. One as the anointed of God and the other as enlightened through an awakening of consciousness. Both states take us out of contingency and help us embrace the oneness of existence. Jung, in summary, considers that Christ is the quintessential symbol in the West of the archetype of the Self, that is, the "God within us," the "divine spark" that is the source and center of the psyche that gives meaning to life. It is the treasure the hero must recover by facing the inner dragons, that is, the defects and weaknesses of their human condition.

When the energy of The World is mischanneled, our minds darken, and we find ourselves blocked in various aspects of our lives (health, money, love, spirituality). Immersed in crises and conflicts, we are unable to find the vital mobility necessary for change, healing, and evolution. For this reason, our soul is unable to achieve the true realization of being. The discomfort in our lives is an expression of the wounded soul seeking to manifest in our consciousness to attend to the true urgency of existence: the becoming of the soul that allows us to transcend. The soul's greatest impulse is to transcend, in a kind of natural survival instinct that supersedes the superficial interests of the ego. The soul seeks to reach its immortal nature, escape the repetitive cycles, free itself from worldly ties, and finally find true freedom.

22- The Fool

Arcane Myth: Dionysus or the void. Key Phrases: absence of prejudice, renewal and evolution, transcendence, the superconscious, the spirit of free will, the transcending soul, the return to Light, the Crown of Life.

The Fool is the cosmic agent, the quantum jumper, the interdimensional spy of The Emperor who comes into our lives to indicate through intuition a new path. Our future self is looking at us right now through our memories, dreams, and intuitions. When a human being awakens, all of humanity moves closer to evolution. Each being has their own thoughts, which have the great power to make changes in the stars with repercussions on humanity. Each of us is called to become the hero of time and contribute to the great cosmic plot through the development of consciousness. Our individual being is the form the universe has taken to become conscious of itself through our life experiences. We are all called to nourish the universal mind and finally become one with the whole.

According to the mysticism of the tarot, the arcana number 22, or the unnumbered arcana, is associated with the quantum and the duality of time/space. The Fool connects everything everywhere at the same time. At the end of the process, his madness transforms into a cure. The journey of The Fool represents the great transformation of the ego, the transcendence of the soul, and the eternal nature of the human spirit. The Kabbalah's Tree of Life is an ancestral mandala representing the human being on all levels: physical body, personality, soul, and spirit. The ten spheres of the Kabbalah, plus the 22 major arcana, mark all the steps a human being must take from their primal state in the sphere of the Kingdom (Malkuth) to reach the sphere of the Crown (Kether), to achieve their full expression and spiritual realization.

Papus states in his book *The Tarot of the Bohemians*:

> This deck of cards called the tarot that the gypsies possess is the bible of bibles. It is the book of Thoth Hermes Trismegistus, it is the book of Adam, it is the book of the primitive Revelation of ancient civilizations. This game, under the names of tarot, Torah, Rota, has successively formed the basis of the synthetic teaching

of all ancient peoples. Where the common man sees only a means of amusement, the thinker rediscovers the key to this tradition so unknown.

In the 22 paths that connect the ten *sephirots* of the tree of life, the 22 major arcana of the tarot are placed in a specific established order. Each path shows a movement of the soul in the search for Enlightenment and the encounter with its spirit.

Chapter 3
Tarot as a Guide to Personal Development.
The Minor Arcana

The privilege of a lifetime is to become who you truly are.
Carl Jung

As we've seen through the journey of the Major Arcana, the Tarot facilitates a process of self-discovery, enabling the development of the ability to shape instincts, emotions, thoughts, and actions in a way that allows for the achievement of one's personal goals (health, money, love, spirituality). Creativity is the artistic language with which we can connect with ourselves to engage with the creative energy that enables us to materialize our desires. This process is one of the Tarot's greatest qualities.

No problem can be solved from the same level of consciousness that created it. When we modify something in our way of acting, whether it be our thoughts, emotions, energy, or intentions, something in our life changes. The inability to progress occurs when one of these channels is blocked. When energy does not flow freely, our capacity to create cannot find a way to manifest, and for this reason, we are unable to improve our existence. When the energy of the Aces is mischanneled, there are limitations to thinking clearly or planning intelligently. Consequently, problems with health, money, and love arise as a result of poor management of one's internal resources. Faced with adversity, our spirit becomes impoverished, and we react with impulsivity and resentment. When this happens, we find ourselves acting from a place of lack, attracting even more negativity into our lives.

When we find ourselves stuck in a situation, whether internal or external, frustration and emotional tension drag us into mental states where it is not possible to see a clear solution to our conflicts.

Fears, disappointments, and despair limit our ability to act. To escape this state, it is necessary to rely on a force that allows us to reorganize our resources towards a different direction. In this sense, the Minor Arcana are auxiliary forces that can advise us in our day-to-day to transform all those situations that limit our life.

These changes are achieved by establishing a channel with the deep intelligence of the soul, with that wisdom that transcends our consciousness and connects with a whole beyond time-space. The quantum field is an invisible space of energy and information available to everyone; there, everything is possible because your thoughts and emotions create your reality. Through this process, our thoughts and desires have to match the sensations and emotions we are feeling. Thus, we are changing our brain waves to a state of creation. Our nervous system aligns with the frequency of the field. When we visualize the future we want and experience those emotions in the present moment, this becomes our reality, now. In this way, we can start to focus our efforts on creating that future we are capable of envisioning. When we set a real goal, we can plan and act in that direction so that in the future we reap the fruit of the seed we sow in the present. For this, it is necessary to till the soil, that is, to work on our past and lighten the load to move quickly on our path.

The quantum field is the infinite potential where we can tune into the future we wish to live. Every frequency carries information. So think of the quantum field as full of infinite amounts of energy vibrating beyond the physical world of matter and beyond our senses: invisible waves of energy available for us to use in creation. What exactly can we create with all this energy swimming in an infinite sea of potentials? That depends on us because, ultimately, the quantum field is the state in which all possibilities to change limiting beliefs exist, to face situations that seem to define us, it's the space where miracles happen. Your future already exists as infinite potential, what stops you or separates you from it is your past.

In this context, the Ace cards appear as in the Judgment card from a higher sphere symbolized by the celestial world, the hand of God intervening in human affairs to assist us. In the Ace of Swords, divine intelligence manifests in our minds to indicate what to do in the form of ideas that emerge from the collective unconscious to provide us with innovative solutions to our greatest conflicts. In the Ace of Cups, the intelligence of intuition allows us unity with the heart, guiding our decisions to successfully start a project. In the Ace of Wands, we find the impulse of the spirit that motivates us to take determination through the necessary action to undertake and leave the comfort zone imposed by our limiting beliefs. In the Ace of Pentacles, we find the strength of our will as a means to strive and give our best effort to work for our goals. All the Aces are related to the power of the Magician to channel energy and establish clear goals that allow us to achieve fulfillment.

The four Aces represent the Creator, the unmanifested beginning from which any event derives. They symbolize primary energy, the divine breath. Active and dynamic, they mark the prelude of something that God contains within Himself: creation. Numerically, the Aces represent unity, considered as a starting point that contains and summarizes the meaning of nine consecutive numbers. All the Aces seek and contribute to realization and fulfillment. Both in Jewish and Muslim religion, visual representations of God are prohibited because, being God eternal and supreme, He cannot be reduced to any form conceived by man. Due to such prohibition, as well as the fact that the divine does not have a single and defined form, art history has often represented God as a hand in the sky. In the Ace cards, we see that the Wands show the palm of the hand (action), while the Swords show the back of the hand (protection). In the case of Cups and Pentacles, the symbol is carried rather than held (strength).

Collectively, the Minor Arcana represent the evolutionary path of the different spheres that make up the being. They are the experiences and needs that must be met by humans on a material, emotional, spiritual, and intellectual level, and they are also the decisions, actions, and projects that we must undertake to achieve such ends. The court cards are the messengers that communicate the realm of the soul with the practical world, helping us through intuition to achieve our goals and objectives. These cards are related to the synchronic principles that can assist us in connecting with the resources, people, or situations that can help us succeed.

Four Aces: Swords, Cups, Pentacles, Wands

- Swords represent intellect. Upon reaching the final stage of their development, they will discover the existence of the other and will require the emotional energy of Cups.
- Cups symbolize emotional energy. When they reach the final stage of their development, they will produce a new life or act in the concrete world, needing the energy of living matter, that of Pentacles.
- Pentacles stand for living matter. At the highest degree of their development, they will transform and face the need to reproduce, thus requiring the creative energy of Wands.

- Wands represent sexual and creative energy. Upon reaching the final stage of their development, they will duplicate and discover androgyny, which is the essence of thought, then requiring the intellectual energy of Swords.

In the Minor Arcana, we observe cards that are very optimistic and others not so much. However, the entire conjunction of cards represents the challenges we must overcome, the crises we must mediate, and the resilience we must develop. There are moments of light and darkness, joy and suffering, mistakes and successes that must be treated with impartiality. From this perspective, the negative appears as something to be transformed into positive. Therefore, we must develop our personal power. Mistakes are pathways to perfection. The Tarot offers us the power to recognize, accept, and correct everything that prevents us from achieving full happiness. Each set of cards of the Arcana represents a level of learning and evolutionary development.

These two energies, Swords and Cups, are placed in the sky quadrant, implying an extroverted consciousness:

- Swords, "knowing how to be": represent intellectual energy, language, thought, concepts, ideas, the activity of intelligence. Air element. Part of the body it represents: the brain, consciousness, ideas transmitted by culture, learning, language as a weapon or as a prayer.

Shadow: confusion, ignorance, paranoia, distortion of perception. Cards (1-9): represent mental evolution, intellectual level, technical development, prefrontal brain, logic, objectivity, initiative, struggle, power, beliefs, judgments, doubts. At the end of the journey lies supreme intelligence as that planning ability that, through superior knowledge and cunning, empowers us to solve problems that arise in our lives.

Many of us may begin the journey of Swords with a certain degree of innate intelligence. The development of our intellectual quotient stems from early life experiences and genetic characteristics; moreover, early stimulation and the evolutionary learning process are crucial to unfold intellectual potential, though often we may become blocked halfway by our own mental structures, old repetitive patterns, limiting beliefs, fears, and a series of obstacles that prevent us from connecting with our full mental capacity. In the Minor Arcana, we see all that we must develop and also what we must overcome to achieve continuous learning in life. The ability to reflect represents the possibility of reaching a higher level of thought thanks to the assimilation of divine principles that grant us ancient wisdom.

- Cups, "knowing how to love": represent emotional energy, the heart, love, primitive feelings, the gift of forgiveness, generosity, adoration. Water element. Part of the body it represents: limbic system, heart, the soul's energy. In shadow; hatred or emotional blockage. Cards (1-9): represent the evolution of the human spirit, the emotional level of consciousness, subjectivity, faith, feelings, connection, relationships, human development, empathy, and emotional expression. Most of us start our life from the nourishment of maternal love, but as we grow, we can lose that connection, stagnate, suffer from emotional wounds, traumas, masks, complexes, disappointments, mourning, distrust, broken dreams, lack of love, toxic attachments, envy, resentments. All this limits our potential to manifest love and achieve fulfillment.

The Cups cards indicate that to connect with the heart's potential, we must overcome our internal blockages through love, forgiveness, and faith. From the heart, we must purify our intentions, develop empathy, compassion, and altruism to reach our true potential. When we manage to transcend our negative emotions, we can transmute and heal our perception to connect with a universal love that transcends our earthly existence. When we are able to express our love through kind acts, we contribute to collective well-being, which has enabled the evolution of our species.

These two energies, Wands and Pentacles, are situated in the earth quadrant, forming the foundation of all living species and representing an introverted consciousness:

- Pentacles, "knowing how to live": represents material energy: the body, health, money, physical appearance, living place, territory, clothing, food, home, profession, economic life, prosperity, money, position in the world, social relationships, the planet Earth. Element: earth. Part of the body it represents: limbs, cells, atoms, molecules that constitute us. Shadow: scarcity, diseases. Cards (1-9): represent the body, physical health, ego, self-image, material goods, work, commercial activity, state of abundance, success. We all start our journey in this world with a healthy body, within a more or less favorable context where we receive food, a place to live, clothes, toys, etc.

However, as we develop, we can become fixated on an attitude of scarcity and competitiveness and can develop a compulsive obsession with acquiring as many resources as possible or constructing an image of perfection through economic status, clothing, plastic surgeries, etc. The Minor Arcana remind us that true abundance is not found only in economic goods; there are wealthy individuals who achieved fortune by sacrificing quality time with their families and celebrities who missed the best moments of their lives to achieve success.

Similarly, there are individuals who greatly deteriorated their health by indulging in carnal passions. Wealth is not solely expressed in material terms; there is also spiritual progress, vital satisfaction, physical health, peace, and tranquility as expressions of wealth, which are measures of the true value of wealth we can achieve in all senses. The material is just a means to develop the spiritual dimension. A state of scarcity limits spiritual development, but this often has nothing to do with material resources, but rather with the management of personal resources (emotions, thoughts, spirituality).

At times, the obsession with generating resources leads people to neglect valuable aspects of their life. Material is only a vehicle to experience the most transcendental aspects of existence. By wisely using resources, it is possible to generate a state of true abundance. We must engage in business that allows us to achieve financial freedom. It's necessary to manage our time intelligently to spend more time with our loved ones. To achieve well-being in life, an individual must develop healthy habits (exercise, diet, positive attitude). Health is the greatest treasure we can possess. Thus, our body should serve us to outline a life project that contemplates harmony, peace, balance, and happiness as the true measure of success in life.

- Wands, "knowing how to do": represent sexual and creative energy, the instinct for reproduction, fecundity, desire, drive, creative energy, imagination, both conscious and unconscious production, the ability to create and invent, vital impulse, healing force, instinct, and the vocation to populate the planet. Element: fire. Part of the body it represents: pelvis and reproductive system. Shadow: lack of energy, vitality, and life vocation. Cards (1-9): represent creative energy, enthusiasm, joy, pleasure, sensuality, determination, strength, action, the primitive brain, our drive for achievement, energy, dynamism, the seeds from which things sprout, the spiritual level of life.

We all begin our lives thanks to an erotic impulse (libido); this is, in a way, the central battery that activates our being, the divine spark that ignites the life impulse. From infancy, we seek to satisfy our demand for desire through an external object (mother, bottle, toy, recognition, belonging, sex, etc.). However, we often have internal blockages that prevent us from connecting with vital energy, repressing enjoyment, or, on the contrary, living in hypersexualization viewing women as mere sexual objects, without understanding that the opposite pole of instinct is spirit. In today's society, we see sexuality portrayed in the media as a wild impulse toward satisfying our needs, thereby losing sight of the meaning of sexuality as a means to achieve human connection.

Rarely do we understand that the most pleasurable sex involves commitment, intimacy, interest, loyalty, honesty, and mutual support. The Minor Arcana remind us that sexuality is just the beginning of a long journey, at the end of which we will unite all sexual, emotional, intellectual, and spiritual experiences into a single direction. By transcending the sexual and spiritual, we encounter a level of depth, intensity, trust, and mutual respect. Love becomes a force to transcend towards eternity. Sexuality is stronger than love, yet love enhances a higher level of sexual pleasure. The most pleasurable orgasms come from intimacy. Over time, empty sexuality transforms into a mere muscle cramp. Sexual energy is intimately related to the creative capacity to transform libido into cultural manifestations or life projects.

The Court Cards

The sixteen court cards of the Minor Arcana represent people, which can reflect ways of being and acting of the querent, or external individuals. According to their rank, they can be identified as:

Kings and Queens: They master their element and represent the principle of passive movement, indicating a moment of pause. They embody the paternal and maternal complex.

- Kings represent active, mature individuals or those with responsibilities. They are associated with the Emperor Arcanum, symbolizing the Animus, the solar consciousness projected externally through the paternal archetype. Kings are linked to power and authority.
- Queens symbolize powerful femininity, creation, and conception. They are associated with the Empress Arcanum and the maternal archetype, symbolizing the Anima, the inner soul, and Lunar identity. Queens signify submission, the desire to protect or care.

Knights and Pages represent quick movement and the fluidity necessary to progress and conquer. They are the impulse, growth, and communication. Symbolizing a state of change, they can be related to complexes of superiority and inferiority.

- Knights symbolize agile, strong individuals who bring about change. They are associated with the Chariot Arcanum and the Hero archetype. They are symbols of communication and overcoming their elements (Pentacles, Wands, Swords, Cups). Knights add dynamism and restart the cycle because they act, advance, and take risks, transforming thoughts into action and surpassing the perfection of their element. The energetic functions (emotional, mental, sexual, physical) are phenomenological forms of libido or psychic energy that remains constant. These are the four functions of consciousness. Knights are about action, strength, movement, everything that always puts us at risk (they are reckless). They possess the practical intelligence always required to pass the tests imposed by the Queens.

- Pages symbolize practical personality. They represent young people, employees, servants, workers, officials, and children. They are associated with the Magician Arcanum and the Puer Aeternus archetype. Symbolizing the principle of initiating action, Pages represent the energetic processes through which consciousness aligns itself through the four functions or intelligences, serving as channels to connect with the environment. They express the doubt or uncertainty of to be or not to be, to love or not to love, to do or not to do, to save or to spend. They express the desire to live, create, love, and be. Pages always need support from other figures, whom they take as learning models, just as a squire admires and constantly relies on the Knight he serves. They symbolize the uncertainty at the start of any activity.

The court figures represent certain archetypes, and their traits are grouped in familiar ways. What we understand as solitary individuals, dreamers, or life of the party are just qualities of individuality. Analytical psychology proposes a personality typology to study personal differences. Tarot, too, has its own system of personalities, represented by the sixteen court cards. Each card shows a side of the personality that is being expressed or seeking expression. It may be a valued trait or a neglected one. It may be a recognized aspect or a repressed one. This dynamic is reflected in the questions of inquiry. The cards reflect a situation of the human dimension, so a certain personality typology is always involved in a spread. The court figures of the tarot are characters with personal stories: understanding them is understanding our life. Their past and their dreams help us understand our own life.

Tarot and Psychological Types

With the aim of establishing differences and characterizing humans psychologically, Jung proposed four psychological functions of the psyche, which differ in how people can perceive and characterize the internal and external world. These are perception, intuition, thinking, and feeling. The first two correspond to non-rational functions that are accepted without any evaluation, without judgments, without reason, just perceptions of things as they are. Perception is produced with the help of the senses, and intuition is internal hunches without immediate influence from the external.

The other two functions are purely rational, evaluating experiences, categorizing, and organizing them, working with estimates. Thinking corresponds to a conscious judgment of truthfulness about an experience, true or false. Thus, thinking corresponds to a psychic function expressed through thought via intellect and logic, aiming to understand the surrounding world and its subsequent adaptation. Feeling manifests as taste, pleasure, or dissatisfaction, acceptance, or rejection. One of the functions is more relevant than the others. Jung called this the superior and inferior function.

Individuals are characterized by a predominance of either rational or irrational tendencies, among which one dominates, enabling them to channel their life actions in the present, orienting and adapting to the real world. One function becomes the most developed, serving as the dominant adaptation function, providing the conscious attitude with direction and quality. This is why it's called the differentiated or superior function. The superior function is more accessible to the threshold of attention. The lesser or inferior function is situated in the unconscious stratum. It can only be differentiated relatively and constitutes the function opposite to the main one. Its corresponding compensation would form a duality called the superior and inferior functions.

Meanwhile, the remaining two—called auxiliary functions—stay on the side and are relatively differentiated. Thus, psychic energy can be directed and oriented inwardly towards oneself or outwardly towards the exterior. In the case of extroverted individuals, who are social and outwardly oriented, they tend to find validity through the collective; conversely, introverts focus on themselves, behaving according to their own subjectivity. This, represented in tarot, would denote the quality of inner development and the unfolding of all the experiential possibilities an individual has throughout their life cycle. The inferior function is the most primitive and unconscious part of our psyche. We all have strengths and weaknesses, areas more developed and others that need to be explored. For example, more intelligent people tend to have less contact with their feelings; more sensitive individuals may have significant difficulties thinking logically. If we manage to identify our inferior function, we will know what we need to develop and what we need to strengthen.

Queens and Pages are associated with introverted personality types:

1. Introverted Thinking: They ask questions and try to understand their own being, retreating into the realm of their ideas.
2. Introverted Feeling: Inaccessible to others. They give off an impression of autonomy and harmony and often have a passion for music and poetry.
3. Introverted Sensation: They nourish themselves with sensory impressions and live immersed in their internal sensations. They are often modest and quiet.
4. Introverted Intuition: Dreamers, they surrender to their internal visions and strive to convey a unique esoteric experience.

Kings and Knights are associated with extroverted personality types:

1. Extroverted Thinking: They govern themselves and others according to fixed rules and principles. They are interested in reality more than material facts.
2. Extroverted Feeling: Conventional, well adapted to their era and environment. They are interested in personal and social success. They are fickle and conform to trends.
3. Extroverted Sensation: Interested in external phenomena. They are practical, stubborn, and accept the world as it is.
4. Extroverted Intuition: Their intuition gives them a nose for anything new. They often resolve disputes and are charismatic leaders.

Jung emphasized the importance of therapeutic work dealing with the inferior function through the individuation process, representing a task of great importance for personal growth. If we ignore our inferior function, we remain incomplete, and complexes will act with greater autonomy. Through work with tarot, we can explore the different functions through analysis, reflection, metaphorization, and the querent's own questions. Together with the response that the arcana offer, they are a great tool to expand the field of vision and achieve wholeness. A theme can be approached from the intuition and sensation it generates. Its content can be explored through the various thoughts and feelings that emerge to finally achieve a broader field of vision.

Tarot: Myth, Symbol, and Dream

> *Dream is the small hidden door in the deepest and most intimate sanctuary of the soul.*
> Carl Gustav Jung

As we have mentioned in the work, Jung classifies people into primary types of psychological functions. In this sense, the tarot allows us to explore through its arcana the four main functions of consciousness. Two of them are perceptive functions, also called irrational (sensation and intuition); the other two are judging functions, also called rational (thinking and feeling). As mentioned, the functions are modified by two main attitudes: introversion and extroversion. Within the psyche, there exists a compensatory mechanism that regulates the tension between opposites. The compensatory tendency is expressed not only in life but also in the dynamics of dreams and is one of the main foundations of Jung's theory of dreams.

If a person has a unilateral attitude during their waking life, the dream sends messages trying to compensate for it. For example, a person who is too optimistic about a situation in their dream might see that same situation pessimistically. In this way, the psychic energy produced by the tension of opposites manages to self-regulate. In dreams, the inferior function is often represented by animal, wild, or exotic figures. The shadow also appears in dreams as a snake, dragon, monsters, or figures of the same sex as the dreamer. The form the shadow takes will depend on the attitude towards it: if it is accepted or repressed, it will become an ally or an enemy. The Anima is personified in dreams through images of women ranging from seductresses to spiritual guides. The Animus, on the other hand, tends to appear as a male representation in the form of a Sage, Knight, King, etc. The archetype of the Self, for its part, tends to manifest in dreams in the form of a mandala or quaternary figures.

Marie Louise von Franz in this regard mentions:

> In dreams, the inferior function, whether it be thinking, feeling, sensation, or intuition, refers to the shadow, to the Animus or Anima, and to the Self, and gives them a certain quality or characteristic. For example, the shadow in an intuitive type will often be personified by a sensation type. The inferior function is contaminated by the shadow in each type: in a thinking type, it will appear as a person of primitive or relatively inferior feeling, and so on.

The union of opposites (Self, Shadow, Persona, Anima, Animus) is the main motive of dream dynamics. Like the Tarot, it is a dialogue formed between the parts that make up the psyche, whose ultimate goal is to integrate the contents into consciousness through the archetype of the Self, represented by the mandala or the World card. Jung often used the expression *coniunctio oppositorum* (union of opposites), taken from alchemy, meaning the union of masculine and feminine, the Sun and the Moon, heaven and earth, old and young, life and death, and all the opposites expressed in the myths of peoples and also manifested in dreams.

There are also prospective dreams, which anticipate future situations. This does not imply that they are divinatory dreams, but rather the unconscious stages events that can be anticipated given the life situations of the dreamer. Jung also mentioned the existence of parallel dreams, those whose meaning coincides with or supports the acts of waking life. These can appear when the person is on the right path; but when he doubts himself, then the unconscious sends the message that he is on the right track. The unconscious is, therefore, intelligent, and according to analytical psychology, it possesses a profound wisdom that is absent in consciousness. Dreams are expressed metaphorically and symbolically to help us face the problems of daily life.

Dreams bring messages from the unconscious; they are messengers of the realm of the soul that seek to mobilize the necessary resources to transcend. Mind and body form a unity, and just as the nervous system seeks to maintain its homeostasis through self-regulation, similarly the unconscious and consciousness constantly interact to maintain balance. The collective unconscious has a transpersonal character that links it to concrete reality. It possesses a type of intelligence capable of analyzing a large amount of data. Dreams are, therefore, sources of wisdom that connect with a whole beyond time-space and whose regulatory function with respect to the subject's life is to enable an approach to the totality of their being.

In Jung's work *Psychological Types,* from 1921, we see that Friedrich Schiller talks about a psychic split, which has been generated by culture itself:

> The rupture of harmony between instinct and reason is a wound that never fully heals. When the collective makes the superior function the measure of the subject for the sake of good order, the preferential use of a single function eradicates any possibility of individuality. Unilateral development leads to a reaction of the inferior functions that cannot be repressed forever. No integrative exercise will be

successful if there is not the capacity to release the energy of the inferior functions to carry out differentiation successfully. It is necessary to honor the energy laws by creating a slope that gives the latent energies the opportunity to manifest their effects.

The difference between extroversion and introversion lies in the different points of localization of libido. When there's a damming up of libido, the opposites that kept the vital flow united disintegrate. From this conflict and the energy released by it, the third element is generated, which is the beginning of new change, hence "only by gathering all the energy of our spirit into a single focus can we go beyond the limits that nature seemed to have imposed. The basic impulses confine man within the limits of time-matter. In human beings dwells the need for nature and culture."

David H. Rosen, in The Tao of Jung: The Way of Integrity, from 1998, describes Jung's conception of the Tao, an ancient Chinese philosophy. In that work, we can understand how the Tao is equivalent to the Self, which maintains a direct connection with the soul of the world unknown to the individual, with respect to Jung's conception. Regarding the dynamics of the unconscious, he states:

> But if we understand something of the unconscious, we know that it cannot be swallowed. We also know that it is dangerous to repress it, because the unconscious is life and this life turns against us if we repress it, as happens in neurosis. Conscious and unconscious do not form a whole when one of them is repressed and injured by the other. Both are aspects of life. Consciousness must defend its reason and protect itself, and the chaotic life of the unconscious must also be given a chance to have its way, as much as we can bear. This means open conflict and open collaboration at the same time. Evidently, this is how human life should be. It is the old game of hammer and anvil: between them, the patient iron is forged into an indestructible whole, an individual. This, in broad terms, is what I mean by the process of individuation.

Jung allows us to understand the following:

> The symbol stands in the center of the opposing functions as a mediator of one-sidedness. The transcendent way cannot be understood intellectually, but symbolically, its function is creative and comprehensive. The transcendent function aims to integrate

the contents of the unconscious into consciousness introducing a change of attitude. Thanks to this function, man can achieve his highest purpose: the full realization of the potential of his individual Self. Thus, what we call symbols of transcendence are those that represent man's struggle to reach that goal.

For instance, the image of the animal sacrifice is a symbol of the refinement of emotion. Marie-Louise von Franz notes how in many folk tales, although the animal functions as a helper and guide, it turns out that in the end, it is mutilated or sacrificed. Von Franz, who deeply explored the symbolism of fairy tales, proposes interpreting the animal sacrifice as "the sudden revelation of the spiritual meaning that seems to lie behind the correction of the animal instinct." She also highlighted how people need to follow their internal drives, but at a certain point in life, there is also a demand for these drives to be somehow sacrificed. In the tarot, we see reflected in many of the cards symbols associated with nature and animality. In the arcana of the Wheel, Strength, Temperance, the Devil, and the World, we see this dynamism of the psyche where facing one's own shadow is properly a process that allows access to the hidden treasures of the soul.

In the same vein, Barbara Hannah suggests that to extract the gold from the emotions that are in the instinct, differentiation with that emotion is necessary, to avoid succumbing to identification with them. If we cannot master our impulses through willpower in life, we often find ourselves turned into a wild animal divorced from consciousness, dissolved in the unconscious. When a deep psychological work of differentiation is carried out, we can extract the gold from the heart of the instinct, accessing the spiritual power present in nature. Instinct and spirituality are poles of totality. The author also reminds us that the desire to control instincts is an illusion. What we can do is "learn to accept them and disidentify from them, thus extracting the essence of their archetypal meaning."

The sacrifice of instinct allows the revelation of its spiritual, subtle aspect. The renunciation of immediate or literal satisfaction is what allows us access to the transformative symbolic. In nature, we see attitudes of sacrifice, unconditional love, harmony with the ecosystem. These behaviors often far surpass human traits. On the other hand, in civilization, we see unnatural behaviors. In this sense, humans can be worse or better than other species.

Animals are faithful to their instincts, to the internal patterns that regulate them and promote the necessary experiences for their fulfillment.

Therefore, they are not affected by the notion of progress or history. They have no cravings for accumulation or prestige. They do not deviate from their predestined path. They live in harmony with nature and in sync with universal cycles. Barbara Hannah suggests that the animals in our dreams and active imaginations are those that can lead us to the natural source of life. The author emphasizes the importance of being on good terms with the animal within us. It is proposed that the fact that some contents appear in dreams in animal form indicates that the aspects they allude to are not assimilated or integrated into human consciousness. Images of mammals would reflect aspects closer to consciousness. Cold-blooded animals, somewhat more distant, and invertebrates and insects would be related to deeper and unconscious strata of the psyche.

Ancient cultures related certain personality traits to a spiritual animal, which accompanies the human being from birth and manifests in dreams, something similar to the Greek concept of daimon. For ancestral wisdom, power animals were messengers of the gods, part of the spirit of the earth that granted man the necessary qualities to survive. Meanwhile, the soul corresponded to a divine factor from the cosmos that gave humans the imaginative faculty to create and think. René Descartes believed that animal spirits would assimilate to the "corporeal soul," although its nature, in Descartes' opinion, would be of a luminous character.

Hillman, on the other hand, highlights how our culture considers that the animal is something inferior, susceptible to being exploited and oppressed by a false sense of intellectual superiority, while for some traditional cultures, "animals impart the secrets of the cosmos. They are the masters in cosmology, that is, they mediate between the gods and humans; they possess divine knowledge. In polytheistic cultures, they are divinities themselves." Hillman then proposes considering animals in dreams "as gods, as divine, intelligent, indigenous powers that demand respect." Animals follow the rhythmic patterns present in nature, observed in the symbolic function of certain archetypes.

Hillman states, "An animal is an eternal form that walks among us, the palpable presence of time regeneration, adaptive life, and survival. Each animal is a sensual display of eternity, and thus, stars, the most enduring of all images, were imagined with names of animals." It is then proposed that animals appear in our dreams at times when we are required to descend to our instinctual level to connect with the "chthonic gods of the underworld."

Regarding this, Jung affirmed, "The animal figure indicates that the contents and functions dealt with in the tale are still on an extrahuman terrain, that is, beyond human consciousness, and therefore participate, on one hand, of the demonic-superhuman, and on the other, of the animal-infrahuman."

As we have mentioned, in this sense, man is a symbolic animal. Interestingly, animals also express a symbolic function through certain representative acts, such as penguins gifting stones to females, or birds that sing, dance, and create art to attract their mates. In nature, we observe fish that design geometric representations in their mating rituals. Other species use the combination of certain colors to capture attention. Thus, the symbol appears naturally as a universal archetypal expression, which leads us to suppose that the symbol's effect on the unconscious is due to its biological and cultural connection that forms part of the psychic structuring of man.

For this reason, we see that in the tarot there is a symbolic relationship with animal or humanoid figures. Practically, from the card of The Fool to that of The World, this connection with the natural part of existence is present, and it is presented as a representation of the biological part or the reptilian and limbic brain, where the phylogenetic heritage of all humanity lies. In the arcana of Strength, The Devil, and The Moon, we see more clearly this symbolism, as an indication of the reconciliation that humans must make between their divine and shadowy parts.

We also see in some cards like Temperance and Judgment the androgynous being as a symbol of the supreme identity present in most religious systems. The figure of the androgyne represents the higher level of the unmanifested being and corresponds numerically to the number 0, the most enigmatic and dynamic. The sum of the two aspects of unity, androgyny is then the starting point, the approach to totality through the integration of opposites, of light and darkness, of the feminine and the masculine. For alchemy, the androgyne represents the conjunction of opposites, in a cosmic principle that, both in Eastern and Western thought, is exemplified and symbolized erotically, as libidinal energy in its pure state. The androgyny of God only appears in Kabbalah, as a manifestation of the sexual act that gives light to life.

A legend about the 14th-century German mystic Meister Eckhart tells that one day a girl arrived at the monastery's doors, claiming she was his daughter and that she had no name. She also claimed she was neither maiden, wife, nor widow; neither knight or lady, nor slave nor lady. The mystic wanted to know more, so his daughter explained that, in relation to God, she was all these things and their opposites. This is the principle of the tarot. Through its cards, we see that we, regardless of our sexual identity, are all the elements that make up the tarot, both masculine and feminine traits, both animals and divine beings. We cannot deny, repress, or displace such aspects, because they are part of our nature. When humans lose connection with their own nature, they artificially create their own hell. Paradise is a beautiful garden where all species coexist in harmony and balance.

Therefore, in the tarot, we see a clear indication of how we must transmute this duality within ourselves to form a conscious unity. The internal and external aspects must be regulated by the emergence of a higher state of consciousness, represented by the Christ archetype. Consciousness can only develop as our capacity for symbolic understanding increases. This is the knowledge that allows us to free ourselves from suffering, which arises from the ignorance of not knowing the place we occupy in the universe.

Chapter 4
Quantum, Geometry, Number, Color, and Alchemy

In all chaos, there is a cosmos; in all disorder, a secret order.

Carl Jung

The tarot shows us a quantum process described in antiquity as alchemy, operating through a series of basic principles: geometry, number, and color. The universe is a vast mind that functions according to an established order. Amid cosmic chaos, there is an order that is accessible to the conscious mind. Therefore, since the tarot, as a book of wisdom, is based on these cosmic principles and is governed by the laws of the universe, it is understandable to access the information contained in energy. We understand with solid bases that it is possible to modify events that transpire through space-time.

In this area, the tarot ceases to be a therapeutic tool and becomes an energy key that opens dimensions that, in ordinary states, are hidden from common sense. The tarot turns us into time travelers, interdimensional explorers; we step out of the three-dimensional or linear mind to become part of the universal framework, recovering information from our own cellular, unconscious, and cosmic memory. Through this connection, we can become an instant that remains in the supraconsciousness as part of the harmonic order, like a chord tuned to a harmonic vibration that resonates in synchrony with the universe.

With this key, we can open the door to the mystery that the symbolic language guards for our perception of the micro and macro universe. By opening both the physical seals and those of the subtle bodies, we find ourselves more and more in our essential image, with which, by identifying, projects us into an experience beyond all mental perception, and we connect with the fact that we are a vibration that expands and contracts within itself. At this point, we cease to be form and transform into a vibration in its pure state, then passing through manifestations of the most beautiful cosmic geometries, which turn into numerical forms and alchemical colors. Finally, through vibration, we become the artistic manifestation of the consciousness of the cosmos. Time and space conjugate in eternity to create art, transforming life into a succession of images and symbols that weave a reality through which our mind can find itself to transcend.

Whoever manages to transcend the multiple universes that exist within and outside oneself through inner alchemy is able to make contact with the creative energy, a mystical experience that changes the entire inner world, restoring the capacity for wonder, re-establishing the lost connection between heaven and earth, between the individual and the collective. From that moment arises the certainty of being and the responsibility that comes with taking charge of one's own destiny through internal development.

Quantum Tarot

At any point where we focus our attention, time and space converge in the total activity of the universe. This means that, in retrospect, for us to be aware of a thought, a whole series of synaptic circuits have had to move, whose origin dates back to the formation of a cosmic order. All activity is connected to an origin that scientists have named the Big Bang. The infinity of preceding causes has a close relationship with each other, just as when something moves in the present, at that precise moment, something is moving in the future. The effects of the causes are moving at this precise moment as a whole uroboric interconnected to a network of events that connect past, present, and future, and whose synchronicities expose the great external reality of internal contents. If we consider space as the place of simultaneous exchange of all parts, time becomes a mere illusion, as the absolute oneness outside of space-time is always present.

From this conception, life itself is only the vision of a projection. Nothing exists except empty space and the Self. Everything we call reality starts in the vacuum that precedes thought. Our mind is capable of constructing reality with the attention we give to that empty space. Therefore, matter is more *nothing* (energy) than *something* (particles). New scientific discoveries indicate that the atom is composed of 99.99999 percent energy and 0.00001 percent matter. Quantum experiments demonstrated that electrons exist as an infinity of possibilities or probabilities in an invisible field of energy. Only when an observer focuses on any location of an electron does that electron appear.

The power of our mind lies in the way we can experience our imagination through the management of our thoughts and feelings. By nature, everything that exists in the physical universe is made of subatomic particles like electrons. These particles are in a wave state until they are observed. They are potentially everything and nothing until observed. We are a consequence of the creation of our attention, so it is of utmost importance to be aware that by focusing our attention on the power of 99% of our intentionality, we can shape what we conceive as destiny. Behind every act, a reaction is generated as a consequence of our initial intention. Photons of light dance in harmony with the permanent atom shaping our reality. From this perspective, we can see the tarot as a quantum instrument where the observer structures an electron at a specific point in space and time.

According to these discoveries, a person is creating and forming their future and reality, so knowing privileged information through reading allows the consultant to bring the necessary energy from their personal and collective unconscious to potentiate the probable futures they can access. The tarot acts in the present to facilitate the reception of information that enables a consciousness awakening. To achieve this objective through the tarot, the past is evoked to release blockages, traumas, beliefs, habits, and all factors that may impede the flow of necessary energy to manifest the desired reality. Knowing the tarot is to know our creative power, which lies beyond physical reality and beyond all linear thought limitation. When we delve into our internal system, illusion schemes that limit our evolution are broken.

Given that little is left to chance nowadays, or rather, nothing is by coincidence. Everything has a purpose which, in the end, is the consciousness awakening. Nothing escapes energy, life is a continuum, the world is part of the universe of vibration, and the human being is a co-creator of their own destiny. The old conception of the material and physical world through formulas and rules has been changed. Everything that was formerly conceived as magic, we now know has an empirical foundation.

Between each subatomic element lies the quantum vacuum field, a sea of vibration altered by fluctuations, translating into virtual activity within the empty space. The quantum vacuum is a sea of creative energy composed of matter and antimatter that annihilate each other, giving rise to null energy, thus maintaining the essential property of the vacuum. The importance of virtual particles lies in their role in transmitting information and energy, being responsible for the fundamental forces of nature (gravitational force, electromagnetism, strong and weak nuclear forces). Hence, they are called "the messengers of the subatomic universe."

According to superstring theory, an electron is not just an element or point without dimension or structure, but a coiled string that vibrates in a spacetime of more than four dimensions. Those that shape matter have a practically infinite number of material states, and only by measuring their state do they stabilize in a specific one. Since it's not possible to measure or calculate their real position or speed, a wide range of probabilities in multiple dimensions is created. Since galaxies, like quanta, create energy vortices in the multidimensional universe, they give rise to the state of spin, which is a rotation movement of particles that, by creating a torsion wave, generates a vortex where information travels instantly to the other side of the universe, where a similar event occurs. This is known in the scientific field as entangled states or twin particles. The interesting fact about this is that both particles share this state simultaneously, regardless of the distance between them. It's as if they were connected by an invisible thread, by a powerful force that binds them. This entanglement of quantum particles is the basis of quantum teleportation.

It's possible to perceive and know through our connection with the surrounding whole that we are energy, we have an electromagnetic field in our body and our thought, which belongs to the subatomic level. Fluctuations are the source of creation. Our brain acts in all dimensional energy fields, and the waves through which it communicates (brain, heart) also function as particles. Therefore, we are linked by a collective quantum vacuum that synchronically connects us with all planes of existence.

Recently, researchers from the School of Medicine at the University of Washington (USA) show how brain areas in the motor cortex responsible for movement are connected to specific neural networks involved in thinking, planning, controlling organs like the stomach, or involuntary bodily functions such as blood pressure and heart rate. This demonstrates the relationship between thoughts and actions. Our brain creates and receives torsion waves. When the spin state in thought is maintained or sustained, the ordinary state of rational mind shifts towards a new conception of oneself, giving rise to what we know as a quantum leap. Quantum psychology does not consider mental illnesses as possible but views them as a disharmony between the body and mind. The differentiation between mechanistic thinking and quantum thinking is to move from *cause and effect to causing an effect*. The former (mechanistic thinking) wants something external to cause an internal change; the latter (quantum thinking) is for something internal to produce an external change.

The human body is composed of approximately 50 trillion cells, forming a network in which everything is interconnected. Neural networks interact through a constant exchange of synaptic energy to create cerebral maps, which, once encoded in memory, can be revisited through imaginative recall. Psychic energy manifests itself in the form of images. These images are universal and can be recognized across different cultural expressions, in speech, people's behavior, and, of course, their dreams. Symbols and myths, which seem to exist in all known cultures, indicate to Carl Gustav Jung that all human societies think and act based on a cognitive and emotional foundation. Jung believed that understanding the unconscious required taking his theory beyond the functions of an organism. Jacobo Grinberg developed the synergetic theory, explaining how the brain interacts with the informational field some call the quantum field, and others, like David Bohm, refer to as the implicate order.

After the significant contributions of Newton and Descartes to science, Albert Einstein's famous formula ($E = mc^2$) demonstrated that energy and matter are the same, forever changing our view of the universe. To broaden our perspective on quantum physics, it's necessary to consider the three laws of energy:

1. Everything is vibration.
2. This energy must flow and to do so must be in a slight state of imbalance.
3. Energy of a particular quality or vibration attracts qualities or vibrations of the same type.

For quantum physics, absolutely everything in the universe is composed of atoms, vibrating at different frequencies. Likewise, a company is a set of frequencies vibrating in coherence to create a single body. Everything, from its brand, workers, material goods, shareholders, as well as customers and suppliers, all form a single quantum field. The internal states of the employees reflect the *health* of the company, and this in turn determines the external effect that it will have on society.

Joe Dispenza, biochemist and neuroscientist, is one of the main proponents of quantum reality. Dispenza asserts that "the mind determines the external experience, because everything boils down to fields of energy, so our thinking constantly alters our reality. Most people are thinking about their problems instead of thinking about the possibilities." Dispenza insists that what prevents us from creating our future is a series of thoughts, behaviors, and emotional reactions that we have repetitively memorized. Therapy based on quantum psychology operates on the most unconscious levels, changing programming through affirmations, meditations, guided visualizations, therapeutic dialogues, etc. For all the above, we see in the tarot a quantum tool capable of modifying the reality of the consultant through its base elements: geometry, number, and color.

Geometry

As we have mentioned, everything in the Universe is made of matter and energy. Energy causes atoms and molecules to be in constant movement, spinning around themselves, vibrating, and creating life. A vibration is the propagation of energy waves. It can be considered as an oscillation or repetitive movement. A frequency is the number of times it oscillates (goes up and down). An energy wave is measured in hertz or Hertz (Hz). Basically, frequency is *music*. From the beginning of the universe with a big bang to the beginnings of human life, when at times in the womb, the mother's and fetus's heart rate (BPM) are synchronized, sound remains present through movements and vibrations. Within the *I Ching*, Hindu mantras, and the Gospel, the relevance of sound is evident. Some recent studies even suggest that cells emit harmonious sounds when they are healthy and chaotic sounds when they are sick.

Binaural sound therapy is a non-invasive form of brainwave entrainment that works by helping synchronize both hemispheres of the brain. Meanwhile, resonance is the phenomenon that occurs when an internal frequency matches an external one. Everything in the Universe has a molecular vibration, nothing is at rest, everything moves, vibrates, and circulates at different frequencies that communicate with each other. People vibrate because they are made of atoms and molecules that respond to energy. As mentioned, the frequency of a wave is a magnitude that measures oscillations per second in a vibration. Both in sound and in the manifestation of light in the form of colors, they obey a geometric ordering pattern, so we can point to frequency, vibration, and energy as the basic architectural structures of the universe.

When we analyze sacred geometry, we observe a metric system that reveals the measure of things through patterns, systems, codes, and symbols, which we observe both in the macrocosm (galaxies, planets, Earth's ecosystem) and in the microcosm (atomic nucleus, neutrons, protons). Since ancient times, Plato postulated the five Platonic solids as the ways in which energy solidifies and constructs matter through the four elements, and a fifth force called ether. From Plato's perspective, the universe must contain a suction force capable of maintaining nuclear force and performing toroidal movements of implosion and explosion, which would be responsible for shaping the material universe.

The toroid, or torus, is a geometric figure constructed with golden spirals inscribed in a sphere, similar to a donut or an apple. The toroid is the shape that atoms, photons, and every minimum constitutive unit of reality take. In the figure of the toroid, all the principles of sacred geometry are gathered: the Great Void, the Law of Unity, the Law of Duality, the principle of self-sustenance, the three mathematical pillar numbers of sacred geometry: Phi, Pi, Euler.

Toroids are classified into sexual, motor, emotional, intellectual, and instinctual toroids. The psychological dimension of these figures is transcendent; in it, the dynamics of opposites converge simultaneously. Its geometry comes from the great void, which is literally a point in space from where everything emerged. These pairs of opposites are shaping the psychological notion of interaction with reality, through which the human being comes into contact with matter or loses contact with it.

It's important to mention that of the five Platonic solids, only three of them contain the golden ratio: the octahedron (intellectual toroid), the icosahedron (emotional toroid), and the dodecahedron (instinctual toroid). The other two Platonic solids, the tetrahedron and the hexahedron or cube, do not have the golden ratio in their construction. Their function is related to the potential to generate structure. The toroid graphically represents the process by which all energy, when properly aligned, is continuously in harmonic, cyclic motion up, down, and around, representing the movement between spirit and matter.

As we've discussed, in the universe nothing is still, everything moves, everything vibrates. Matter and energy are merely the results of vibratory states. Spirit is a polar extremity of higher vibration, and matter is a denser polar extremity. Between both extremes, our thoughts and emotions act as intermediate frequency vibratory states. All matter is formed from tiny particles called atoms, which in turn are made up of even smaller particles called subatomic particles (electrons, protons, and neutrons).

The so-called law of attraction is the way our thoughts and emotions harmonize with certain vibratory states, increasing the likelihood of evoking specific experiential situations.

Interestingly, everything in the universe is made of matter, and matter is composed of atoms and molecules. These particles are made up of quarks, and quarks, in turn, are composed of photons of light. String theory posits that if we were to observe a subatomic particle under a very powerful microscope, we would realize that it is not actually a point, but a small loop or string vibrating in space-time. In other words, these strings are vibrational states, and what causes them to vibrate is energy. Therefore, according to this theory, we can assume that absolutely everything is energy. Hence the importance of focusing our attention on configuring the intentions of our quantum field, rather than on the consequence of our own actions. The purity of our intentionality determines the final outcome. The only thing we can truly control in this universe is how we react and manage our own internal resources.

Exploring sacred geometry, we discover that shapes are directly related to Earth's geometry. From the golden ratio in the arrangement of continents to the geometric patterns in the Earth's magnetic fields, creation is a cosmic dance between energy and matter. Every seed, mountain, river, and forest reflects an order that reveals a connection between nature and the cosmos. This same order is present in the human spirit and mind when we observe that mandalas were used in different cultures: Egypt, China, India, America, Europe, etc. It is evident that they emerged from a collective mind as a manifestation of the structure of the human spirit. In our daily life, we find mandalas in the concentric circles generated by a drop of water, the pattern formed by the petals of flowers, in the interior of a kiwi, an orange, and many other fruits and vegetables.

Mandalas are present in nature and in ancient civilizations from the beginning of human life on Earth. One of the oldest mandalas is the circle of giant stones at Stonehenge, in Salisbury, England. Even in crop circles, these mandalic forms appear mysteriously. In North America, numerous tribes, such as the Lakota, create mandalas using colored threads and feathers (dreamcatchers). In the Huichol culture of Central America, the eyes of God or *si'kuli* serve to see and understand the unknown. In Hindu and Chinese culture, these geometric forms likewise hold great symbolism.

When we analyze great works of art, such as the *Madonna of the Goldfinch*, Botticelli's *Venus*, or Da Vinci's *Vitruvian Man*, we see universal mathematical constants emerge. These mathematical proportions are present in great historical monuments, such as the Great Pyramid of Giza in Egypt, the Parthenon in Greece, and Notre Dame Cathedral in France, geographical locations that are aligned with celestial positioning. In the present era, these same architectural principles are used in the construction of the most sophisticated skyscrapers, allowing for detailed construction of window placement, ceiling heights, and column proportions. These principles reflect the harmony, symmetry, and balance present in nature and are associated with principles of divine beauty.

Some people who work with sacred geometry claim that these symbols stimulate both hemispheres of the brain: the right side relates to artistic and spatial skills; the left to mathematics and logic. With new computer and neuroscientific tools, it is possible to propose a relationship between sacred geometry and the divine proportion, and from this to the Fibonacci sequences, which represent the fundamental algorithm of creation, the source code of the universe, and its mechanism of self-adjustment. In this way, we can understand how geometry shapes our perception and grants us, through the symbolic function, a way to understand the organizing principles of the universe. This has been evidenced in the work of Dr. Lauretta Bender, who created the Bender-Gestalt Test, using a series of geometric figures to assess visuomotor gestalt function in both children and adults.

Within the area of sacred geometry, the triangle symbolizes balance, harmony, and realization; the square represents the foundation of stability; the spiral expresses the connection of the body with the higher self, relating to kundalini and the flow of energy; the cross embodies the principle of the union of heaven and earth. Other universal geometric symbols include the Seed of Life, Flower of Life, Tree of Life, Metatron's Cube, Star of David, Merkaba, Vesica Piscis, etc. Thus, geometric figures, like numbers, are a way to understand the relationship between matter and energy. They personify archetypal principles that confer a universal sense of organization among the universe, nature, mind, body, spirit, and soul.

In tarot, we primarily find the six spheres of the universe in the major arcana. First are the cardinal virtues (Strength, Justice, Temperance, and the Hermit represents prudence). These virtues have a divine force, guiding us towards cosmic principles (Moon, Sun, Star, World). Once this force and contact with nature in a divine and virtuous form are established, the possibility of finding external and internal balance emerges, through the spiritual and material dimension (Emperor, Empress, High Priestess, Hierophant). With these pillars, we build our personality (Fool, Magician, Lovers, Hanged Man). To complete our evolution, we must confront fate (Devil, Death, Judgment), for which we have three points of support (Chariot, Wheel, Tower). These symbols confer a depth of dimension that allows us to understand through their cards the cosmic principles that grant man the power to transcend his life.

Thus, tarot readers and alchemists are tasked with exploring and expanding the spirit of their time through artistic work (tarot), a work that, if conceived from the creative impulse, would exceed the scope of conscious understanding. The language of the unconscious is symbols whose essence does not lie in the personal history of the individual but in the collective history of humanity, according to Jung in his work *On the Phenomenon of the Spirit in Art and Science*, 1966:

> The symbol is structured as a language perceptible to reason. As a language, it can be accessed, but as a symbol, it cannot be fully grasped. The unconscious expresses itself through symbols. The symbol is not a closed, unequivocal, or essential concept but ultimately an unlimited reality, an open horizon, and a language of which the human being only knows its yields.

Number

For Jung, our psyche is part of nature and expresses itself according to these organizing principles (archetypes) described by the sages of antiquity. The quaternity and mandalas are the forms in which the psyche managed to structure itself through an organizing principle present in nature and the cosmos. In the initiation centers of ancient Egypt, various disciplines such as numerology, astronomy, astrology, symbology, and tarot were taught. In these schools, it was demonstrated that there was a harmony between the cosmos and an intimate connection between the macrocosm and the microcosm, recognizing at all times that the disharmony of some parts affects the general harmony of everything.

The Pythagoreans established precise relationships between arithmetic, geometry, music, astronomy, and astrology, all considered numerical sciences. Everything that happens in the cosmos is based on vibration, rhythm, and cycles, which can be studied and interpreted through the tarot. Regarding this, Nikola Tesla mentioned, "If you want to understand the Universe, think in terms of energy, frequency, and vibration." Numbers are representations of conscious force fields. We can say they are conscious entities since, as energy fields, they are at the base of everything. They are connected with everything that exists. They allow us to explain the origin and manifestation of all creation. Like sacred geometry, it has two sides: a contemplative and a practical side, an intuitive and an intellectual side, a quantitative and a qualitative part. In popular culture, the Matrix could well exemplify this ancient knowledge about a symbolic code that precedes everything we define as reality.

To perceive the so-called reality, the mind needs a logic to structure it, while creative sensitivity needs the intuitive and contemplative part. The cerebral hemispheres must work in synchrony, activating and balancing all the neural circuits that allow encoding and decoding the synaptic impulses that form our image of the world. Each arcana we work with, like numbers, colors, and geometric figures, are representations of fields of consciousness.

Numbers, as fields of energy, are the foundation of all creation and are intimately connected with the workings of the universe. In every figure, a part of creation itself is represented, always containing the archetypal energy of numbers. Here, we are not talking about measure or quantities, but about the essence of numbers as conscious entities. In the cosmos, everything is related to everything else. What happens in one part of this whole affects everything that happens in others. From the moment we are born, we are part of this cosmos and are influenced by the energies of the closest celestial bodies around us. But in reality, we are influenced by all parts of the cosmos, just as everything that happens to us in some way influences the entire cosmos. Thus, understanding numbers as organizing matrices of the universe's energy becomes the master key to accessing knowledge that remains hidden from the senses.

The first thing we need to know is that the tarot is like a calculator: if we can understand the meaning of numbers 1 through 9, we will have done much of the work. The digits from 1 to 9 symbolize the stages through which an idea must pass before it becomes reality. Pythagoras believed that the universe is subject to progressive and predictable cycles, and to measure and understand these cycles, one had to use frequencies ranging from 1 to 9. The correct application of the vibratory code possessed by numbers invites us to a direct reading regarding the underlying intelligence of the universe. Through numerology, Pythagoras constructed the possibility of understanding the characteristics and faculties possessed by all individuals, along with life events, since he saw in numerical and geometric patterns the explanation of all natural phenomena.

Each number functions as the result of a specific vibratory manifestation, just like a musical note. The meaning of the numbers was interpreted by

Pythagoras from 1 to 78 through the tarot. They represent a story of conscious and correlative evolution of existential experience on the earthly plane. Most religions talk about what the soul and spirit must learn. And this map is expressed in numbers. Like a language where each word has an empirical representation and both an objective and subjective meaning, the same happens with the semantic expression of each number. The entire Bible could be summarized in a simple mathematical formula (3 + 1) (Paradise, Sin, Salvation, Paradise).

Each number will have both a positive and negative aspect, and it is the interpreter of the card's job to explain the work that each frequency demands: one cannot and should not make cuts within numerological readings, as it deals with a totality that constructs the whole. If in making a chart, a person has many number 2s, one is dealing with a sensitive, empathetic individual, who always seeks another, who will be insecure, fearful, and will have to work on their fears and insecurities to generate a different emotional matrix. Numbers have certain archetypal qualities that, as we have explained, have a philosophical precept: 1 not only represents a quantity but unity; 2 is not just the sum of 1 + 1 but represents the duality of experience; 3 symbolizes a dimension of height, the Logos as an expression of internal thought; 4 represents quaternity as a manifestation of concrete reality accessible to consciousness... Thus, each number has a quality that goes beyond a simple numerical value.

The knowledge of the tarot is based on understanding the hidden meaning of numbers. This knowledge is one of our greatest allies when we want to learn to interpret the meaning of each card, for which we must address both the qualitative and quantitative meaning of each number to achieve a correct interpretation:

Zero. Represents nothingness, that is, where everything emerges. It can be the beginning or the end, there are no limits, and it represents infinity.

One. It is the starting point. It signifies unity, action, independence, motivation, the capacity to give, creation, will, and beginning.

Two. It is the beginning of something from two. It signifies balance, contrast, opposite poles, association, communication, negotiation, selection, distribution, intuition, the need to seek a balance.

Three. It is creation itself. It symbolizes imagination, what is neutral, the middle point, harmony, charm, fecundity, grace, the gift, time, variety, mystery, intuition, and the link between will and feeling.

Four. Space, the tangible, matter, the body, the four extremities, stability, endurance, functionality, the physical, humility, simplicity, the fruit or product, the son, the cross, the cardinal points, the elements, and practicality.

Five. Represents the environment, roots, family, people as a collective, the gateway or a window to something, the bridge that connects the interior with the exterior, thought, communication, adventure, and movement.

Six. Signifies a crossroads, choice, work, sacrifice, renunciation, vocation, growth, adventure, attraction of opposite poles, emotion, love sensation, free will, trust, and sincerity.

Seven. Perfection, imagination, awareness, understanding, healing, courage, decisiveness, valor, sagacity, self-discipline, independence, individualism, rebellion, and originality.

Eight. Signifies opportunity, observation, intention, abundance, repetition, justice and norms, law, order, balance, stability, serenity, and responsibility.

Nine. Represents a goal, the end, principles, aspirations, ideals, philosophy, experience, wisdom, the end of the path, abandonment, loneliness, and doubt.

Ten. Represents the end of a cycle and the beginning of a new one, therefore, rebirth.

You might wonder why we explain the meanings only from 1 to 10. Well, because, according to the numerology of the tarot, in every figure there is a root number. For example, 16 sums up 1 + 6 = 7. Since antiquity, great thinkers from Plato to Leonardo da Vinci were amazed by the theory of the golden ratio and the regular polyhedra, also known as Platonic solids. One of them, the dodecahedron, held a prominent place in the arithmetic mysticism of the Pythagoreans. For the Pythagoreans, the number was the essential material of all things. From their own experiments with the monochord, they proved that numbers described the theory of musical sounds and also explained the movement of the planets, as the mathematicians of Babylon already knew.

Pythagoras was one of the first to discover both the quantitative and qualitative qualities of numbers, relating them to metaphysical aspects. It seems that in many cultures, numbers were ways in which gods communicated; for others, they were the source code of the universe. In addition to Pythagoras, great geniuses in history delved into the mystery of numbers. Tesla believed that 3, 6, and 9 were numbers that connected with the frequency of your desire and could attract it into your reality. 3 represents the connection with the source or the universe, 6 represents inner strength and harmony, and 9 represents internal rebirth.

Even Carl Jung and Wolfgang Pauli were fascinated by the mystery of the number 137 and the principles of synchronicity. Pauli argued that a theory was needed to determine the value of the constant and "thus explain the atomic structure of electricity, which is such an essential quality of all atomic sources of electrical fields that occur in nature." One of the uses of this curious number is to measure the interaction of charged particles like electrons with electromagnetic fields. Alpha determines the speed at which an excited atom can emit a photon.

The number 137 is a magical figure that has intrigued physicists for over 50 years. Physicist Richard Feynman believed that there is a number all worthy theoretical physicists should be concerned about. He called it "one of the damn biggest mysteries of physics: a magical number that comes to us without man understanding it." This magical number, known as the fine-structure constant, is a fundamental constant with a value equivalent to 1/137, or 1/137.03599913, to be exact. It is designated by the Greek letter alpha (α).

What makes alpha special is that it is considered the best example of a pure number, which does not require units. In fact, it combines three of the fundamental constants of nature: the speed of light, the electric charge carried by an electron, and Planck's constant. Delving into the associated information, the inverse value of this number, that is, 1/137, is a universal constant of electromagnetism called the "fine-structure constant"—it's not necessary to go into much detail here.

It's only important to note that the mystery lies in the fact that such a constant does not have associated units like the rest of the physical constants, which, according to science, means it is a pure number. This would imply that it is a constant that does not depend on the system of units being defined. Thus, this characteristic sharpens its significance because the mystery of any law of physics or natural law is always rooted in its constant values.

Analogously, in tarot, all the knowledge of the deck is contained in ten numbers, plus one unnumbered card. We can establish a dual relationship between the arcana that allows us to understand the relationship that exists between all the cards: the Fool and an unnumbered card of totality; the

World, which brings together the major arcana with the minor arcana and is one of the important cards representing total realization. From a Jungian perspective, the World card is related to the archetype of the Self, the central archetype of the collective unconscious. The image of the totality of the psyche, the center that gives meaning to life, and in this sense, the central axis of the tarot that represents the journey of the Fool as the hero's journey.

According to Alejandro Jodorowsky's methodology, the tarot deck is conceived in 78 cards as follows:

- The Fool: Represents essential energy, without anything to limit it. It is zero.
- The World: Represents indivisible totality. "All is one," it is 21.
- Number 1, The Magician (rational world) and Strength, 11 (unconscious world). Both cards symbolize a beginning.
- Number 2, The High Priestess (rational world) and The Hanged Man, 12 (unconscious world), both cards symbolize an accumulation of knowledge and experience.
- Number 3, The Empress (rational world) and Death, 13 (unconscious world). Both cards symbolize an action of transformation.
- Number 4, The Emperor (rational world) and Temperance, 14 (unconscious world). Both cards symbolize external or internal manifestation.
- Number 5, The Hierophant (rational world) and The Devil, 15 (unconscious world). Both cards symbolize a temptation to change level, in the light (5) or in the dark (15).
- Number 6, The Lovers (rational world) and The Tower, 16 (unconscious world). Both cards symbolize an emotional discovery (6) or a creative discovery (16).
- Number 7, The Chariot (rational world) and The Star, 17 (unconscious world). Both cards symbolize the conquest of the external world (7) or the conquest of the internal world (17).
- Number 8, Justice (rational world) and The Moon, 18 (unconscious world). Both cards symbolize inner balance (8) or outer balance (18).
- Number 9, The Hermit (rational world) and The Sun, 19 (unconscious world). Both cards symbolize a spiritual understanding (9) or an understanding in the material (19).
- Number 10, The Wheel of Fortune (rational world) and Judgment, 20 (unconscious world). Both cards symbolize a realization in the world (10) or a realization in the beyond (20).

In the Minor Arcana, we observe that the whole has four doors:

Swords, representing the intellectual; Cups, representing the emotional; Wands, representing the sexual; Pentacles (Coins), representing the material.

When grouping the Major and Minor Arcana together, we can see that there are groups that form the structure of the tarot:

- Degree 1
  Seed, totality, beginning, origin, unity
  1 The Magician "to channel energy"
  11 Strength "will"
  Ace of Swords "potential of the mind"
  Ace of Cups "potential of love"
  Ace of Wands "potential to create"
  Ace of Pentacles "material potentiality"

- Degree 2
  Gestation, accumulation, inaction, union, duality, stability
  2 The High Priestess "gestation"
  12 The Hanged Man "meditation"
  2 of Swords "accumulation of thought"
  2 of Cups "union and connection"
  2 of Wands "accumulation of energy"
  2 of Pentacles "preparation and agreements"

- Degree 3
  Action, balance, harmony, creation, discovery
  3 The Empress "powerful and creative action"
  13 Death "changes and transformations"
  3 of Swords "mental activity"
  3 of Cups "love, triumph, abundance"
  3 of Wands "creation, decision, determination"
  3 of Pentacles "new work, clients, earnings, success"

- Degree 4
  Stabilization and power
  4 The Emperor "laws, authority, order"
  14 Temperance "harmony"
  4 of Swords "comprehension"
  4 of Cups "emotional stability"
  4 of Wands "repetition of creation, routine"
  4 of Pentacles "good health, good salary"

- Degree 5
  New ideal, crisis, communication, transition
  5 The Hierophant "guide and communicator a bridge"
  15 The Devil "temptation, passion"
  5 of Swords "new knowledge"
  5 of Cups "idealizations"
  5 of Wands "desire"
  5 of Pentacles "expansion, remodeling, change"

- Degree 6
  Pleasure, discovery, harvest, passivity, wisdom, enrichment
  6 The Lovers "union, addition, creation, doing what one loves or desires"
  16 The Tower "independence, opportunity for growth"
  Six of Swords "joy of thinking"
  Six of Cups "union and decision"
  Six of Wands "creative and sexual pleasure"
  Six of Pentacles "prosperity"

- Degree 7
  Action in the world, transitional state, desire, instability, intelligence
  7 The Chariot "movement and decision"
  17 The Star "creation, hope"
  7 of Swords "thoughts finding their action"
  7 of Cups "altruism, kindness"
  7 of Wands "action towards others"
  7 of Pentacles "materialization of the spirit"

- Degree 8
  Perfection and receptivity, harvest, tranquility, karma, action, and reaction
  8 Justice "consequence of action"
  18 The Moon "intuition, femininity, mystery"
  8 of Swords "meditation"
  8 of Cups "fullness of the heart"
  8 of Wands "concentration of energy"
  8 of Pentacles "prosperity and health"

- Degree 9
  Crisis and evolution, obstacle before a great learning
  9 The Hermit "wisdom, solitude, introspection"

19 The Sun "success, true love, fraternity"
9 of Swords "enlightenment arising from a crisis"
9 of Cups "leaving one emotional world for another"
9 of Wands "leaving one thing to do another"
9 of Pentacles "birth, reward"

- Degree 10
End and beginning of a cycle, fulfillment, change
10 Wheel of Fortune "fulfilled destiny, concluded cycle"
20 Judgment "awakening of a new consciousness"
10 of Swords "intellect filled with love"
10 of Cups "fulfilled love life"
10 of Wands "creativity reaches the spirit"
10 of Pentacles "prosperity that begets creativity"

We can view the different groups of tarot cards as a multiverse. To understand this, we can imagine that our existence is a conjugation of different universes, starting with the most obvious, the galaxies, and terrestrial ecosystems. Looking closer, we find within each person a universe made up of molecules, cells, bones, organs. In another universe, there are viruses, bacteria, antibodies. In another, synaptic energy, and so on, until we reach the universes of the spirit, instincts, emotions, and consciousness (Pentacles, Cups, Swords, Wands). However, all these dimensions together are part of the same reality at different levels of existence and are correlated with each other by forces beyond our understanding.

Commonly, the expression "breaking the fourth dimension" is used to mention the limits that separate the real from the imaginary. The fourth wall is, figuratively speaking, what separates the audience from what occurs on stage. Talking about the fourth spatial dimension sounds like science fiction. And not without reason, even among mathematicians like Ludwig Schläfli, the fourth dimension has long retained its mysterious aspect. Popularly, the fourth dimension is associated with paranormal events or sometimes with Einstein's theory of relativity. We can understand the fourth dimension as that reality which is only accessible through psychism, through a specific language like that used by scientists to explain the functioning of the universe. This can be exemplified by the recent creation of the metaverse, where a space constructed by mathematical symbols enables the conjugation of a reality that goes beyond the material, where through the projection of holographic avatars, a common space for interaction is formed.

Color

Thanks to M-theory, theoretical physicists like Stephen Hawking have postulated that our universe could contain up to 11 dimensions, 10 of space and one of time. One of the most significant advancements in science that could prove the supposed existence of these hidden dimensions is the Large Hadron Collider, which has enabled experiments that were previously impossible.

Analogously, in the tarot, there are 11 colors considered from the alchemical system as the brush that brings life to the tarot: black would be the so-called nigredo (manure, putrefaction, fertilizer), while violet represents the philosopher's stone (the spiritualization of matter). The colors represent principles: the first is black (matter) and the last is violet (spirit). The colors represent an ascending journey of the being:

- Black: chaos where order begins, fertility, growth, depth, represents harmony or the effect of cosmic movement on us.
- White: purity, fidelity, sanctity, soul, virtue, and simplicity, the bright light of the moon, represents higher planes.
- Flesh: humanity, matter
- Dark Green: temporal nature
- Light Green: eternal nature.
- Red: animal kingdom, activity
- Navy Blue: receptivity to earthly forces
- Sky Blue: receptivity to celestial forces
- Orange: receptive intelligence, energy, joy, happiness
- Bright Yellow: active intelligence, development of the intellect, represents sunlight
- Violet: wisdom

Many people have believed since ancient times that colors possess some kind of magical power. Even tarots, such as the Rider-Waite tarot and the Tarot of Marseilles, are composed of highly colorful cards. Mood is fundamental to all facets of our lives, and color is a way of expressing the energy of the soul. In nature, color has a function of utmost importance. Similarly, in culture, color is used by brands as a means to reach the consumer. According to the Color Marketing Group, a company specialized in the use of colors, nearly 85% of the reasons why a person chooses one product over another have to do with the perception of color. Color psychology is also applied in branding. For example, the color red is used to stimulate appetite; McDonald's, Pizza Hut, KFC, and Wendy's use this color in their logos and facilities.

Vasily Kandinsky is considered one of the fathers of painting. He was convinced that colors could be used as a universal language capable of speaking directly to the soul. For Kandinsky, the use of certain colors could provoke a specific emotional response in the viewer. It was only necessary, according to the artist, to find the right key to unleash the strings that oppress the soul. Kandinsky stated the following: "Color influences the soul directly. Colors are the keys, the eyes are the hammers, and the soul is the piano with its numerous strings. The artist is the hand that plays, pressing one key after another, to cause vibrations in the soul." In Kandinsky's paintings, influenced by theosophy, geometric shapes and colors reflect thoughts, intuitions, sensations, and defined emotions.

Vasily Kandinsky, in his book *On the Spiritual in Art* from 1911, addresses the two effects that color has on the viewer: the physical effect of color, which can be assessed through chromotherapy, and the effect of color that acts on the nervous system, not only by association but by physical repercussion. And an effect when, by association, the color is linked to personal and cultural meanings, or to objects and shapes. Color, says Kandinsky, has enormous power. Harmony and the use of color are based on the principle of contact with the human soul. A resonance in which the inevitable relationship between color and form is involved leads us to observe the effects that form has on color.

Art throughout history has shaped civilization. We can affirm in a sense that art created the world. When the first Paleolithic decorated caves were discovered at the end of the last century and the beginning of this one (Altamira, 1879; La Mouthe, 1895; Les Combarelles and Font de Gaume, 1901), the scientific world discovered in art one of the most important functions of the human being, manifesting that capacity to encode the world through mental maps. The magic art hypothesis posited that the first works of art were the result of transpersonal experiences. Art in the caves represented the first records of abstract signs, the fundamental thing about this discovery would be the complementarity and alternation of two principles, the masculine and the feminine, as derivations of the representation of the sexual organs (pubic triangle and penis), and on their frequent association with certain animals, assimilated to a woman equivalence (or female sign) bovid and man (or male sign) horse. Nowadays, the presence of oval and phallic forms in hundreds of commercial products is not a coincidence.

Kandinsky speaks of that canvas, which the artist turns into an ideal, where the first great abstraction occurred, by abandoning three-dimensional modeling and turning reality into a composition of two-dimensional elements, such as color and line. On that same canvas, it is possible to combine through contrasts and harmonies the play of graphic pictorial compositional elements freed from the object. Art, for Jung, has the capacity to make visible archetypal images of the collective unconscious in which the era becomes aware of itself. Jung proposed the technique of "active imagination" as one of his major contributions to the therapeutic field. Regarding art, he mentioned the following:

> Art is a kind of innate drive that seizes a human being and makes him its instrument. The artist is not a person endowed with free will who seeks his own benefit, but art itself allows its purpose to be realized through him. Literature constructs worlds, real or fantastic. Through narrative, human phenomena are accounted for, and in the best cases, it manages to express part of reality.

For his part, Freud thought that the work of art had the same origin as dreams: both were the manifestation of an unconscious desire and were created in the same way. The same mechanisms operated both in dream construction and in artistic creation, hence it was possible to extend psychoanalytic discourse towards the work of art as a way to access the depths of the mind where the soul resides.

Alchemical Tarot

In antiquity, alchemists used art as a tool for transmutation: the Great Work (Magnum Opus). Today, alchemical texts are known mostly for their illustrations. The content and operations they describe are wrapped in symbolism that requires deep study of an entire universe of symbolic correspondences. Among the books of alchemy that modernity has rescued, we must mention *Aurora Consurgens*, a text dating from the 13th century, but whose illustrations, for which it is famous, are from a 15th-century edition. Professor Raimon Arola mentions that the relative notoriety of this book is due to Carl Jung seeing in alchemy a precursor to the processes of spiritual integration of the human psyche. He found a compilation from 1590 titled *Artis Auriferae*.

In his study of Hermetic science, Jung found the other part of the manuscript in the library of Zurich. It is this part that has become more well-known, under the impulse of Jung and his disciple, Marie-Louise von Franz, who published an edition of the *Aurora Consurgens* in 1966, with commentary on the Jungians' favorite theme: the conjunction of opposites. This work consists of 37 images, in which the alchemical process is represented alongside a profuse symbolism characteristic of alchemy. There is the trinity of mercury (the son, a serpent), gold (the father, the Sun), and silver (the mother, the Moon), in addition to the different animals associated with each stage of transformation. The process to achieve this, according to Jung's comparative reading, involved extracting a celestial spirit from matter through dissolution, separating the pure from the impure, circulating it to activate its original splendor, and then coagulating it. This spirit was the quintessence, the eternal and incorruptible aspect of the body, a *corpus glorificatum* that could unite with what the alchemist Gerhard Dorn called "the *unus mundi*," the Adamic state of divine unity. The entire process is about separating to reunite, materializing the spirit and spiritualizing matter through the work of art, one through the other.

Spiritual alchemy proceeds in this same manner. This is why Jesus tells us to elevate our souls towards God by praying and reincorporating them again by exercising charity, thus becoming one, as He was one with the Father. The alchemists used the figure of Christ, according to Jung, because Christ is the archetype of the perfect man, of the complete man. Jung states:

The lapis, which is born from the dragon, is praised as the savior and mediator, as it represents the equivalent of a redeemer that has emanated from the unconscious. The Christ-lapis parallel wavers between a mere analogy and a profound identity, but generally, it is not thought of as a logical conclusion, hence a dual approach remains. This is not surprising, as many of us today have not yet come to understand Christ as the psychic reality of an archetype, beyond his historicity.

We find mythological references of great similarity between Christ, Quetzalcoatl, Osiris, Dionysus, and other deities that are primordial ideas transcending humanity. For Jung, "these archetypes are not devised by man, but man is an incarnation of these archetypes." The alchemists sought to complete Christ's victory over worldly powers, and therefore they wanted to obtain the universal remedy against suffering and death. They were the continuators of creation, the restorers of paradise, of a redemption that has not been fully effected or that, at least, must be effected in each individual. This identification of Christ with a chemical factor, with a medicine or elixir obtained from nature, has unconsciously, given that alchemy is the precursor to chemistry, elevated the status of matter, that is, transformed energy through a continuum into another plane of existence.

This image appears with some constancy in the comparisons made of the philosopher's stone with the phoenix, the bird that rises from its ashes, sometimes, like Christ, on the third day. The axiom of Maria the Jewess expressed a *leitmotif* (metaphor) through a numerical equation, 3 + 1, which represents the path of restoration from duality to unity and the possibility of returning from the exterior to the interior towards the lost paradise through the manifestation of Christ consciousness.

In *Symbols of Transformation* (1952), Jung highlighted the symbolic analogies between the mythical Solar hero and Jesus. In Psychology and Alchemy, he demonstrated the symbolic similarities between Christ and the alchemical lapis; in Aion, he revealed the synchronism of the Age of Pisces with the symbolism of Christ as a fish and as an archetype of the Self that evolves over two thousand years, while reflecting on its complement, the Antichrist of the Apocalypse. Jung says that the imitation of Christ causes man to develop and elevate internally.

To transform the shadow, the Sun must be introjected into the heart's center through discernment of cosmic principles. Christ is obviously connected with the Sun and with the regal, triumphant, and luminous aspect of consciousness. Without the experience of opposites, there is no experience of totality, nor is there internal access to sacred figures; without original sin, there is also no possibility of salvation. Christianity raised the antinomy of good and evil to a universal problem and, through the dogmatic formulation of opposites, elevated it to an absolute principle. Good is equivalent to the unconditional imitation of Christ; evil, its impediment.

In the path of the tarot, we see that true human development corresponds to spiritual birth. This birth can only occur through the manifestation of a symbolic life. For this reason, the archetypal images represented by the arcana propose a rebirth, which happens when all the chemical elements have been given in the correct proportion and all physiological events have developed to their complete realization. The movement that the Fool begins reaches its climax; then it is time to return home. From that moment, a door opens, that of the promised land (the World). This represents the final work, which allows, from the symbolic perspective, to liberate the wisdom of the feminine spirit trapped in the materialistic view of the world, represented by Christianity as the Holy Spirit, in popular culture as *exiting the Matrix*, or also in psychology as *becoming aware* of the illusions in which the ego is submerged.

The Fool is also known as the Mat. If we add it to the World card, the result is the Metaworld, a term used by Cristóbal Jodorowsky as an analogy for psychological integration and a means of personal empowerment that allows us to be creators of our own reality. Through the development of attention and purpose, we discover that this universe is moved by a greater purpose. When we are aware of this fact, we can orient our lives towards such a purpose, this cosmic destiny is represented in the tarot as the path of the Fool and the World.

The tarot cards are an instrument that gives us direction, as they are structured like a true treasure map. This means that the tarot will show us the way to this integration, as defined by Jung. Archetypes are innate energies common to all human beings, transmitted through myth or manifested in dreams, stories, legends, rituals, and works of art. In the tarot, archetypes can act as guardians of our behavior when the individual needs to solve an existential difficulty. For this reason, Cristóbal Jodorowsky mentions:

> The arcana of the tarot are doors to contact the universal energy within oneself. These doors, when activated, allow a profound change in our psyche, so that our soul can express itself in total freedom, allowing the person to be in contact with their deep needs.

For C. Jodorowsky, a healthy being is one who no longer lives imprisoned by the past or influenced by fear of the future, but lives in the present (in the here and now). A person who has undergone a process of individuation no longer lives as a victim or a villain but is free from self-destructive forces. An integrated being does not live conditioned by dogmas or limiting beliefs. Through hard inner work, they have managed to unify the three brains (reptilian, mammalian, human) and integrated the two hemispheres (logical and artistic). In this way, their body, mind, and soul find the necessary congruence to live in harmony with the cosmic principles present in nature.

The realization of the World represents the concept described by Abraham Maslow as self-actualization, referring to the personal development process in which a person strives to reach their maximum potential and satisfaction in life. It is a state in which a person feels fulfilled and satisfied with themselves, with a strong sense of purpose and meaning in life. According to Maslow, self-actualization is a continuous process and a goal that must be pursued throughout life. This path represents the power to achieve congruence between thinking, saying, and acting. Maslow describes the characteristics of a self-actualized person: skill development, growth mindset, healthy relationships, physical and emotional well-being, deep sense of life, and personal transcendence.

Chapter 5
Psychotherapeutic Readings of the Tarot

Now that we have knowledge about the tarot deck and a solid epistemological approach, we can use the tarot to guide a therapeutic process from the perspective of analytical psychology. The act of meditating and reflecting on each arcana represents the possibility of analyzing our life (childhood, adolescence, adulthood, personal relationships, beliefs, etc.), as well as the various situations we face throughout our life cycle. This in itself is a method towards the development of consciousness.

We can see in the arcana a ladder to ascend to a different way of thinking. When, after a long process of reflection, we finally reach the top, it will be possible to contemplate a deeper meaning of our existence and change our way of acting and reacting, acquiring from that moment the ability not to identify ourselves with all those masks that tie us to certain social roles. All the hidden potential of our personality lies beyond that comfort zone when we manage to integrate all the parts that make up our being. When we access totality, we transcend our individual ego, becoming more understanding of our surroundings, developing the necessary responsibility to take charge of our destiny, and contributing our greatest talents to the world.

The current crises we face as a society are due to this inability to find a healing method that allows us to become aware of our actions. The world is immersed in major conflicts: wars, terrorism, totalitarianism, environmental crises, mass shootings, stress, suicides, addictions, etc. All these events have as their root the lack of development of a higher level of consciousness. The division and lack of empathy among humans can only be addressed by illuminating our wounds. Recognizing our differences and understanding the individuality of each being represents a significant evolutionary leap for the current civilization and is part of a necessary process to remedy the current condition of humanity. The ability to connect with universal love can be achieved through any religion, philosophy, belief, book, movie, or, as proposed by this work, through the tarot.

Traditionally, the tarot is used as a system of questions and answers where, in most cases, the attempt is to forecast a situation, predict the future, or resolve a doubt, which can often be quite complicated. For example, when a tarot reader claims that the querent's partner is cheating with a lover of a certain physical description, or when suggesting that someone close is stealing money, or that bad news will be received soon. This generates a series of suggestions that, far from helping the querent, can be harmful.

Truly making use of that kind of information should be a task guided by an ethical code. No matter how well one knows the tarot, responsible use should be limited to conveying the information that emerges from the querent's own unconscious. The questions asked in a consultation can serve to identify a projection or a problem that can be worked on. For example, a querent asks if their ex-partner is still thinking about them: we really cannot know this for sure, but what we can know is that the querent is thinking about their ex-partner, and therefore it is likely that there is an unresolved mourning process in the background. This indicates a guideline for initiating a therapeutic intervention. What is not closed in a previous relationship will be projected onto the next one, so it is important to properly conclude one cycle before starting another.

If a querent asks if they will get married soon, we can discern an underlying need that may complicate their interpersonal relationships and rush things. Thus, that question can be an opportunity to address what a wedding or an engagement ring represents for the querent. Clearly, what can most help the querent formalize a relationship is to shift from a state of lacking to a state of completeness. Developing self-love and healing emotional wounds is a process that can help the querent improve their relationship and delve deeper into a sentimental commitment.

When a querent asks if they will get the job they desire, we can understand that there are doubts about their own abilities to secure that job, so we can start working on self-confidence and developing the necessary skills to increase their chances of achieving that goal. In reality, nothing is defined; there are multiple futures, and where the querent places their attention and energy is where they will mobilize their potential to take action. However, the tarot can help us indicate which characteristics or traits increase or decrease the probabilities of achieving that goal.

Thus, every question has an underlying issue that reveals the concerns disturbing the querent, thereby establishing a pattern for intervention. Similarly, doubts arising at an intellectual level can serve to delve into the emotional issue. When doubt comes from an affective layer, it can help manage thoughts that allow for better coping with a situation. When intuitions lead down an uncertain path, it can help structure more functional beliefs. Every question indicates a positioning and a function that is present, so each querent's question is valuable information that enables a course of action within the therapeutic space.

If a patient asks us if they will become a millionaire or famous, we can understand there is an unsatisfied desire for recognition or a state of lack, so we can take the opportunity to explore what the relationship with money symbolizes for the querent or what social recognition represents for them. In this way, we can help them reach their full potential through work on their spiritual sphere to help them connect with those needs that must be met to achieve a state of fulfillment.

If in a reading there is a concern for issues related to mystical experiences, divine knowledge, and spiritual evolution, we can help the querent see beyond fanaticism or religious dogma by allowing them to realize that their life will prosper in all aspects as long as they can develop empathy, compassion, understanding, and faith in themselves. When the querent discovers that to progress on the spiritual path, they must take responsibility for their interpersonal relationships and develop a commitment to the planet and their own life's vocation, at that moment, they will be able to discover on their own that spirituality arises from communion with their own inner self, and from the contact they can establish with their own soul. Thus, understanding this will make it more feasible for them to evolve spiritually. To achieve their spiritual goal, the querent will not need to perform magical rituals nor pray hundreds of Our Fathers for each sin committed; their spiritual progress can be translated into the simple commandment of becoming aware and loving their neighbor as themselves.

The knowledge of the Minor Arcana allows us to know that true satisfaction is found not only in satisfying a specific aspect of life but in achieving harmony among the four elements. This way, the possibility of transcending to the higher spheres of life emerges. Most people tend to orient their questions around health, money, and love, without recognizing that often there is a hidden desire to develop their spirituality and find a deeper meaning to their existence. All human beings have an unconscious desire to leave a legacy in this world in the form of a family, a job, a work of art, or anything that allows us to be part of the history of this world. Not even wealthy, attractive, famous people or spiritual guides escape existential voids, sadness, and the frustrations that come with living.

Working with the Major Arcana offers us the possibility of an evolutionary development of consciousness. In this sense, the tarot offers more than simple answers; it is more than an oracle of divination or a means to obtain what we desire. We are all seeds with the potential to become great trees that can bear fruit over time, but few of us find the right conditions (sun, water, fertilizer, etc.) that allow us to flourish in all our splendor. We constantly ignore what our true desires are, confused by societies that stimulate success. We are indecisive about what actions to take to achieve personal well-being.

According to Erich Fromm in his book *To Have or To Be?* (1976), the current formula for success suggests that we must *have* in order to *be*. If we don't have, we are not. However, within deep philosophy, we find that we must *be* in order to *do*, which eventually leads us to *have*. Finding a deep meaning to existence is an essential part of personal growth. Having a clear vision allows us to direct our life mission towards what we really have to do (will, discipline, perseverance, etc.) in order to have abundance (health, money, love, and happiness).

For Fromm, the compulsion to have increases our frustrations and is a fundamental cause that still leads us to harmful or frankly self-destructive behaviors, both individually and collectively. Fromm outlined a broad panorama of the conditions necessary to generate authentic change in human life and, with it, significantly improve our relationship with the world, nature, and the planet in general. According to Fromm, if human beings want not only to survive but also to live in harmony with their environment (with their fellow humans and with nature), they must first learn to *be*.

Victor Frankl stated, "Life is not primarily a quest for pleasure, as Freud believed, nor a quest for power, as Alfred Adler taught, but a quest for meaning. The greatest task for any person is to find meaning in their own life." This call to develop and cultivate certain essential qualities for life can be found within the tarot, as a path towards spiritual fulfillment that implies an evolutionary journey. Spirituality is a function that arose with evolution as an integrative platform for civilization. We can only ensure the continuity of our species in space-time if we educate ourselves in the art of being more human. The next evolutionary leap for our species is not wings or longer necks but the possibility of transforming into beings with a higher level of consciousness.

Tarot Spreads

To start a reading session, first, we look for a quiet place, our peace corner. We should visit it again and again. We will sit with our back straight in a comfortable chair. Close your eyes and practice complete breathing, also called long and deep breathing. It basically involves inhaling air through the nostrils in four equal cycles, holding it as long as possible in the lungs, and then exhaling it also in four identical cycles through the mouth, trying to visualize the journey that sigh makes from the inside of our being to the outside of us, until it integrates with the cosmos. We will attempt this over and over again until we are completely calm, and then let ourselves be carried away by imagination to that place in the past that pleases us the most. Subsequently, we will let childhood memories envelop us, dialogue with the inner child, and ask for its help. And we will go even further, towards those universal forces (God, Jesus, Buddha, angels, etc.). This is an indisputable preliminary step to being a good interpreter of this oracle. Once meditation has allowed us to clear our mind of obstacles, we will take the tarot deck.

Why is this preliminary step necessary? Because it's related to the principle of correspondence, which explains that the vibration of the spirit is of infinite intensity. For the ancient Egyptians, reality was nothing but a replica of what remains hidden. For this reason, we must level and synchronize our brain waves to the same state. It's important to establish a good communication link that allows connecting mind, heart, and spirit, calming our body in the process. Performing a prior meditation practice allows us to achieve such a state. Now we know why it's important to fully identify with the deck of cards to be a good interpreter of this oracle. As therapists, empathy is our greatest instrument of work. We do not reveal the mystery of an invisible spirit, but rather, we connect with the synaptic vibration of the present time, which sharpens all our senses to be able to channel our intuition with whatever the querent needs from us. The healing process with the tarot is an accompaniment through a healing process that the querent must undertake. The therapist merely guides the querent in their own healing process.

The session or card reading should never last more than 45 minutes, at most we can extend it to an hour. We see in this item that the structure of attention is being respected. It's difficult to maintain high concentration for longer than that. Following the style of suggestions we have been making, the reader will already foresee what the answer is. However, as long as we can have the office well-ventilated, illuminated with natural or artificial light, and clean, we will be in a position to do a good job. We can put on some relaxing music, light some incense and candles to create an atmosphere of tranquility.

Now that we have a conducive space for healing, we can propose some card readings from a therapeutic approach. The proposal of these spreads is a basic example of how to start a reading session, but it's necessary to understand that this sequence of cards can be expanded to delve deeper into the meaning. In the tarot, nothing is definitive, and when there are doubts or there doesn't seem to be a clear message, more cards can be drawn. It's also not necessary to throw the whole deck. The session concludes when the necessary information is obtained to work on a theme, or when a message emerges to provide clarity on some personal issue from which the reason for the consultation derives.

The proposal of this approach is to use tarot readings to guide a psychological accompaniment process. For this reason, a reading can serve as a preamble to a series of sessions. If, for example, in the first session we observe an emotional wound or mourning, we can plan a therapeutic plan of several sessions where we work on a specific theme using various techniques such as therapeutic dialogue, letter writing, art therapy, music therapy, psychocorporal massage, active imagination, guided visualization, metaphorization, the empty chair, neuro-linguistic programming, channeling emotions, etc. Now that we have this clear, we can contemplate the different types of readings that we can perform with the tarot.

It's important during a reading to delve into and ask the querent for relevant information about their life, to have a broad overview of their situation, rather than trying to guess. It's vitally important to achieve emotional accompaniment that facilitates the expressive integration of all those experiences that are painful for the querent. During the session, it's important to allow the querent to express what memories, sensations, and intuitions each card generates for them, allowing them to project their inner world and introject the lessons that each arcana has for them. At all times, we must practice active listening and try to connect with their emotions. The querent and the tarot reader must construct a narrative or clinical history to establish a path of healing with clear objectives.

Reading of the World

In this reading, we can analyze our relationship with the four main needs of human beings: emotional, material, intellectual, and spiritual. The center, the World card, represents our Self. Cups, Pentacles, Wands, and Swords will be the space where the cards that emerge will indicate what we need to work on and integrate to improve each aspect of our life.

This reading can be approached from the humanistic perspective. The pyramids of human needs can serve as a guide to explore our biological and safety needs with the Pentacles, social belonging and affection needs with the Cups, recognition needs with the Swords, and finally, self-realization needs with the Wands.

Basic needs will be covered by the Pentacles and Cups, while higher needs, by the Swords and Wands. The cards that appear in the reading in each space should be interpreted as the tarot's message regarding that need, according to the meaning revealed by the arcana.

Reading of Time

Past Present Future

This reading can be useful for structuring a sequence of time in which we can analyze what we need to heal from our past, what we need to accept in the present, and the challenge we have to face to create our future. These three times can propose an action plan to transform our situation and allow us to locate our perception of both the past and the future. Thus, we can identify limiting beliefs, fears, emotional blockages, incomplete cycles, and deficiencies that could limit our evolution in the present. Normally, disappointment, sadness, and guilt come from the past from all those situations that we cannot change and that constantly fill us with complaints. Anxiety, on the other hand, comes from all those situations that have not yet happened and fills us with expectations and fears that cause us emotional tension.

The only thing we have is the here and now. Focusing on the present is the best opportunity we have to modify our reality through responsible actions. This reading can be approached from a Gestalt perspective, allowing us to manage our resources in the here and now to have all the intellectual, energetic, emotional, and spiritual capacity at our disposal to visualize a better future. In this way, we will realize what we need to do to reach that prosperous future we desire so much. This reading offers the opportunity to integrate and express the parts that make up the narrative of our life. If we are capable of changing our internal script, we will be able to find a new path filled with hope and possibilities. According to Epictetus: "It's not what happens to us that affects us, but what we tell ourselves about what happens to us."

Reading of Emotions

Joy

Sadness

This reading helps us explore our emotional management and delve into which thoughts or beliefs are associated with that emotional expression. Being able to identify our emotional rationalizations allows us to find a means of expression to validate and modify them. Each emotion plays a role in our lives. An emotion is an internal state that influences our external actions. Emotions guide our behavior with the goal of increasing the probability of survival and ensuring our well-being. This reading can be approached from a cognitive-behavioral perspective or through NLP (Neuro-Linguistic Programming). An emotion is closely associated with a thought. An emotion releases a series of neurotransmitters that in turn influence a certain way of acting, which perpetuates a cycle in which behavior feeds back into a belief that fosters a thought, which in turn reinforces a feeling about a specific event in our life that gives rise to a belief. The way we process information and how that processing influences us determines our behavior.

The involuntary reaction that occurs in the autonomic nervous system and the endocrine system causes variations in breathing rhythm, blood pressure, muscle tone, pupil dilation, etc. The emotional state reflects the emotion externally: voice tone, body gestures, facial expressions, etc. When our ability to cope with this reaction is overwhelmed, we live in a prolonged state of stress. Over time, these emotions can become somatized, generating symptoms or diseases. Unexpressed emotions have negative consequences on our organism. The inability to process affective states such as fear, guilt, or pain significantly affects our lives.

This reading allows finding, through the analysis of the arcana, those beliefs and emotions that identify us. At the same time, these same archetypes are attached to our psychic biology, so that we can restructure these beliefs to free ourselves from such emotions. Working with emotions can be approached from the recognition of physiological symptoms. When an emotion arises, a series of neurotransmitters released into the bloodstream activate certain bodily sensations that make us feel a certain way. It's as if we drank ten cups of coffee in one gulp. Understanding these mechanisms can be useful for channeling emotional states by understanding the usefulness of that emotion:

- Sadness: Sadness appears in the perception of a loss. From it derive other secondary emotions such as loneliness, pessimism, disappointment, or guilt. Its function is personal reintegration. It motivates us to ask for help, reflect, and make changes in our life.
- Fear: Fear appears in the face of threatening situations or stimuli. That threat can be real or imagined. From this emotion arise states of insecurity and anguish. Its function is to protect us both physically and psychologically from situations that endanger our integrity.
- Joy: Joy arises when we achieve something we desire. It generates security, a feeling of well-being, and leads us to reproduce those behaviors or actions that make us feel good. Its function is affiliation, and its reproduction allows us to orient ourselves towards activities that generate well-being for us.

- Anger: Anger appears when we perceive that something we want or desire does not go as expected, or when we perceive that someone intentionally interferes in the achievement of our goals. It is related to annoyance or frustration. Its function is self-protection. It allows us to establish boundaries that protect us from adverse situations.

Other emotions like disgust and surprise help us protect ourselves or stimulate us towards those experiences that can benefit or harm us. All the situations we live are associated with an emotion that guides us towards a certain way of acting and reacting. To manage emotions correctly, we can formulate phrases that consider the function of each emotion. For example, in fear and anxiety, we can repeat to ourselves: "I know this emotion is a protection mechanism. I am safe, no one can harm me, regardless of how I feel. Soon I will regain balance, and everything will return to normal." If we also combine these phrases with breathing exercises, music therapy, art therapy, and visualization, we can intelligently manage our emotions, avoiding impulsive reactions.

According to Daniel Goleman, emotional intelligence is the ability to recognize both our own and others' emotions and to manage our response to them. We can define it as the set of skills that allow greater adaptability to the environment. An emotion provokes an action, a response, which is usually automatic, or in other words, a reaction to a stimulus. Emotions carry considerable energy, which propels us into action. We can say that emotions are the bridge between thought and action. According to Daniel Goleman, emotional intelligence has five key elements:

- Self-awareness
- Self-regulation
- Self-motivation
- Empathy
- Social skills

The central axis of emotional intelligence is to be able to "think with the heart and feel with intelligence." In this sense, this tarot reading offers the possibility to modify thoughts to change emotions, or on the contrary, to manage emotions to structure more functional thoughts. When we change a thought, we change an emotion; when we modify a feeling, we can think differently. Between these two aspects, beliefs can serve us to achieve such action. If we believe that we are victims or villains, it's logical to feel defenseless, demotivated; however, if we go beyond our limiting beliefs and see ourselves as people capable of recognizing our own mistakes and learning from them, we will have the capacity to manifest other kinds of emotions with more positive effects in our life.

Reading of Family Constellations

Paternal Grandparents Maternal Grandparents

Father Mother

Older Siblings Younger Siblings

In this reading, the positioning of paternal figures is on the left side, while maternal figures are positioned on the right side. Siblings are placed according to the order of birth: older siblings to the left and younger siblings to the right. Likewise, the cards that appear will be the message that the tarot has about the projection one has on grandparents, parents, and siblings. This way, this reading enables exploring the family system dynamics to establish a healing process.

Every family system has a structure. Often, these systemic orders cannot be structured in the most appropriate way: there are mothers who have to be fathers, children who have to take care of their parents and siblings, grandparents who have to be parents... Families are often marked by tragic events: deaths, abortions, abandonments, fights, wars, migrations, etc. For this reason, it is necessary to structure the unconscious disorders that bind us to the family to understand our origin and place in this life.

If we know where we come from, we can clearly know where we are going, no matter how painful our life story is. The recognition of these events allows us to create a healing narrative. Despite our deficiencies, we can structure the elements of a family dynamic by honoring our past. No matter what we have lived, no matter how dark our past has been. Only when we connect with the root of our past can we heal our present and design our future. We are all heirs to a past we cannot change. At the same time, we are responsible for creating a better future. Happiness cannot be known without knowing sadness; life cannot be valued without the presence of death. Thus, the recognition and acceptance of all life experiences from childhood to the present are the only possible path toward the emergence of a complete being.

The second part of the constellation reading is done with one's own family dynamic if we have a partner or children, placing grandparents and parents in the same way but adding the partner and children to the family system.

Paternal Grandparents Maternal Grandparents

Father Mother

Querent Partner

Children in order of birth

Healing occurs when we are capable of recognizing, accepting, forgiving, and transforming everything that causes us pain. Our life experiences are a source of knowledge that, with a bit of luck, can be transformed into wisdom. Everything we did not like or wish we had experienced differently can be modified in our own life story. We can become the parents we always wanted to be by changing our behavior patterns and making conscious the wounds and traumas that exist in our family tree. These memories of pain are transmitted through epigenetic mechanisms. This emotional energy often manifests in our life as a form of unfinished destiny, which is marked in our family tree.

When in our life we feel affected by emotions that do not have a logical explanation or pains that do not correspond to an observable event, it is likely that we are affected by events experienced by our ancestors or unfinished destinies that marked our family system. To free ourselves from the memories of pain, it is necessary to honor our great-grandparents, recognize the suffering of our grandparents, the sacrifice of our parents, and understand the place occupied by present and absent family members. The dead live within the living: our great-grandparents are part of our mind (Swords); our grandparents live in our heart (Cups); our parents, in our sexuality (Wands); finally, the absent and present, in our body (Pentacles).

To heal the unresolved issues of the tree of life and honor the family destiny, it is necessary to close cycles by recognizing the pain and accepting the family gifts. The relationship with our family system is a bond that comes from the soul. We must understand our hierarchical order in the tribe. We must give each member their place and restore balance by closing all unfinished cycles. For this, it is necessary to:

1. Recognize the emotion (fear, anger, joy, sadness).
2. Understand the mission of such emotion.
3. Recognize the function of the emotion by integrating it.
4. Let go and be thankful for the learning.

In the Tarot, Temperance balances emotions by looking at the past, The Star honors ancestors indicating a path of healing; in the Judgment card, we see in the family dynamic a process of integration; finally, The Sun indicates fraternal love, love towards children, and the union of the family system as a whole.

The Arcana 1 and 10 represent the healing process. If we observe the image of Arcana 10, we see that it is just a wheel left to its fate (family destiny). There is no one to make it work using the handle, there is no fortune there for the moment. But if it is followed by The Magician, a character appears who makes it spin, indicating with his wand in his hand his will to make fortune come, and in the other hand, he has a gold coin to define the type of gift that is being awaited. However, if we change the order, first The Magician and then The Wheel, a catastrophe occurs because The Magician is concerned with obtaining another type of treasures looking into the void, The Wheel remains unused and for that reason, it is not possible to change the family destiny.

The Lovers Arcana represents emotional connections and the family system. If we add Arcana 6 and The Emperor = 10, The Wheel of Fortune emerges. This Arcana allows us to intervene with love and modify the unfinished matters of the family destiny that could affect the structure of our genealogical tree and the own family lineage. According to Ismael Sánchez's methodology, to heal we must:

- Recognize the emotion: fear, disgust, anger, sadness, shame, joy.
- Give a place to the emotion, what is its function: protection, boundaries, reflection, remorse, joy.
- Integrate and be grateful for the function of the emotion that allows us to grow and advance.

In this way, we can conclude unfinished cycles with our genealogical tree, using healing phrases like now I see: _____ I recognize that: _____ despite: _____ thanks for_____ now I decide to live_____.

People with an intellectual personality type are usually more prone to fear and their insecurities due to a lack of vision. Emotional people suffer sadness due to their sensitivity. The visceral ones are more given to anger and rejection because of life's injustices. The corporal ones are more prone to succumb to their weaknesses and temptations. However, they can also develop great strength. All personality types have strengths and weaknesses, blind spots, and areas of opportunity.

Healing the bond with parental figures allows us to structure unresolved unconscious disorders. Whether we have a close or distant relationship with our parents, healing the connection with Father and Mother allows our soul to find inner peace by recognizing our hierarchical order within the tribe. The Arcana 0 represents that unconscious search to find our place, the internal positioning. The Arcana 3 and 4 represent our earthly parents. If we add 3 + 4, the Arcana 7 appears, which symbolizes our place in space-time. We are

50% Father Sun and 50% Mother Moon. We are composed of mind and soul. Healing the relationship with our parents grants us the possibility to introject the Sun and Moon as representatives of our masculine and feminine energy, which reflects a highly functional personality structure where we are capable of manifesting logical, orderly thinking, but also being sensitive to our inner self, finding a sense of joy in life. If we summarize the work with the genealogical tree, we could say the following:

- I become aware that what I carry is not mine.
- What I carried was a movement of childish love, which at its core is a way of interfering in the destiny of my ancestors.
- I honor the burden because it helped me move through life for a long time. I honor the origin because that is where it belongs.
- I return the burden to my ancestors with love, because I understand that is where their experience and wisdom lie, not trying to save anyone.
- I take responsibility for my own burdens and become an emotionally adult.

In life, we sometimes carry unresolved situations from our ancestors because we manage them from a place of childish love. From the ego, we tell ourselves the story of "I have to save"; however, adult love is understanding that everyone must take responsibility for their own happiness. I honor my ancestors when I leave their burdens with them and transform their experience into learning. Within a family constellations reading, we can ask during the consultation: What do I need to know to heal and improve my family relationship? What does my family need to be at peace? We can reinforce our reading with phrases like:

- I connect with my ancestors.
- I connect with my family.
- By order of love, my family is here represented.
- I accept, learn, and transform to heal.
- From now on, peace and love will be mine.
- I deserve, desire, and manifest happiness in my life.

To conclude, we can meditate by visualizing an image of our family, focusing on a memory that generates tranquility for us. Whenever we remember our loved ones with love, they will live in our minds and hearts as an altar that rises through time over the eternity of an immortal dream. We must work on an image of parents that allows us to heal regardless of what our relationship with them has been like. It's necessary to understand that we were created by a universal love that transcends our own parents. We should imagine our parents to project a healing image that allows us to introject a positive memory, thus making it possible to structure a healing narrative. Our parents become a gateway to our own mind and soul; for this reason, we must heal the bond with parental figures, to find peace and achieve well-being in our lives.

We must accept all our life experiences so that we can stop struggling with everything we cannot change. When we leave behind childish claims, we are more capable of moving forward with maturity, lightening our baggage of unnecessary burdens by re-signifying all life experiences. Pain becomes part of our inner wisdom, ceasing from that moment to represent limiting situations. When we honor and respect our past, we gain the power to take charge of our own destiny. When we become our own parents, we take care of our inner child.

This tarot reading is of vital importance to remove the blockages that hinder our personal development by correcting one dimension (Pentacles, Cups, Swords, Wands). It influences the other aspects of our life. If we are capable of mobilizing the energy of our family system, we can structure more functional thoughts. When we mobilize our internal resources, we can heal grief, emotional wounds, deficiencies, limiting beliefs, repetitive behavior patterns, complicated relationships, unconscious loyalties, self-sabotages, and childish reproaches.

By recognizing the hierarchy and belonging within the family system, we find our corresponding place, such that we can give and receive in equity, finding balance in our system. By establishing family roles, we can structure a healthy partnership that facilitates unity and order in our family system. To evolve, we must heal individually, regardless of whether we are accepted or not. As long as we are capable of loving without limitations, we can progress. The Tarot allows constellation work by enabling emotional support and accompaniment necessary to intimately and personally express everything that needs to be managed for healing. Within systemic therapy, we find the following elements:

- Facilitator: Tarot reader
- Support Group: The Tarot cards (arcana)
- Constellator: Querent

In this way, with the constellation of this Tarot reading, we can manage the elements and guidelines necessary for a therapeutic approach where it is possible to direct a process of modifying the internal narrative and structuring a new family order that allows the querent to free themselves from pain. When we reach this point in the reading, we can add more cards if there is a situation that needs to be expanded upon. Similarly, cards can be moved or reversed ones flipped as a representation of the action to transform a situation. This is a message to the unconscious that enables change. The constellation only happens individually as a personal process in which one can only heal their own perception of the family to leave behind states of lack, defenselessness, and orphanhood.

Birth Reading

When we take the date of your birth year and just add it to the digit of the current year, for example, 5 + 2023 / 7 = 5 + 7 = 12 = 3, we find the digit of our year's destiny, that is, the assigned task for this year in which we can evolve if we are aware of it:

1. Magician: To imitate or develop talent
2. High Priestess: To care for or serve others
3. Empress: To let go or to bind
4. Emperor: To ground or to wander
5. Hierophant: To attend to or to burden
6. Lovers: To love or to reject
7. Chariot: To integrate or to separate
8. Justice: To question or to harm
9. Hermit: To attend to or to burden
10. Wheel of Fortune: To change or to repeat

The history of our civilization began thousands of years ago in the spirit of our imagination when our ancestors started to envision shapes in the skies. Ancient sages through their myths narrate how the human soul came from the great dark night and our consciousness arose with the first rays of the sun, our current condition being a historical journey between the soul and consciousness. In our male and female lineages is found all the information of the tree, meaning all the experiences, good or bad, all the knowledge and discernment capable of solving any situation in our lives. This biological information is encoded and decoded within our genes and quantum field as a mechanism to ensure the continuity in space-time of our species.

Recognizing our place in the evolutionary fabric allows us to understand that we have a mission that forms our sense of life and gives us the possibility to transcend. We must not only integrate our light and shadow but also heal ancient wounds that precede us. We must transcend the memories of pain to know our destiny, like that sense we establish when we have a clearly defined vision and mission in life. All of us are preceded by a story that somehow programs us at an unconscious level: difficult fates, deep wounds, unfinished cycles, so the only way to stop repeating these family patterns is by illuminating the wounds that were not recognized at their time. Our birth comes endowed with a unique and unrepeatable destiny, which could translate into the responsibility to continually improve the human condition.

Reading of Destiny

Within the Tarot, there are four destinies or types of existential tasks, according to the destiny of our birth date, ranging from arcana 1 to 9. To know our destiny, we must individually add all the digits of our birth date, for example: $2 + 5 + 8 + 1 + 9 + 8 + 8 = (41) (4 + 1) = 5$. Once we have obtained our destiny number, we can consult it in the Tarot in the following way:

- 1-6-8: To be Roots, to help others connect with their interior, wound, shadow, but also to recognize their potentials, talents, and love. The mission of these people is to connect with their emotional, intellectual, sexual, and spiritual body.
- 2-5-9: To be Portals, to care, accompany, and guide others in the transformation of their suffering into wisdom through understanding, their mission is to illuminate their wounds.
- 3-4-10: To be Wings, to motivate and mobilize energy to help others rise and open their wings through empowerment, but for this, they must first leave their comfort zone and overcome all their internal blockages.
- 7: To be Integrator, their function is to synthesize, gather, and connect all disciplines, feelings, and ideals of the collective to give meaning to destiny, but for this, they must understand that everything is important for human evolution.

Reading of Death

The dead live within the living, influencing their decisions. When someone from our family system dies, they release an information field where all their life experience is encoded, just as genes are transmitted. Depending on how this ancestor lived, their fate will be a force or a burden, leaving a healing or destructive legacy for their descendants, depending on whether they had the chance to fulfill themselves, if they lived as victims or perpetrators. The descendants who humbly accept the unresolved issues of their ancestors are freed and can take the light, strength, and wisdom of their ancestors, honoring their destinies. On the contrary, when we deny our past, there remain unconscious mourning, unclosed cycles that steal our energy and can make us feel fatigued without an apparent reason, as well as great existential voids. Even if in the professional or personal sphere we consider ourselves successful, beneath the surface lie unresolved issues.

Often, there's a tendency to follow, care for, or replace the dead. Therefore, we must invoke them consciously. For this, we can carry out the following exercise.

We start by relaxing in a place without external noises. We choose a place that gives us warmth. We breathe deeply and momentarily nullify all internal dialogue. It's normal to feel a sensation of cold (a symptom of death). Then, we invoke and imagine our deceased loved ones in front of us. Once we have evoked their memory, we look at them attentively and repeat the following phrase: "Thank you for your legacy. I recognize and respect your burden. I take your light. You can rest in peace, now I choose to live."

Now we imagine a white light where they are heading. If we notice that someone resists, we repeat the phrase: "Now you can rest in peace, I choose to live." Finally, breathe deeply again, silence your mind, and focus your attention on what changes within you, become aware of the sensations running through your body. Slowly open your eyes and write down the first thing that comes to mind.

This exercise can be performed for thirteen days and would be the equivalent of telling a lullaby and turning off the light in the sacred sanctuary where our deceased rest in peace. The imagination allows the inner child to honor the memory of loved ones. The dead need the living to enjoy life so they can rest. According to the day of the month a person passes away, just like the birth destiny, there is a specific energy that can help us identify the unfinished destiny of the deceased, allowing us to transform their departure into a life lesson:

- 1, 6, 8, 15, 17, 19, 24, 26, 28 = root death
- 2, 5, 9, 11, 14, 18, 20, 23, 27, 29 = portal death
- 3, 4, 10, 12, 13, 21, 23, 30, 31 = wing death
- 7, 16, 25 = integrative death

- Ace of Cups. Root legacy of love/fear. Their task in life was to open their heart, learn to love by developing acceptance and understanding, transcend the fear of loving and being loved. Healing phrase: "With love, I leave your fears with you. Thank you for opening your heart and feeling love. Now you can rest, I choose to live."

- Ace of Swords. Portal legacy of joy/unhappiness. Their task in life was to open the intellect, learn to be tolerant, understanding, reflective, take care of their mental health, transcend suffering, control their mind to build their happiness. Healing phrase: "With love, I leave your unhappiness with you. Thank you for opening your mind and expanding your beliefs. Now you can rest, I choose to live."

- Ace of Wands: Wing legacy of satisfaction/anger. Their task in life was to open up to creative energy, materialize dreams through empowerment, and carry out professional projects by taking control of their life through concrete actions. Healing phrase: "With love, I leave your anger with you. Thank you for opening your creativity and dreaming of great changes. Now you can rest, I choose to live."

- Ace of Pentacles: Integrative legacy of gratitude or distrust. Their task in life was to open their body, appreciate life, time, health, to be grateful for life's gifts, and to live in the present from a place of abundance. Healing phrase: "With love, I leave your distrust with you. Thank you for opening your body to abundance. Now you can rest, I choose to live."

Chapter 6
Tarot as a Clinical Instrument

When we have not healed our past, we live for money, external pressures, we do not listen to our interior, we fall into perception errors that interfere with the development that maturity brings. Therefore, it is necessary to undergo a process where we separate light and shadows, to heal old outstanding issues and release a new field of information towards our descendants. This process should be a ritual prior to any couple deciding to form a life project. Alejandro Jodorowsky states: "When the foundations of a couple are demands instead of gifts, a building doomed to collapse is being constructed. A couple is two complete beings who miraculously unite to create, enjoy, share, and expand."

Healing as a couple means leaving behind the sins of the world towards the construction of a new Garden of Eden, where the genealogical tree can be sown anew. We all have the duty to take charge of creating a better future. This will largely depend on what we do in the present, so it is important to reflect on our past, analyze our life story, and modify our own narrative to not repeat dysfunctional patterns. With awareness, we can take and let go of what best suits our path.

Looking at our childhood and adolescence with acceptance and responsibility places us in a state of emotional adulthood. To position myself as an emotional adult, it is necessary to integrate Dad and Mom, but it also implies making peace with two stages of development: childhood and adolescence. The illusion of living in the adult is anchored in childhood. The passion and pleasure of living in the adult are found in the memories of adolescence. When we are not aware of our unconscious programming, we are victims of our own shadow, projecting unresolved internal conflicts into our interpersonal relationships.

The shadow of our wild nature is an unconsciousness preceding the emergence of consciousness. For thousands of years, we were wild beings, amoral, trivial warriors, doing what was necessary to survive; with the emergence of altruism, we began creating the social skills that allowed us to transition from wild tribes to more civilized communities. In this process, myths managed to unify different individuals under belief systems that would shape the family, religion, society, government, etc. However, the rise of solar consciousness created a lunar reflection in the lower part of our personality, where all those survival instincts that allowed us to get here still dwell. This shadowy part is the cause of our flaws and most irrational impulses. When we integrate the shadow, we acquire the power to transform consciousness. Forgiveness is a gift that allows us to heal and move forward without burdens. Forgiveness is towards ourselves. Forgiving others places us in a position of superiority or inferiority. If we all forgive ourselves individually, the whole world could heal by taking responsibility for its own wounds. For this, it is necessary:

- To forgive from the body for not being perfect.
- To forgive from the heart for not loving the family.
- To forgive from the spirit for not being faithful to our life mission.
- To forgive from the soul for not having a responsible relationship with the collective.

Forgiving ourselves frees us from the guilt lodged in the depths of our psyche. Recognizing my actions and assuming the consequences allows me to appreciate the experiences that enable us to grow. We must forgive ourselves for our human condition, which makes mistakes. When we do not forgive ourselves, we become fixated on neuroses that take us out of the present, abandoning our essence, and remaining tied to unfinished family destinies, bound to the wounds of our ancestors, victims of the pain of our lineage. Nonetheless, this pain is something greater that pushes us to heal until we are at peace with ourselves. Forgiveness grants us the power to help and serve others. When we serve both the individual and the collective, we strengthen our inner authority.

- The authority to take charge of my inner child to not project my childish complaints towards my parents onto others. In this way, we manage to avoid unnecessary suffering in our interpersonal relationships.
- Authority to take charge of my role as victim, perpetrator, and savior. By acknowledging that it is I who place myself in these roles, I can position and forgive myself beyond the duality of victim or victimizer.
- Authority to laugh at myself, my self-image, self-discourse, suffering. I don't take things personally and flow freely.

Individual Fears

We all have fears. Most of them stem from ideas shared by the majority of us. Fears represent a mental prison; recognizing and finding their root is the first step to overcoming them. Various reasons can cause a person to stop living out of fear. The experiences that each person goes through can lead to losing the excitement for life, achieving goals, or reaching dreams, thus adopting a passive attitude. The fear of life is so limiting that it turns a person insecure, dependent, distrustful, isolated in all their personal relationships. Fear is a prison that prevents the development of the true potential we have to live life fully. Steven C. Hayes, in his book *Get Out of Your Mind and Into Your Life*, 2013, mentions that to overcome the suffering generated by fears, it is necessary to develop awareness, acceptance, commitment, and values. Through tarot, we can address these fears:

- Ace of Swords: fear of being judged. We believe we are wise or ignorant.
- Ace of Cups: fear of not being loved. We become very emotional or cold.
- Ace of Wands: fear of being rejected or not desired. We believe we are attractive or ugly.
- Ace of Pentacles: fear of being abandoned. We create attachments where we become dependent or independent.

The four Aces represent the main fears we have to face in our life. Jung stated: "What you resist persists; what you accept transforms you." When we learn to accept what happens in life, we can move towards learning that ultimately leads to conflict resolution. Having the ability to accept what we cannot change is an essential step to be able to move forward with our lives. Going against reality will entail an emotional drain that not everyone is capable of handling.

Acceptance also relates to the emotions we experience. Rejecting or avoiding them doesn't help us move forward; in fact, it makes it harder. Proper emotional channeling also aids in the acceptance and management of our fears. Not everything in life will be likable, and this shouldn't mean frustration. On the other hand, if we want to start living without fear, perhaps one of the questions we should ask ourselves is: where do my fears originate? This way, we can begin to understand what led us to our current situation.

The mind often sets traps for us. The ego constantly lies to us, presenting a series of intrusive and irrational thoughts that aren't entirely real. There's a way to face them: living in the here and now. The experience of living in the here and now will act as a protective factor for our mental health. Wayne W. Dyer, in his book "Your Erroneous Zones" (1976), states: "There is only one moment in which you can experience something, and that moment is now." Living in our minds can play tricks on us, such as overthinking the past (what I could have done, would have done differently...) and the future (constant uncertainty about what will happen). The best way to connect with the present is to focus our attention on what truly allows us to improve our lives. When we focus our attention on who we are, what we have, and what we can achieve, we gain a greater degree of self-confidence to face and overcome the fears that limit our lives.

Paternal and Maternal Archetypes as Structuring of Thought and Feeling

When we carry Mom in our hearts, we feel the fullness of life. When we carry Dad in our hearts, we see life clearly. When we do not place ourselves in our rightful place, we are not well-positioned in any area of our life. There are two archetypes or ways to position ourselves from the child's consciousness in a relationship: the saved and the savior. When I try to save Mom or Dad from the child's perspective, I will try to save everyone, and this would be equivalent to meddling. As the adults we are, we must respect everyone's processes, honoring the difficulties each being experiences from the soul, understanding that in these difficulties lies their learning, their experience, and that they are capable of bearing and carrying it within themselves. However, often we prevent ourselves from showing the world who we are for fear of criticism, fear of what others will say. When a descendant comes from a male lineage of belittled men, they will unconsciously strive for society's acceptance, that is, their attention will be on others instead of themselves.

At the core, when we seek societal acceptance, our inner child is seeking acceptance from Dad. The father is our most immediate connection to the real world, the material, the practical, what we can touch. Dad is the ancestor who governs our relationship with profession, studies, the path we take, our actions. He also rules the organs on the right side of our body and the left hemisphere responsible for logic and formal learning. If you notice that any of these areas of your life is stagnant, talk to your father, whether he is alive or not, whether you knew him well or barely remember him, whether he is in front of you or miles away. In tarot, the figure of the Father is represented by the Emperor, the Hierophant, and the Sun.

The Mother figure, from an astrological viewpoint, is represented by the Moon, symbolizing life-bearing energy and the gateway to the inner world, the need for affection. Thanks to the maternal archetype, we can engage in self-observation, contemplate dreams, and experience imagination. It governs the organs on the left side of our body and the right hemisphere responsible for intuition and creativity. Within tarot, the Mother card is represented by different figures, such as the High Priestess, Justice, and the Moon; however, the card that represents our biological mother is the Empress.

The descendant who does not take Dad may find it difficult to show themselves to the world as they are. Often, we experience moments in life where we are either asked to retreat or stay, that is, to look more to the Father (retreat) or more to the Mother (stay). Neurosis arises when we fail to discern between one moment and another, when the strength of Dad is needed and when the openness of Mom is necessary. When Dad's strength was missing, the descendant will have problems with willpower, self-discipline, jobs, and formal situations. When Mom's openness was missing, the descendant will then find it difficult to manage emotions, relate to partners, friends, and thus adopts a behavior in which they do not allow themselves to enjoy life.

Knowing our wounds is to monitor the narration of our inner discourse. To heal, we must observe the internal dialogue to see our mask, whether as a perpetrator or victim. Our personal narrative shapes our internal image of the world and the self. Working on our Maternal and Paternal complex, in turn, allows us to work on complexes of superiority and inferiority. When we face the childish complaints of our ego, we can take charge of our own destiny. The adult stands on their own, needing no permission to be; however, the adult we are still coexists with our child's soul. In moments of neurosis, when life feels like a burden, it's actually the child within needing our attention. If, as adults, we become aware of these childish complaints, we will realize that every neurotic state (whether implosive or explosive) is essentially a child throwing a tantrum.

The Five Wounds of the Soul

We all come into the world with wounds that we must learn to accept. Suffering has different levels of intensity, depending on the individual, and most do not know where it comes from or what to do to stop it. All we know is that many people and situations make us react and, therefore, suffer. This is why it is interesting to discover the source of our sufferings. Our soul suffers differently depending on the wounds that are active. The saddest part is that we let our ego convince us that it is helping us to suffer less through the mask when, in reality, the opposite happens; the ego will always try to maintain an image; on the contrary, the soul will strive to express a truth.

The ego's favorite method to prevent us from feeling the suffering generated by a wound is to incite us to put on a mask every time the wound is activated. When we assume a mask as our identity, all we do is maintain and nurture our wounds. The more a wound is fed, the more it hurts. For this reason, in our society, there is a large number of cases of suicide, irrational violence, and pathologies. From this perspective, we can see addictions and hyper-consumption as an unconscious desire to connect with one's inner self. In our society, existential voids largely contribute to the increasing number of divorces, toxic relationships, and unhappiness every day. To this we can add the deterioration of the social fabric, discrimination, wars, and environmental destruction, which makes it clear that something is not right in our society.

In some psychological theories, it is said that we develop all our beliefs during the first seven years of our life. Most of our thoughts, beliefs, fears, feelings, and decisions are experienced unconsciously. We all have a genetic memory inherited from our family; we all carry the pains and frustrations of our ancestors. When Eve ate the apple from the tree of knowledge (mental dimension), they became imperfect and problems with women began. By eating the forbidden fruit, we turned into gods judging others through moral dictates. When Cain killed his brother Abel, humanity began to use its intelligence for perverse ends. These symbolic stories remind us that, although we cannot change the past, we certainly have the power to choose our future. We are the only creators on Earth who have free will.

Unfortunately, we have ended up forgetting that the only real power we have is that which wisdom grants us. It is very important to remember that the ego is made up of mental energy. Our mental dimension is essential for thinking, reasoning, planning, organizing, memorizing, etc. The ego is a wholly human creation. It feeds on our mental energy to survive, and when its image is affected, it tends to distort reality. However, ego and soul need each other to transcend: one holds the key, and the other the access door. Together they represent our lunar and solar energy. For this reason, only the unification of opposites can restore wholeness to the human being.

Despite this, the ego constantly seeks to paralyze the progress of things, to distract us, to capture our attention in trivial matters, in a constant internal dialogue; on the contrary, the soul tries to create a connection, its impulse is to transcend, evolve, and find continuity beyond space-time. In mythology, it is said that the presence of Sophia was captured from the supreme heaven by the archons and taken to the dark worlds, imprisoning her in the shadows, until Christ finally descended into the depths of creation to free her. This is a representation of the existing disintegration between the soul and the ego. For this reason, many times in our life, we can all feel a call that goes beyond the ordinary. That force is Christ, who, to experience his presence, we must silence our mind and allow his spirit, which is beyond space-time, to act in our quantum field.

Sophia is the Yin force and Christ the Yang force acting within us. If we do not rescue Sophia (reason, feeling, intuition), we will never be complete nor feel integrated. Without her, Christ does not act in our hearts to enlighten us. Artists called her "the inspiring muse."

Alchemists, through their work, achieved the *Opus Magnum* by the process of creating the so-called Philosopher's Stone, which granted the elixir of life, the Holy Grail represented in the Tarot cards of The Fool and The World. Sometimes our wounds are due to a truly traumatic childhood past. Other times, however, they are due to distortions in the interpretation of reality by the inner child.

Many of our behaviors and reactions are programmed by one of these five fears, or rather, by the emotional wounds we have suffered since childhood, which is why it is fundamental to heal them in order to heal the world. The causes of these wounds are due to specific traumatic experiences or events over time. Lise Bourbeau, in her work *The Five Wounds that Prevent Being Oneself* from 2021, mentions that the five wounds of the soul can summarize all human sufferings. These five wounds are: rejection, abandonment, humiliation, betrayal, and injustice. Therefore, to hide our wounds from ourselves and others, we put on masks, which over time lead us to identify with certain social roles that ultimately make us forget who we really are. Each wound corresponds to a specific mask:

- **Rejection.** When your wound of rejection is activated, you put on the evasive mask. This mask prompts you to flee from the situation or the person you believe is the cause of the rejection; all for fear of feeling panic or feeling powerless. This mask can also make you as invisible as possible, withdraw into yourself or, on the contrary, have an obsession with obtaining social recognition at all costs. To heal this wound, it is necessary to accept ourselves unconditionally, with our flaws, weaknesses, and shortcomings, avoiding comparisons, judgments, or self-blame. We must work on self-esteem and recognize those valuable virtues that are part of our being. We must connect with our achievements and recognize ourselves for the successes and goals met that can motivate us towards constant evolution.

- **Abandonment.** When your wound of abandonment is activated, you put on the dependent mask. This makes you like a small child who needs attention and seeks it by crying, complaining, or being submissive to what happens. This wound manifests as a wounded orphan who is constantly a victim of circumstances. This wound is healed when we take care of our needs and prioritize our personal well-being, setting clear boundaries, avoiding mistreatment. When we give ourselves permission to enjoy life, play, be free, laugh, and dream, we become the parents of our inner child and motivate ourselves to heal further.

- **Humiliation.** When the wound of humiliation is activated, you don the mask of a masochist, making you forget your own needs to think only of those of others. The goal is to transform yourself into a good, generous person, always ready to lend your services, even beyond your limits. You also manage to take on the responsibilities and commitments of those who seem to have difficulties fulfilling what they must. You do everything possible to be useful, especially to avoid feeling humiliated or diminished, pleasing others excessively. This wound heals when we recognize our place in this world and balance giving and receiving. When we recognize our worth, we can transform. For this, it is necessary to develop humor and to some extent learn to laugh at ourselves, overcoming our personal importance. When we recognize our personal limits with humility, we feel motivated not to take things too personally and to flow more freely.

- **Betrayal.** When you experience the wound of betrayal, you put on the mask of a controller, which makes you distrustful, skeptical, defensive, authoritarian. You do everything possible to prove that you are a strong person and that you do not easily let yourself be swayed or manipulated. Above all, you try to show that you do not allow others to decide for you. Often, this leads you to adopt a hostile attitude, attacking first rather than getting hurt. You do everything possible to maintain the ego's image to the point of lying or manipulating. You project an image of self-assuredness, though it may not correspond with reality and you doubt your decisions or actions. This wound heals when we develop a sense of responsibility for our own well-being, when we are true to our principles and clearly understand our life's mission. We must trust in our own abilities, finding the balance between what we say, feel, and do. This grants us the consistency necessary to act in favor of our true well-being. Healing requires us to humbly recognize our vulnerability and not try to control the world around us, showing openness to changes in our life. Healing requires cultivating faith in ourselves and humanity, learning to trust and openly cooperate with others. Our society depends on the ability to combine efforts and fight together for collective goals that benefit us all.

- **Injustice.** When your wound of injustice is activated, you put on the mask of rigidity, which makes you a cold, harsh, brusque person. Your body and attitude become cutting. This mask makes you very perfectionistic and live with feelings of anger, impatience, criticism, and intolerance towards yourself and others, manifesting prejudices and labels that seek to avoid emotional closeness. This wound heals when we develop the flexibility and resilience necessary to face suffering without fear. When we cultivate faith in humanity and trust in the universe, our life lights up, and we can leave bitterness and fear behind, to embrace the opportunities to connect with other people. When we build healthy relationships, we find the motivation necessary to be more just with ourselves and others, which motivates us to act according to ethical principles.

To heal emotional wounds, we can engage in meditation, focusing on our breath, clearing the mind of intrusive thoughts, concentrating on a sound, a color, a scent. Subsequently, we can bring to our mind the image of our inner child, visualizing it as an innocent, fragile being. Once we have a clear image of it, we can repeat the following phrases: "I am now safe," "No one will hurt me," "I am free." Later, in front of a mirror, we can declare the following, connecting with the energy of each phrase: "I am loved," "I am valuable," "I am beautiful," "I am intelligent," "I am brave," "I am capable," "I am strong," "I deserve to be happy," "I wish to be happy," "I have faith in myself and am confident that I will succeed." This exercise can be repeated every day until we feel motivated to recover self-esteem, faith in ourselves, and the personal power to act. This exercise enables structuring an internal discourse that projects an image of empowerment to face life with more resources.

A Clinical Approach from Tarot

I know it's not easy to look at oneself, that defenses, fears, and resistances are activated, preventing it. It might be simpler to close the eyes to the soul to not see its wounds, because they hurt too much. But covering them with masks does not heal them, only perpetuates them. A life of openness to consciousness, opening ourselves to see, to feel, to identify, to accept, and with all that to heal. It may not be the shortest path, but it is the one that will take you further. Self-knowledge and personal development are key to a fulfilling life. This process begins with healing our childhood wounds, in recognizing our deficiencies. Once your inner child manages to heal, you will be able to overcome your fears, regaining confidence in your gifts and talents.

When we open our hearts to love and self-understanding, we connect with the possibility of transformation. An ancient Buddhist saying goes: "It is not what happens to us, but what we think, feel, and do about it that causes us suffering." In the ephemerality of existence, everything is learning, and only in the acceptance and understanding of ourselves can we rest in the eternal here and now. This is the beginning and the end of all spiritual practice. We live in a wonderful place, the Earth, we are immersed in a collective journey to know the immensity of the universe. The elements that make up creation combine in an endless number of forms. In each of our atoms and expressions, a sense is coded that transcends our existence and grants us a glorious life purpose.

These are the words of Jung: "The symbol is not only an expression but also has an effect. It reacts upon its author. Ancient magical effects are associated with that symbol (...). And only through the symbol can the unconscious be reached and expressed, for which reason individuation can never do without symbols." In this sense, therapy through the tarot emphasizes the importance of symbols and the symbolic. Synchronicity is embodied in the collective and individual unconscious. A good therapeutic system shows the nature of the human being, its structure (physical, astral, mental, and spiritual), the place it occupies in the world, the peak to conquer, the path to walk, and also explains the work to be done on oneself. Fate, the trials, are good for us. We must see the difficulties in life as heroic tests that lead to the development of our true potential.

Visiting the world of the archetypical is a process of psychological exploration that allows us to delve into the depths of our own mind to establish a direct connection with the soul, hence the necessary meditative reflection of the tarot to improve the life of the consultant. The 22 archetypes are like an instinctive tendency that, as described by Jung in his book *Man and His Symbols* from 1964, are above all archetypal forces that lie within each of us and are like pieces of life itself; that is, images connected to the individual through the bridge of psychic energies that are distilled from the microcosm view of our limbic system, or second brain, called emotions, to the rest of our powerful brain, with the intention of understanding ourselves and everyone around us.

Whether we are aware of these unconscious forces or not, myths and archetypes live through us and within us in many ways; hence the importance of exploring the oceanic and almost infinite world of the unconscious as if we were avatars of a metahistorical psychic tendency that sees itself. This highlights the critical importance of paying attention to these archetypes or 22 primordial images that invade us, sometimes even in our nocturnal or diurnal dreams, or in the form of synchronized events. They serve as a kind of initiation ground or a rite of passage in our psyche-soul, elevating us to a new stage that may allow us to resolve the questions we all ask: Who am I? Where do I come from? Where am I going? Questions that have pursued us since the dawn of humanity.

Access to this alchemical wisdom is a treasure that only the ego can unearth. This event is only possible when the person (ego, mask) manages to make peace with the archetypes lying within themselves. When a process of hemispheric integration and unification of the cerebral trinity, with its multiple intelligences, is carried out, one begins to live a life more at peace with oneself. This is the central axis of tarot, the hero's journey as a process of unification, integration, transformation, and evolution, which requires time and effort. For the ancient alchemists, the so-called Major Arcana or 22 archetypes of the tarot were like the seeds of any plant, which only when planted in the darkness of the earth wish to grow and develop, and eventually emerge into the light by their own will, thereby transmitting a certain order in the chaos of the mind of the one who consciously elaborates this.

The archetypal comes to act as a kind of holographic projector in the womb of the inner world, like a seed that must open. The tarot acts as a germinal projector showing a world to come, which curiously exists within each and every one of us. And we must come to a logical understanding of who we really are by deciphering this archetypal code through the elaboration and work of all these visions of the unconscious. This is why it is said in some tarot texts that the 22 Major Arcana speak to us of the transcendent (the inside), and the 56 Minor Arcana, of the outside (the world), but both, the inner world and the outer world, are there to be integrated into each other.

Our biological birth enables a symbolic birth. This, in turn, is a means to have a spiritual birth. Often, we are not aware of these powerful unconscious forces that Jung and others termed archetypes, which operate within the laws of the universe to help us manifest our greatest dreams. Or, as we might say in terms of quantum physics, we can create our reality by changing what is observed and becoming the observer who observes itself, and in such observation, is capable of transforming its reality. Tarot, as a clinical tool, is capable of organizing reality. An individual evolves by realizing that it is the balanced relationship between these two worlds, the physical and the spiritual. With tarot, we realize that everything is dual. Duality is composed of opposites that are the two sides of a path; they form it if they unite, but it is our tendency that divides it. Without one of the opposites, there would not be the other; without the possibility to hate, the ability to love would hold no merit.

Every aspect of life has a good side and a bad side; what really matters is to find a middle point that enables learning. Wisdom is not in the extremes but in the middle path, in knowing how to unite opposites, in recognizing pain and love as part of life. Dualism can only be transcended when we recognize that both light and shadow are forms that allow us to glimpse reality and access wisdom. When there is no light, darkness hinders our vision, but when light exceeds its threshold, it blinds us. Whenever we identify with a quality, no matter how good it seems, there is a risk of falling into totalitarianism, subjectivity, and projection. On the contrary, when we are aware of our vulnerability, we are more capable of strengthening ourselves, introjecting values, and contemplating the opportunities that allow us to grow. Tarot is a method of deep psychoanalysis, truly effective in expert hands. Therefore, you must learn its meanings in depth, and there will come a day when tarot and you are one.

The true spirit of tarot is revealed only to those who approach it with pure intention and a true desire to know. Each tarot card is like a portal of light and a source of healing and wisdom. Have you ever wondered what intelligence is, physically speaking? While you can delve deeper by consulting books on neurology, the process that shapes our intelligence quotient begins in the first year of your life, and it is until approximately six years of age that the greatest development of the subconscious occurs in the human cerebral cortex.

Curiously, in card number 6, known as The Lovers, it is revealed whether we have well-established the principle of maturity or the opposite. Meditating on this card, we see if we choose things out of whim or through reflective aptitude that help us grow, or if we only value those we wish to obtain; hence the myth of the Judgment of Paris, with his misguided choice of Helen of Troy and its consequences, is reflected in this card. Sometimes, it is not good to choose without thinking of the consequences. Therefore, it is crucial that, in the learning period from zero to six years, we are trained in the best human values, as the density of our neural network will increase dramatically in the first six months after birth, followed by a constant increase in the connections of brain cells until the age of six.

Afterward, what is inscribed or memorized in our brain will most affect our adult life. So, if in the early years of life we do not have certain experiences regarding essential values, some connections about them will not be adequately established. In this initial stage, a kind of basic network is prepared on which we will have to organize our existence later. If some specific synaptic links are missing, in adult life we will have more difficulties establishing these connections, thus we struggle between what is right and what is not.

In analytical psychology, we assume that the collective subconscious is present in all of us at birth, and only later do we develop what we know as the conscious mind. As children, we are connected to our parents and the rest of the world through our brain. Initially, there is no mechanism of repression in us to deal with things that are unpleasant. But over time, these barriers appear, forming complexes, beliefs, perceptions, mental structures, attachments, character traits, habits, etc. Carl Jung said about this: "The things that most strongly affect a child at an early age do not come from the conscious state of their parents but from their unconscious background; therefore, it is important for parents to study their children's problems in light of their own problems as parents." Generally, what has a powerful effect on a child's psyche is also everything that the parents or ancestors have not lived or to which they have renounced with unconvincing excuses.

Therefore, in current psychology, we can find various factors linked to the anxiety and repression in the adult's hidden inner child, sometimes recognized when investigating the family model, which can be attributed to a very early interaction with the parents' unconscious. In an interaction between cells, neurons, etc., the axon and dendrite create a synapse, which is a bridge or conducting thread to unify multiple connections and give rise to certain patterns of thought that manifest specific behaviors and attitudes. However, this does not define us; according to neuroplasticity, we always have the power to create new connections. Changing attitudes, habits, and manifesting new behaviors create new synaptic connections and give the individual the possibility to renew and evolve.

Now, ask yourself, how many cellular bodies do you still have unconfigured in your life? Tarot is a tool that enables the expansion of the cerebral field, to perceive the world around us and ourselves clearly. For this, we need a practical method to facilitate personal transformation, and here I propose one. Always start by observing the 22 tarots and asking yourself deep questions like: Who am I? Where do I come from? Where am I going? Then choose one of the 22 cards. After choosing the one that attracts you the most, you're going to draw it. Then color it for about twenty minutes. After reading the key questions and choosing the one that attracts you the most or best fits what you are looking for, you will write it down as part of a script or story that relates to the situations you face in your life. Each card will help you to deepen and reflect on some aspect or situation in your life. The analysis should help you transform the experience into knowledge and the knowledge into a change in attitude. Finally, this change should motivate you to take actions that allow you to improve.

Next, it would be appropriate for you to read the story that goes at the beginning, under the key phrases that I will show below. After reading the story, synthesize the meanings of those cards and the possibilities of acquiring them by drawing and meditating on them, write everything you feel and comes to your mind in your notebook, and leave it there for a few days. After two or three days, look back and reflect on everything felt and written, and meditate on it again. After three to eight days, you will see that the answers will come directly from you to whatever was oppressing you. In some way, they will emerge within you or will already be there in your meditations and notes, and gradually you will see everything more clearly. The unconscious will become visible to you. With what emerges in your notebook, you must construct a script or a story of your life, in which you will be the main character. It will depend only on you whether the story you write will be one of drama, terror, or pain, or if, on the contrary, your story will be filled with love, hope, humor, joy, optimism, and faith.

Through this method, you can manage your own heroic journey, illuminating your shadows and integrating the qualities that allow you to unfold all your evolutionary potential. The phrases for meditating with the arcana according to Vianey Torres's methodology are a way to reprogram thoughts and structure an internal narrative that empowers your life. Its elements are key phrases that represent a decree, an emotional rationalization that enables the combination of new beliefs. These phrases should be completed with our imagination as a means to modify a specific situation (love, work, health, money, etc.). For instance, with The Fool, we decree to free ourselves from (guilt, anger, victimhood, suffering, fears, frustration, addictions, toxic relationships, the need to control, compulsive obsessions, etc.).

Moreover, they can be combined with another arcana to form a sentence, for example, The Fool + Wheel of Fortune. I free myself from the need to control, I trust in the changes in my life to (open myself to new work opportunities, heal a relationship, travel freely, learn something new, find happiness, etc.). How we complete the sentence will largely depend on the context we wish to use it for. This phrase will be the result of the reading we choose, which we will have to repeat constantly, after meditation, upon waking, before sleeping, or at those moments when tension or anxiety invade us. To enhance this activity, you can visualize the arcana paying attention to their symbols, colors, and shapes. These guide phrases are an example of how we can complete and combine sentences:

0-The Fool. I free myself from (_____);_____

1-The Magician. I trust in my talent (to create);_____

2-The High Priestess. I recognize the wisdom within me (to heal);_____

_____

3-The Empress. I have the necessary creativity (to visualize); _____

_____

4-Emperor. I have the necessary personal power (to materialize); _____

_____

5-Hierophant. I am at the service of God's spirit (to transmit); _____

_____

6-Lovers. I decide to act with my heart (to achieve); _____

_____

7-Chariot. I direct my will with intelligence (to advance); _____

_____

Sinuhe Ulises García Reynoso _____

8-Justice. I seek to balance my life with justice (to succeed); _____
_____

9-Hermit. I illuminate my path with wisdom (to guide); _____
_____

10-Wheel. I humbly accept the changes that come into my life (to learn); ___
_____

11-Strength. I master my impulses and develop my spirit (to take responsibility);
_____

12-Hanged Man. I am willing to make the necessary sacrifices (to overcome);
_____

13-Death. I face the death of my ego, vanity, and pride with detachment (to transform); _____

14-Temperance. I transmute my emotions (to understand); _____
_____

15-Devil. I confront my shadow (to accept); _____
_____

16-Tower. I release old thought patterns (to change); _____
_____

17-Star. I have faith in my ability (to shine); _____
_____

18-Moon. I connect with my intuition and creativity (to reveal); _____
_____

19-Sun. I heal my inner child (to flourish); _____
_____

20-Judgement. I am reborn as a new being (to integrate); _____
_____

21-World. I transcend my soul (to evolve); _____
_____

22-Fool. Now that I am free, I have <u>the power to transform my life and materialize my dreams by connecting my body, mind, and soul with the universe.</u>

This method is as simple and straightforward as you can complete by drawing and coloring the chosen card in such a way that you internalize the principles of each arcana. Thus, you will gradually begin to transform. Over time, your consciousness will manage to expand. This in itself is the essence of healing. No therapist can heal you if you do not want to improve. Healing occurs when you contact your own inner wisdom and act in that direction. The symbolism of the tarot speaks directly to our psyche (soul). Therefore, it is no coincidence that when we ask a question, we are drawn to or a specific card appears that is governed by a specific color, a Hebrew letter, a number, a geometric figure, a myth, etc. The synchronicity present in the tarot reminds us that there is a universal order that watches over our evolution. We are never alone; we are always in direct connection with the source. We are part of a whole, and the whole is part of us.

Final Reflection

Upon concluding this book, perhaps not all concepts will be crystal clear, given the complexity of tackling tarot on its own, and even more so, understanding the various therapeutic approaches and branches of science considered in this work. Therefore, it is advisable to review this text a couple of times to fully comprehend its content. The reader is also encouraged to independently delve deeper into the authors and concepts mentioned throughout the text, to further expand their knowledge. Likewise, having a dictionary of symbols is recommended to achieve a total understanding of this text. The central axis of this book represents a transition from myth to logos, a point of unification between the scientific method and spirituality. It is a path to integrate all the wisdom of the past into the present, connecting with the cultural roots of our history, to enable the design of a better future. This work is a method towards self-knowledge that leads to inner healing through a science of the soul that seeks to elevate the reader's quality of life. This work is a tribute to the first scientists who were considered witches by a world that was not yet able to comprehend the magnitude of their discoveries or the wisdom of their knowledge.

If you know nothing about your own mind, all your efforts will be in vain.
If you want to know your own mind, there is only one way:
to observe and recognize everything that relates to it.
This must be done at all times, not only during
meditation hour but also in daily life.
Thich Nhat Hanh

Bibliography

"Tarot y Arquetipos", Independently published.

Joaquín de Saint Aymour. (2019)." El Tarot Alquímico de Jung".

Sallie Nichols.Alexis Racionero Ragué. (2021)." El viaje del héroe: Mitología, storytelling y transformación personal".Jules Cashford.Barbara H. (1954-1958). *The Archetypal Symbolism of Animals: Lectures Given at the C.g. Jung Institute Zurich.* Wilmette Ill: Chiron Publications.

Hillman, James Estar infestado Traducción Alejandro Chavarria en https://alexchrojo.wordpress.com/2023/10/08/estar-infestado

Hillman, James.(1999) "Sobre el fenómeno del espíritu en el arte y en la ciencia".(2023) "El hombre y sus símbolos"."El libro rojo". El Hilo De Ariadna.

"De lo espiritual en el arte".Berman, M. (1992). *Cuerpo y espíritu.* Edit. Cuatro Vientos, Santiago.

Branston, B. (1960). *Mitología germánica.* Barcelona, España, Edit. Vergara.

Cashford J. (2018). *La luna, símbolo de transformación.* Atalanta.

Franz M. L. von and Boa F. (1997). El camino de los sueños: Dra. Marie-Louise Von Franz, En Conversaciones con Fraser Boa. Cuatro Vientos.

Greene, L. (1990). *Astrología y destino.* Editorial Obelisco.

Hillman, J. (1994). *La cultura y el alma animal.* Caracas, Venezuela: Fundación Polar.

Hillman, J. (1999). *El código del alma.* Martínez Roca: Grupo Editorial Planeta.

Hillman, J. (2004). *El sueño y el inframundo.* Barcelona: Paidós.

Hillman, J. Estar infestado. Traducción Alejandro Chavarría en https://alexchrojo.wordpress.com/2023/10/08/estar-infestado.

Jung, C. G. (1960). *Tipos psicológicos*. Edit. Sudamericana, Bs. As.

Jung, C. G. (1988). *Sincronicidad*. Málaga: Ediciones Sirio S.A.

Jung, C. G. (1990). *Las relaciones entre el Yo y el Inconsciente*. Barcelona: Editorial Paidós.

Jung, C. G. (1991). *Arquetipos e Inconsciente colectivo*. Barcelona: Editorial Paidós.

Jung, C. G. (1999). *Sobre el fenómeno del espíritu en el arte y en la ciencia*. Madrid: Trotta.

Jung, C. G. (2001). *Los complejos y el inconsciente*. Barcelona: Alianza Editorial.

Jung, C. G. (2018). *El libro rojo*. El Hilo de Ariadna.

Jung, C. G. (2023) El hombre y sus símbolos. Editorial Paidós.

Kandinsky, V. (1996). *De lo espiritual en el arte*. Barcelona: Paidós

Monthly Notices of the Royal Astronomical Society, volume 470, issue 4, October 2017, pages 4698–4719, https://doi.org/10.1093/mnras/stx1517.

Nichols S. (1997). *Jung y el tarot*. Nirvana Libros, S.A. de C.V.

Orero A. y Esteban P. (2019). *Tarot y arquetipos*. Independently published.

Racionero Ragué A. (2021). *El viaje del héroe: mitología, storytelling y transformación personal*. Nirvana libros S.A de C.V.

Sagan C. (2019). Life cycle of a star: and the circulation of reputation. Published online by Cambridge University Press.

Saint Aymour J. de (2019). *El tarot alquímico de Jung*. Ediciones Efecto Mariposa.

www.ingramcontent.com/pod-product-compliance
Lightning Source LLC
LaVergne TN
LVHW051216070526
838200LV00063B/4920